MORNING GLORIES

MUNICIPAL REFORM IN THE SOUTHWEST

Amy Bridges

PRINCETON UNIVERSITY PRESS   PRINCETON, NEW JERSEY

Copyright © 1997 by Princeton University Press
Published by Princeton University Press, 41 William Street,
Princeton, New Jersey 08540
In the United Kingdom: Princeton University Press,
Chichester, West Sussex
All Rights Reserved

Second printing, and first paperback printing, 1999
Paperback ISBN 0-691-01009-9

The Library of Congress has cataloged the cloth edition of this book as follows

Bridges, Amy.
Morning glories : municipal reform in the Southwest / Amy Bridges.
p. cm.
Includes bibliographical references and index.
ISBN 0-691-02780-3 (alk. paper)
1. Municipal government—Southwestern States—History.   I.Title.
JS440.B75   1997
320.8'5'0979—dc21   96-45262

This book has been composed in Sabon

The paper used in this publication meets the minimum requirements
of ANSI/NISO Z39.48-1992 (R1997) (*Permanence of Paper*)

http://pup.princeton.edu

Printed in the United States of America

10 9 8 7 6 5 4 3 2

For Richard Gray Kronick ────────────────

FRIEND TO 37 MILLION

EXEMPLARY FATHER

PARTNER IN LIFE

The Reformer

A Reformer is one who sets forth cheerfully toward sure defeat.

It is his peculiar function to embrace the hopeless cause when it can win no other friends and when its obvious futility repels that thick-necked, practical, timorous type of citizen to whom the outward appearance of success is so dear.

His persistence against stone walls invites derision from those who have never been touched by his religion and do not know what fun it is.

He never seems victorious, for if he were visibly winning, he would forthwith cease to be dubbed "reformer."

Yet, in time, the Reformer's little movement becomes respectable and his little minority proves that it can grow, and presently the Statesman joins it and takes all the credit, cheerfully handed to him by the Reformer as bribe for his support.

And then comes the Politician, rushing grandly to the succor of the victor!

And all the Crowd!

The original Reformer is lost in the shuffle then, but he doesn't care—

For as the great band-wagon which he started goes thundering past with trumpets, the Crowd in the intoxication of triumph leans over the side to jeer at him—a forlorn and lonely crank, mustering a pitiful little odd-lot of followers along the roadside and setting them marching, while over their heads he lifts the curious banner of his next crusade!

Richard S. Childs
National Municipal Review, 1927

Contents

List of Tables   xi

Acknowledgments   xiii

One
Southwestern Cities and the Course of Reform   3

Two
Small but Ambitious   31

Three
Setting Forth Cheerfully   52

Four
Sure Defeat   72

Five
The Little Movement Becomes Respectable   99

Six
The Statesman Joins It   125

Seven
And Takes the Credit   151

Eight
The Politician and the Crowd   175

Nine
Morning Glories   207

Appendix: Notes on the Choice of Cases   223

Bibliography   225

Index   235

Tables

1-1	Major Charter Changes in Southwestern Cities	10
2-1	Population of Southwestern Cities, 1890–1920	35
4-1	Turnout in Municipal Elections in Selected Cities, 1920–1945	76
4-2	Percentage of Population Foreign-born in Selected Cities, 1930	78
4-3	Population of Southwestern Cities, 1920–1950	97
6-1	Turnout in Municipal Elections, 1947–1963	133
6-2	Social Characteristics of Selected Cities, 1960	134
6-3	Competitiveness of Elections in Selected Cities, 1945–1963	135
6-4	Demographic Characteristics of Neighborhoods in Austin, Phoenix, and Albuquerque, ca. 1960	144
6-5	Turnout and Voting Returns in Austin, Phoenix, and Albuquerque, ca. 1960	146
7-1	Population of Selected Southwestern Cities, 1950 and 1960	153
7-2	Land Area of Selected Southwestern Cities, 1950 and 1960	154
7-3	Local Government Employment and Spending, 1960	161
7-4	Financing Local Government, 1960	162
7-5	Public Libraries in Selected Cities, 1960	163
7-6	Percentage of Students in Public Schools, 1960	167
8-1	Turnout in Municipal Elections, 1965–1989	179
8-2	Population of Southwestern Cities, 1970–1990	192
8-3	Land Area of Southwestern Cities, 1970–1990	193
8-4	Ethnic Composition of Southwestern Cities, 1990	205

Acknowledgments ————————————————————

I AM the beneficiary of assistance from many sources. The National Endowment for the Humanities awarded me a fellowship early in the history of this project, when I foolishly imagined I could research and write this book in a year. I did not, but I did travel, research, write, and think with the assistance of NEH funds. For their concrete expression of optimism I am most grateful. The Committee on Research of the University of California also provided funds for travel and research.

Portions of chapters 2 and 3 appeared in "Winning the West to Municipal Reform," *Urban Affairs Quarterly*, and are reprinted here with the permission of Sage Publications. Accounts of public discourse in chapters 1, 3, 5, and 6 were published in "Creating Cultures of Reform," in *Studies in American Political Development*, and are included here with the permission of Cambridge University Press.

I have enjoyed the luxury of a corps of able research assistants, some of whom I have not yet met. Tami Waggener (Austin), Tanya Donaghey (Dallas), Trish Oberweis (Phoenix), Erin Hatch (San Diego, San Jose), and Katherine Holsworth gathered election returns, primary documents, and newspaper clippings for too little compensation. Friends and colleagues also helped. Ray Duch, Reta Mae and Vince Kelley, Jeff and Jean Tulis, Ben and Mary Page, and Martin Sánchez-Jankowski helped me find my way in their home cities. Steve Amberg, Michael Dawson, Philip Ethington, Ken Finegold, Marilynn Johnson, Doug Rivers, Heywood Sanders, Rogers Smith, and Ray Wolfinger helped me track down fugitive sources and recruit able research assistants. Joan Kronick shared documents saved from her participation in the War on Poverty in Dallas. Several colleagues shared information from their own research. Robert Dahl sent copies of early New Haven voting returns. Terry Christensen, Peter Lupsha, Howard Rabinowitz, and Heywood Sanders shared unpublished papers, expertise on local data sources, and their own insights into local politics. I owe special thanks to Harry Kinney, Calvin Goode, Vincent Griego, and Louis Saavedra, who graciously provided tutorials in local politics.

Colleagues and friends read and commented on the manuscript, or portions of it, in various manifestations. Gary Cox, Michael Danielson, Harry Hirsch, Gary Jacobson, Richard Keiser, and Margaret Weir pointed me in sensible directions and rescued me from erroneous paths. Arnold Hirsch raised profound questions about the study of local politics, to which I know have made inadequate responses. Stanley Engerman, Arnold Fleischmann, Dennis Judd, and Katherine Underwood read the whole—or as my daughter Emma Rose would say, the whole *entire*— manuscript and provided detailed, smart, and supportive commentary. As every honorable author must, I claim sole authorship of the mistakes.

Martin Shefter, Theda Skocpol, and Ira Katznelson invited me to bring this book to Princeton. Malcolm DeBevoise and Malcolm Litchfield welcomed the book to the press, and Malcolm Litchfield reminded me just often enough that he was waiting that I felt I should stop writing. Beth Gianfagna answered a gazillion questions and helped me keep my sense of humor.

My greatest good fortune is my family. Rick read every revision of every chapter, raised important questions, helped me make sense of election returns, criticized uncertain logic, and offered trenchant praise. He has never inquired about the cost of my far-flung research assistants. Rick saw me off on research trips and welcomed me home on my return. Our daughters Dorothy Jane and Emma Rose cannot remember a time before I was working on this book. They have been patient and gracious beyond their years. Thank you, ladies.

Still, no one is happier than Rick, Dorothy, and Emma to see the manuscript off to Princeton. As a memento of their forbearance I save the undated message, "Mom called from Albequgurky."

MORNING GLORIES

One

Southwestern Cities and the Course of Reform

IN ONE of his most famous remarks, George Washington Plunkitt dismissed municipal reformers as "morning glories" who "looked lovely in the mornin' and withered up in a short time, while the regular machines went on flourishin' forever, like fine old oaks." Plunkitt recalled New York's People's Municipal League of 1890, the Committee of Seventy of 1894, the Citizens' Union, the good government clubs; none had lasted more than a few years. New York was hardly exceptional. Although the municipal reform movement eventually had profound effects on city politics everywhere, in the large cities of the Northeast and Midwest, municipal reformers celebrated few victories at the polls, and when they did win, their time in office was in most places fleeting. So Plunkitt found "college professors and philosophers . . . are always discussin' the question, 'Why Reform Administrations Never Succeed Themselves.'"[1]

In the Southwest municipal reformers enjoyed a different history. In the Progressive Era, and again in the 1940s, municipal reformers celebrated political victories across the region. Just as the big cities of the Northeast and Midwest were commonly governed by political machines, and the cities of the South by Bourbon coalitions, so the cities of the Southwest have in the twentieth century been governed by municipal reformers. Had Plunkitt investigated the morning glory, this possibility might have occurred to him. Plunkitt, of course, was talking about the flowers, which open in the morning and fade as the sun goes down. By contrast, its roots and vines (as anyone with morning glories in the garden has the misfortune to know) are invasive and tenacious. Nowhere is this more true than in the Southwest. There the vigor of the morning glory is so great that other plants are smothered by it. In Arizona the morning glory is considered an agricultural pest, the sale of morning glory seed is banned, and import of plants of its genus (*Ipomoea*) illegal.[2] Likewise, the growth of municipal reform in the southwest choked out its opponents, replacing parties with nonpartisanship, party politicians with a civic elite, mayors with commissioners and managers, competition with political monopoly.

---

[1] William L. Riordan, *Plunkitt of Tammany Hall* (New York: Bedford Books, 1994), 57.
[2] I am indebted to Everett Hall of the Arizona Department of Agriculture for the this information, in conversation, December 1991.

Morning Glories traces the ascent of municipal reformers in the South-west and offers an account of the governments they provided. The book repairs two deficits in our understanding of city politics in the United States. First, it adds new chapters to the history of municipal reform. From the turn of the century to the 1980s, I chronicle the course of re-form from the early, only partially successful institutionalizations of the years before World War II, to the governments of the big cities of the mid-century Southwest, and finally the successful efforts to dismantle city-wide elections in the last generation. Second, *Morning Glories* substan-tially rights the regional imbalance in the study of city politics, in which the cities of the Southwest have been neglected.

The textbook history of reform is a truncated one. Students of city politics are familiar with the mugwumps and party bosses of the late nineteenth century, the muckrakers and progressives of the first genera-tion after 1900, the Seth Lows, Tom Johnsons, Carter Harrisons, and George Washington Plunkitts. These actors dominate the history of their eras as they dominated the politics of the nation's big cities. In later pe-riods municipal reform suggests the profound effects the movement even-tually had on local politics everywhere: the decline of corruption, the replacement of patronage with civil service, the introduction of profes-sionalism and expertise to city government, the growth of ungovernable bureaucracies.

By the middle of the twentieth century, reform governance was, in the textbooks, relegated to the suburbs. In *City Politics*, Edward Banfield and James Q. Wilson explained the "reform ideal" and sketched the kind of community in which it was "nearly realized in practice":

> An example is Winnetka, a suburb of Chicago the residents of which are almost all upper middle class Anglo-Saxon Protestants. Winnetkans are in fundamen-tal agreement on the kind of local government they want: it must provide excel-lent schools, parks, libraries, and other community services and it must provide them with businesslike efficiency and perfect honesty. Politics, in the sense of a competitive struggle for office or for private advantage, does not exist. No one offers himself as a candidate for office. Instead the civic associations agree upon a slate of those "best qualified to serve" which the voters ratify as a matter of course. Members of the city council leave "administration" entirely in the hands of the city manager.

Robert C. Wood's *Suburbia* had shown that the style of politics found in Winnetka was typical of suburbs, where, it seemed, good government advocates had found their greatest success.[3]

---

[3] Edward Banfield and James Q. Wilson, *City Politics* (New York: Vintage, 1966), 140. Robert C. Wood, *Suburbia: Its People and Their Politics* (Boston: Houghton Mifflin, 1959).

The institutionalization of reform politics in the suburbs is presented as the denouement of the history of the municipal reform movement. Contemporary city politics textbooks have shared this reading. Judd and Swanstrom report in *City Politics, Private Power and Public Policy* that city-manager government was "rarely instituted in the big cities, [although] it became common in smaller cities around the nation." Harrigan writes in *Political Change in the Metropolis* "reform-style city government is most likely to be found in suburban cities."[4] The same textbooks discuss the bias of various reform arrangements (citywide elections, for example) but do not offer a portrait of reform governance. Historians have shared this reading; even urban historians as wise as Roger Lotchin and Charles Glaab agreed that "the city manager system 'did not significantly influence big city government and politics' after World War II."[5]

Yet at the moment Banfield and Wilson were writing *City Politics*, Dallas, Austin, Phoenix, San Antonio, San Jose, Albuquerque, and San Diego were governed by nonpartisan city-manager regimes, with city council members elected citywide. In 1960 they were small cities, only Dallas ranking in the largest dozen of the nation's metropolises. In 1990 the same cities were all among the nation's largest dozen cities and still boasted nonpartisan city-manager governments (although city councils were by then mostly elected from districts). If the suburbs are home to the denouement of municipal reform, the movement's greatest achievements were the governments of the big cities of the Southwest. *Morning Glories* provides an account of politics and government in these homes to big-city reform.

The politics and history of the big cities of the Southwest has been the object of remarkably little study. From the study of the machine to urban renewal, community participation, voting, and elections, the urban politics literature has been dominated by the cities of the Northeast and Midwest. With the appearance of competition between the "frostbelt" and the "sunbelt" for federal funds in the 1970s, greater attention was given to southern and western cities, and many monographs and books were written about "sunbelt cities." Attention to cities in the southern tier redirected urban studies away from an almost exclusive focus on the old cities of the Northeast and Midwest. For readers interested in politics,

[4] Dennis R. Judd and Todd Swanstrom, *City Politics, Private Power and Public Policy* (New York: HarperCollins, 1994), 97. John J. Harrigan, *Political Change in the Metropolis* (New York: HarperCollins, 1993), 115. These two books account for 75 percent of urban politics textbook sales in the United States.

[5] Roger Lotchin, "Power and Policy: American City Politics between the Two World Wars," in *Ethnics, Machines, and the American Urban Future*, ed. Scott Greer (Cambridge: Schenkman, 1981), 1–50.

however, these studies were less than wholly satisfying. For one thing, many authors focused on growth and local economies or the shifting balance of influence in the nation's capital rather than on local politics. Second, the sunbelt was most often conceptualized as everything south of the Mason-Dixon line.[6] There were good reasons to think of the sunbelt as the southern tier, but there are substantial political, social, and economic differences between the states of the Confederacy (and their cities) and the Southwest. Third, lacking a shared or comparative focus, the monographs and books about sunbelt cities did little to portray the common themes of political change in the big cities of the Southwest. Even in the Southwest, among historians, political activists, and political observers, everywhere I traveled I encountered insistence that local politics, wherever I was, was unique.

The narratives of municipal reformers in power and city politics in the Southwest are as closely joined as those of the boss and his machine to city politics in the Northeast. It is in the Southwest that the municipal reform movement had its greatest triumphs in the Progressive Era. Since that time citywide elections, nonpartisanship, and commission and council-manager government have been the rule not only for small cities (as in other regions) but for big-city politics. If elsewhere municipal reformers were either confined to smaller cities or condemned to valiant but futile opposition, in the urban Southwest good-government advocates have ruled for generations.

Morning Glories is an essay in both history and political science. The historical contribution is a narrative of political life in the cities of the Southwest. *Morning Glories* traces politics in southwestern cities from 1900 to the present day. "Big City Reform" anticipates the narrative of the book. *Morning Glories* also offers explanations of how that political life came to be. "Explaining the Course of Reform" sketches the historical and analytic puzzles raised by the narrative, and describes my approach to solving them.

Big-City Reform

The nineteenth-century history of machine politicians and municipal reformers is the prologue to this account of big-city reform. Machine politi-

---

[6] This definition of the sunbelt underlies, for example, Kirkpatrick Sale, *Power Shift: The Rise of the Southern Rim and Its Challenge to the Eastern Establishment* (New York: Random House, 1975); Ray Mohl, *Searching for the Sunbelt: Historical Perspectives on a Region* (Knoxville: University of Tennessee Press, 1990); Richard M. Bernard and Bradley R. Rice, eds., *Sunbelt Cities: Politics and Growth since World War II* (Austin: University of Texas Press, 1983).

cians and municipal reformers were the fraternal twins of the antebellum United States, their simultaneous birth beginning a struggle for control of the nation's cities. Hardly had the first party boss appeared in local politics when a municipal reform movement was organized to dethrone him. Baltimore, Boston, Philadelphia, New York, Pittsburgh, Springfield (Massachusetts), and Cincinnati had municipal reform movements before the Civil War. For the rest of the century, and in some places much longer, party politicians and municipal reformers competed for control of city governments.

The rhetoric and much of the program of municipal reform were nineteenth-century inventions. Reformers saw the ills of local government as a consequence of machine rule. "Nothing can be more true than that that modern and monstrous instrument known as the political party machine . . . is the source of these evils."[7] Machines drew their strength, reformers argued, from the unquestioning partisanship of working class, especially immigrant, voters bought with the dispensation of favors and patronage. The corruption inherent in such a system was both shameful and expensive. Were machine politicians to remain in control of city government, Boston's Citizens Ticket feared "a load of municipal taxation and debt more intolerable than the British tyranny, from which our fathers revolted."[8]

Reformers' program followed directly from this analysis. Largely negative, the proposals of municipal reformers were meant to dismantle machines by loosening the ties between voters and officials. The key was depriving politicians of patronage and other resources. First, reformers championed nonpartisanship to erode the ties of party. In Boston the *Daily Advertiser* hailed the election of a reform mayor as "a victory of citizens without distortion of party against a corrupt and proscriptive partisan rule."[9] Similarly, New York's reformers boasted that their candidates were "untrammeled by party pledges."[10] Second, in place of party politicians, reformers offered government by the city's "best men." Reformers would, if elected, replace the rule of muscle with government by men of "spotless integrity, close judgement, and sterling common sense."[11] Reform candidates promised businesslike efficiency in place of extravagance, as when New York's reformers declared, "Retrenchment is the twin of reform."[12] Philadelphia's reform administration claimed credit for lowering taxes and replacing the "evil-minded, vicious, and

[7] *New York Herald*, November 27, 1861.
[8] *Boston Daily Advertiser*, December 8, 1855.
[9] Ibid., December 11, 1855.
[10] *New York Herald*, October 18, 1854.
[11] Ibid., October 18, 1854.
[12] Ibid., October 18, 1854.

depraved in office with men of probity and good business capacity."[13] Later, civil service and competitive bidding for government contracts were proposed to deny the resources of favors, patronage, and corruption to municipal officeholders.

Municipal reformers were often politically allied with nativists, and later, with proponents of eugenics and white supremacy, sharing with them antipathy to immigrants and people of color, and so a desire to tighten controls on voting. From the middle of the nineteenth century through the Progressive Era, reformers and nativists proposed voter registration, literacy testing, extending the residency period required for voting, and the poll tax. Banfield and Wilson identified the same motivations with the city-manager plan later in the century: "Making local government 'businesslike' meant 'getting rid of politics,' which in turn meant curtailing the representation of low-status minorities. In its early years, the [council-manager] plan appealed to a good many people as a convenient means of putting the Catholics, the Irish, the Italians, the labor unions, and all other 'underdogs' in their places."[14]

Reformers recognized that machine politicians won votes not only by providing patronage employment, but also from the provision of rudimentary social services. The reform movement was divided, however, over the appropriate response. Social reformers and the most prominent women among municipal reformers argued for the professionalization of social services, while many structural reformers argued for shortening government's agenda. Jane Addams, for example, believed machine politics "would disappear once the city itself provided the services currently offered by the boss." Women's municipal activism embraced the tasks of public education, child welfare and juvenile guidance (especially for adolescents), charity, and public health ("municipal housekeeping"). When a committee of the National Municipal League wrote its municipal program, however, women were excluded from the committee and their concerns from the reform agenda. The program diagnosed municipal ills "as a problem of institutional structure and governmental machinery." This meant that the National Municipal League not only endorsed model political and administrative arrangements, but also a very limited sphere for local government.[15]

---

[13] [Philadelphia] *Evening Bulletin*, April 9, 1860.

[14] Banfield and Wilson, *City Politics*, 171.

[15] Helene Silverberg, "'A Government of Men': Gender, the City, and the Origins of Political Science," in *Gender and American Social Science: The Formative Years*, ed. Helene Silverberg (forthcoming, Princeton University Press). Silverberg highlights the different approaches of men and women by observing that women saw the importance of street cleaning in its public health consequences while men (in this case Columbia's William Munro) thought clean streets crucial because streets were "the arteries of the city; they carry the life

In the Progressive Era, municipal reformers in the nation's big cities only rarely prevailed against the strong partisan loyalties of machine supporters, not least because so many reformers were hostile to immigrants, who were a large portion of the electorate. By contrast, the municipal reform movement celebrated triumphs across the United States as small cities and towns adopted commission charters. The commission plan gained prominence once it was adopted for Galveston, Texas, after a hurricane destroyed that city. Galveston's successful comeback made the commission plan "the core of urban progressivism."[16] The National League of Municipalities endorsed the commission plan as its model city charter. Armed with the plan, with editorials, speakers, and advice from the National Municipal League, good government organizations in smaller cities across the country campaigned to reorganize local governments.

It is at this moment that the narrative of *Morning Glories* begins. Table 1-1 shows major charter revisions in seven southwestern cities. (A discussion of the choice of cases appears as the appendix.) In the narrative I present politics in southwestern cites in three periods. The first is from the first reform charter (usually a commission charter) to the adoption of city-manager government. The adoption of city-manager charters in most places initiates the period of big-city reform, which is concluded by the adoption of district elections for city council members. These "periods" are not altogether concurrent with major twentieth-century historical markers (say, World War I or the New Deal). Moreover, they are not concurrent across cities. Dallas, for example, may fairly be said to exhibit big-city reform politics from well before World War II until 1976; San Diego, from 1931 to 1988; while in Albuquerque big-city reform is more short-lived, from 1946 to 1974.

The first era of reform government in the Southwest begins shortly after the turn of the century. Chapter 2 sets the regional stage by describing the situation of the small cities in Texas, New Mexico, California, and Arizona, focusing on Houston, Austin, Albuquerque, Phoenix, and San Diego. Cities and towns in the Southwest shared a set of dilemmas and challenges, and chapter 2 presents these as well as efforts at city building at the turn of the century. The natural environments of their towns were not promising, the financial resources of locals were very limited, and prospects for growth were uncertain. The result was that local leaders organized to aggressively seek investment and settlers from

---

blood of urban commerce." The Municipal Program also "delineated the terrain for an autonomous, empirical discipline of political science," relegating social welfare concerns (and the women along with them) to sociology.

[16] Bradley R. Rice, "The Galveston Plan of City Government by Commission: The Birth of a Progressive Idea," *Southwestern Historical Quarterly* 78, no. 4 (April 1975): 366–408.

TABLE 1-1
Major Charter Changes in Southwestern Cities

	Commission Govt.	Mayor-Council	Manager	Mayor-Council	District Elections
Albuquerque	1917[a]	—	—	—	1974
Austin	1909	—	1924	—	—
Dallas	1907	—	1930	—	1976
Houston	1905	—	1942	1947	1979
Phoenix	1913[a]	—	1949	—	1982
San Antonio	1914	—	1951	—	1977
San Diego	1909	1915	1931	—	1988
San Jose	1915[a]	—	—	—	1978

Sources:
ALBUQUERQUE. 1917: Dorothy I. Cline and T. Philip Wolf, "Albuquerque: The End of the Reform Era," in Leonard E. Goodall, ed., *Urban Politics in the Southwest* (Tempe: Arizona State University Press, 1967), 10.   1974: Paul L. Hain, F. Chris Garcia, and Judd Conway, "From Council-Manager to Mayor-Council: The Case of Albuquerque," *Nation's Cities* (October 1975): 10–12.
AUSTIN. Harold A. Stone, Don K. Price, and Kathryn H. Stone, *City Manager Government in Nine Cities* (Chicago: Public Administration Service, 1950), 410.
DALLAS. 1907, 1930: Stone et al., *City-Manager Government*, 262.   1976: Arnold A. Fleischmann, "The Change to District Elections in Dallas," typescript in the Supplementary Information of the Austin City Charter Revision Commission, March 7, 1984.
HOUSTON. Robert D. Thomas and Richard W. Murray, *Progrowth Politics: Change and Governance in Houston* (Berkeley: IGS Press, 1991), 180 (1905), 184 (1942), 185 (1947), 188 (1979).
PHOENIX. 1913, 1949: Paul Kelso, *A Decade of Council-Manager Government in Phoenix, Arizona* (Tuscon: University of Arizona Press, 1960), 17.   1982: *Arizona Republic*, December 2, 1982, X-3.
SAN ANTONIO. John A. Booth and David R. Johnson, "Power and Progress in San Antonio Politics, 1836–1970," in David R. Johnson, John A. Booth, and Richard J. Harris, *The Politics of San Antonio: Community, Progress, and Power* (Lincoln: University of Nebraska Press, 1983), 14 (1914), 22 (1951), 25 (1977).
SAN DIEGO. 1909, 1915, 1931: Stone et al., *City Manager Government*, 134.   1988: Dean Schloyer, "Ethnic Politics in a Sunbelt City: The Case of San Diego" (M.A. thesis, University of California, San Diego, 1993), 39.
SAN JOSE. Philip J. Trounstine and Terry Christensen, *Movers and Shakers: The Study of Community Power* (New York: St. Martin's Press, 1982), 83 (1915), 105 (1978).
[a] These charters also provided for city managers.

elsewhere. Chapter 3 describes local campaigns for municipal reform. Here, in a political and social setting entirely different than the nation's big cities, reformers were very successful. The small towns and cities of the southwest had no entrenched political machines, nor did their citizens demonstrate secure partisan attachments. Reform's appeal lay in its promise to shape government to finance and administer survival and growth. Assisted by the National Municipal League, reform swept the cities of the Southwest as it won supporters in small cities across the country (see table 1-1). The Progressive Era victories of reform advocates in the Southwest mark the beginning of a common political history for the region's cities and towns.

Once reform charters were in place, they proved difficult to bring to life. Chapter 4 traces local politics in the interwar period. In the years between the First and Second World Wars, most often reform government de jure was factionalized (San Diego, Phoenix) or personal, machine-style politics (Austin, Albuquerque, Houston) de facto. Much of reform's agenda was accomplished nevertheless: taxes were low and so was participation, party organizations atrophied, growth strategies were realized. Even so, recurrent efforts at reform were a leitmotif of local politics in the 1920s, 1930s, and early 1940s. San Diego (1931), Austin (1926), and Dallas (1931) abandoned their commission governments in favor of city-manager charters.

Other southwestern cities followed suit between 1945 and 1955. Chapter 5 portrays the refoundings of southwestern cities at midcentury, reviewing shifts to the manager plan in San Diego, Austin, Dallas, and Phoenix. Houston was an exception to the trend, adopting but then rejecting city-manager government; its changes are also traced in chapter 5. The *National Municipal Review* celebrated the advance of the city-manager plan, reporting increasing numbers of manager charter adoptions from 1945 through 1953. New charters were only a part of changing politics in this decade. Everywhere local elites organized anew and were active in the pursuit of postwar growth strategies.

In the years that followed, local leaders saw all the wishes of reformers come true. Chapters 6 and 7 provide a portrait of local politics and government in the 1950s and early 1960s. These years, and in some cities another ten or twenty years in addition, were the heyday of big-city reform.

Big-city reform was characterized by very low participation and little competition at the polls as incumbents (often sponsored by nonpartisan slating groups) could as confidently count on reelection as any machine politician. In the postwar period, southwestern cities grew at a daunting pace; city governments labored to meet pent-up demands for housing, schools, and public services, as well as to recruit industries to stave off postwar recession. The success of these efforts led to a remarkable public consensus about politics and government. Residents of Anglo, middle-class neighborhoods were both good government's beneficiaries and its strongest supporters.

A close examination of elections even at the apogee of big-city reform reveals weaknesses in popular support. Chapter 8 describes challenges to big-city reform in the two decades after 1965. As in cities elsewhere, the civil rights movement and the provocations of federal interventions changed the direction of local politics. There were in addition the stresses of unchallenged growth. The political concessions of the 1960s and early 1970s proved unequal to demands of disaffected constituents, and the succeeding generation sought to change the rules of local politics once again. Chapter 8 describes this most recent reorganization of local politics as citywide elections to city councils were replaced by district elections.

Explaining the Course of Reform

The political history of southwestern cities raises a series of analytic and historical puzzles: Why were municipal reformers so successful in the southwest? How can the progress of reform and the governments of southwestern cities be placed in the larger dynamics of American history? How did the institutional arrangements created by reformers shape local politics and government, policy and opposition? If reformers succeeded in loosening the ties between politicians and their constituents, how did reform regimes organize consent?

The broad outlines of the course of reform may be explained by understanding how the institutions reformers put in place created a characteristic political community, understanding how and why region mattered, and recognizing that race both informed the design of reform politics and became the means of its undoing. Because considerations of rules, region, and race displace familiar emphases on political culture and urban growth, this section concludes with discussions of the political culture of reform and growth regimes in the Southwest.

Institutions

The central analytic story of *Morning Glories* involves not growth, region, or political culture (although attention is paid to each of these), but political institutions. Institutions have regained prominence among quite different sorts of studies of politics. The renewed attention to institutions represents dissatisfaction with approaches that understand politics as a sum of behavioral parts, as epiphenomenal to social change, or as the empirical manifestation of values or ideals.

A variety of "new" institutionalisms have called attention to the causal role of government and politics. The "new institutionalism" proposed by March and Olsen was "simply an argument that the organization of political life makes a difference," "an empirically based prejudice." March and Olsen suggested political analysis begin with a recognition of the causal role of political institutions, arguing that institutional arrangements shape strategies, choices, and even, perhaps, identities for participants.[17]

March and Olsen's argument amplified the case, already well under way, for "Bringing the State Back In." Theda Skocpol, and later Steve Skowronek and other students of American political development developed historical institutionalist perspectives on politics.[18] Yet another impetus to bringing the state back in was the Marxist recognition of the "relative autonomy of the state." Like both March and Olsen and the historical institutionalists, Marxists stepped away from social or structural determinism and increased their attention to the political causes of particular outcomes, the role of "statecraft," and the differences in politics, parties, and policies of advanced capitalist countries.[19] Finally, social-choice theorists' project is to build the "positive theory of institutions." For example, beginning with the observation that how preferences are aggregated shapes collective outcomes, social-choice theorists have studied rules, agendas, voting procedures, and the like as determinant of policies and politics.[20]

The common ground of these approaches is considerably more striking than their differences. The insights of the new institutionalisms are extremely useful in the study of city politics. And conversely, because the organization of local government varies quite a bit and changes more frequently than national and state institutions, city politics provides an excellent object of study for those interested in institutions. Although

[17] James G. March and Johan P. Olsen, "The New Institutionalism: Organizational Factors in Political Life," *American Political Science Review* 78, no. 3 (September 1984): 734–49. Thus, for example, preferences might not be exogenous to politics, but rather, created by political activity or political institutions. The authors called this the "new" institutionalism to signal their recognition that attention to institutions has a long intellectual history.

[18] Among other writings, see Theda Skocpol, "Bringing the State Back In: Strategies of Analysis in Current Research," in *Bringing the State Back In*, ed. Peter B. Evans, Dietrich Rueschemeyer, and Theda Skocpol (New York: Cambridge University Press, 1985), 3–30; Stephen Skowronek, *Building a New American State: The Expansion of National Administrative Capacities, 1877–1920* (New York: Cambridge Unviersity Press, 1982); and "Institutionalism: Ideas, Structures, Methods" (panel discussion, annual meeting of the Social Science History Association, Baltimore, November 1993, typescript), 40.

[19] The initial structuralist argument for the relative autonomy of the state is found in Louis Althusser, *Reading Capital* (London: New Left Books, 1970); and Nicos Poulantzas, *Political Power and Social Classes* (London: New Left Books 1973). Adam Przeworski and John Sprague wrote about political participation from this point of view, examining the logic, for socialist or communist working classes, of engaging in electoral politics.

[20] See for example, William H. Riker, *Liberalism against Populism* (Prospect Heights: Waveland Press, 1982).

most recent students of American political development have focused on administrative institutions or legislatures, my own interest is in popular and electoral arrangements.

Institutional approaches inform the arguments of *Morning Glories*. Although most students of American political development have presented analyses of administrative or legislative institutions, my own emphasis is on the arrangements of politics and elections. Political institutions are understood here as "staging grounds" or "rules of the game" for political action.[21] The analytic effort is to understand how the rules influence both the strategies and tactics of the players, and styles of governance. The choice of citywide or district elections may serve as an example. The requisites of winning elections citywide influence the strategies of both incumbents and opponents, encouraging them to form alliances to win sufficient votes. By contrast, the likely form of opposition in cities with district elections is an insurgent candidacy in a particular ward.

The same empirical example (election to city councils under various rules) provides evidence about the importance of rules determining how preferences are aggregated. The same votes cast in each system might well result in different winners to seats on the city council, a rules issue that has been the focus of sustained civil rights activity.

Rules also determine who may enter political life, and in particular, who may vote. Over the course of U.S. history the rules governing suffrage have varied dramatically, from the dismantling of property requirements for Anglo men or the enfranchisement of aliens in midwestern states in the nineteenth century, to the exclusion of people of color, women, or the propertyless from all or some elections. Fights over rules governing enfranchisement have been viewed as posing very high stakes for most of our history, and for good reasons. Rules governing enfranchisement are also an important part of the history of big-city reform.[22]

An additional consideration is the general configuration of institutions in local politics. The presence or absence of parties, the roles of county government, administrative organizations, and public authorities struc-

[21] Some institutionalists have appropriated a sociological understanding of institutions. Skocpol, for example, says "institutions for me are sorts of relationships that persist. . . . [Institutions] have shared meanings and relatively stable bundles of resources attached to them." I mean by institutions legal or organizational arrangements. The sociology definition seems unsatisfying for two quite different reasons. First, it fails to distinguish between customs (a wake, a baby shower, or a consensus) and governmentally sanctioned events (marriage, a birth certificate, a Supreme Court ruling). Second, because society's more formal institutions (its legal rules and large institutions) may not embrace "shared meanings." For example, one citizen's good government may be another's racial privilege. Skocpol's remarks are from "Institutionalism," 59.

[22] E. E. Schattschneider, *The Semi-Sovereign People: A Realist's View of Democracy in America* (New York: Holt, Rinehart, and Winston, 1960).

ture political life. The existence of these institutions creates more or less accessible, and more or less important, targets for political activity; their presence advantages some constituencies and disadvantages others.

Some authors have observed that institutional approaches tend to present the coherent functioning of the political order to the exclusion of explanations of change.[23] Perhaps because the institutional arrangements of local politics change frequently, it is more apparent in the study of city politics that while communities inherit sets of rules that organize political life, residents simultaneously argue, organize, vote, protest, fight, and compromise over the rules. If they inherit one set of institutions, another (more or less different in different generations) will be their legacy. It hardly follows, then, that an institutional approach presupposes a focus on stability. Rather, attention to institutions may simply be another way to think about the insight that people make history, but not under conditions of their own choosing.

In writing about local government, as in writing about other institutions, the "very fact that institutions can shape behavior and outcomes makes it necessary to explain how they are created and sustained by rational actors who understand their importance."[24] Municipal reformers, themselves very interested in political institutions, saw themselves and their project in just this way. Municipal reformers and political scientists together carved out the shared intellectual territory of municipal institutions at the turn of the century.[25] Just as the twentieth century disciplines

[23] Karen Orren and Stephen Skowronek, for example, argue: "Each framework has cast institutions as the pillars of order and regularity in politics; institutions are seen to integrate the actions of the polity, to coordinate its interests, and to make it cohere as an organized system. Notwithstanding very real differences in approach, institutional politics has consistently been portrayed as normal politics, politics-as-usual, a politics in equilibrium. These images leave the study of institutions cut off from the study of change. . . . The dynamics of the polity are taken to be essentially homeostatic, resolving exogenous disruptions in new institutional settlements" ("Institutionalism," 40). By contrast, I see continuous conflict and renegotiation about the rules of politics.

[24] Morris Fiorina, commentary at "Institutionalism," 71.

[25] For an account of the joint efforts of municipal reformers and political scientists, see Silverberg, "Government of Men." Since Melvin Holli wrote *Reform in Detroit*, students of city politics have distinguished between "social" and "structural" reformers. Social reformers, like Hazen Pingree, opposed machine politics because it was fundamentally corrupt, delivering little to those who most ardently supported it. Pingree and other social reformers hoped to put municipal government in the service of alleviating the inequities of urban life through, among other things, municipal ownership of utilities, housing code enforcement, and public health measures. Structural reformers focused on changing the government organization and administration and the rules of local politics. As Melvin G. Holli recognized, the structural reform agenda also included social goals, since structural reformers aimed to write the rules to decrease the influence of many groups in local politics. It is the structural reformers whose efforts and progress are charted in *Morning Glories*.

of political science and public administration were created, and intent on rearranging the administrative and political life of the nation's cities, municipal reformers offered detailed analyses of the workings of local political institutions. Reformers' concerns embraced both the concerns of contemporary new institutionalists who study organizations, and the interests of those whose interest is in how political rules influence the aggregation of political preferences.

Municipal reformers were prolific in the invention of public organizations and administrative arrangements. The National Municipal League and the Short Ballot Organization were just the beginning. Municipal reformers organized municipal research bureaus and nonpartisan slating groups; campaigned for civil service, commission government, and the city manager; and promoted city planning, the authority, autonomous commission, and special districts to further economic development (of which the best known southwestern examples are the Los Angeles Department of Water and Power and the city's Harbor Commission; the Port of New York Authority shares their progressive origin).

Reformers were also assiduous in arranging the rules of government and elections. Reformers' aims of loosening the ties of politicians and their constituents on one hand, and limiting the number of constituents on the other, informed their designs. To those ends reformers endorsed nonpartisanship, citywide and nonconcurrent elections, selection of the mayor by the city council, and a variety of barriers to registration and voting. The twentieth-century reformer Richard S. Childs counseled the importance of "wieldy constituencies" for the success of municipal reform.[26] Leaders of big-city reform governments understood the principle well. Reform governance worked in part by selectively mobilizing "wieldy" constituencies from the unwieldy societies of their metropolitan settings.

Reform designs worked much as reformers intended. Reform regimes governed a political life of low participation and little public dissent. Thus the solution to the consent problem was, in the first instance, the exclusion of most urban residents from the political system. As a result, the characteristic political community of reform government was relatively small, affluent, and Anglo. Reform governments did not reflect, in their personnel or their policies, the divisions and preferences of their diverse big cities. Reformers wrote the rules to win the game of local politics; their great accomplishment was to create political communities

---

The distinction between social and structural reform is found in Holli, *Reform in Detroit: Hazen S. Pingree and Urban Politics* (New York: Oxford University Press, 1969), chap. 8.

[26] Richard S. Childs, *The First Fifty Years of the Council-Manager Plan of Municipal Government* (New York: American Book–Stratford Press, 1965), 85.

that looked like Winnetka in social settings that were much larger and more diverse.

City and Region

The political life of cities is shaped by their lack of autonomy from their political and economic environments. City governments are dependent on the state governments of which they are, legally, the creatures, and local politics bears the marks of federal policies and politics; city governments thrive and decline with local economies, as connected to the national and even international economy as local governments are to higher governments.

The limited capacity of local governments as well as the potential interventions of state and national governments encourage local activists to pursue their goals in state and national arenas. Early in the century town leaders petitioned territorial and state governments for prisons, schools, or siting of the capital; in the same years town representatives sought railroad connections, federal assistance for flood control, harbor improvement, or other large-scale projects, and negotiated with national companies for improved water, electricity, or public transportation. Later, chambers of commerce sought federal defense spending, local governments pursued programmatic grants, and some citizens tried to change local education, government hiring, or the organization of local government itself by recourse to federal courts. Through these activities, local politics is tied to national politics and the larger economy.

The permeability of local politics also lends significance to region. I began this study with the observation that cities in states from Texas and Oklahoma west to the Pacific Ocean shared a pattern of political development. I was hardly the first to notice the regional cast to city politics in the United States. Region appears repeatedly in studies of cities. Raymond Wolfinger and John Osgood Field, for example, found that "one can do a much better job of predicting a city's political forms by knowing what part of the country it is in than by knowing anything about the composition of the population."[27]

There has been little agreement, however, about why region mattered. Some students of the United States have relied on cultural explanations for regional phenomena. Robert Lineberry and Edmund Fowler, for example, argued that "geographical subdivisions are relevant subjects of political inquiry only because they are differentiated on the basis of atti-

[27] "Political Ethos and the Structure of City Government," *American Political Science Review* 60, no. 1 (June 1966): 306–26. Wolfinger and Field attributed regional differences to the institutions "fashionable" at the time southwestern cities were politically organized.

tudinal or socioeconomic variables." A similar premise underlay Kirk-patrick Sale's discussion of sunbelt politics. Accounting for the right wing character of sunbelt politics, Sale argued that at "bottom is probably the religious fundamentalism of . . . the area . . ."[28]

More recently regions have been understood by attention to histori-cally specific political and economic relationships. To explain progressive successes in the West, Martin Shefter argued that the region had a greater "regional receptivity to reform" than the Northeast because the third party system was not well established in the West.[29] For their part, mu-nicipal reformers were surely advantaged by the absence of strong party organizations; weak opposition eased the way for the passage of reform charters.

Students of economic development have understood region as a rela-tional concept. Beginning with students of "underdevelopment," and fully elaborated by Immanuel Wallerstein, geographical areas were dis-tinguished by their relation to the world economy, and particularly the timing of their initial contacts with world trade.[30] Richard Bensel em-ployed a similar understanding to the study of regions in American poli-tics.[31] Along these lines, I recognize the Southwest's late entry into the national economy, and the absence of sufficient local capital to pursue economic development, as key features of the region.

I propose that "region" is usefully understood as a *historically strate-gic location*. Citizens of the Southwest were latecomers to both economic development and national politics. Although regional differences con-tinue to influence city politics in the United States, it is early in the cen-tury that strategic location of the Southwest most profoundly shaped the pattern of municipal political life.

Historically, strategic location denotes three things in this study. First,

[28] Robert Lineberry and Edmund Fowler, "Reformism and Public Policies in American Cities," *American Political Science Review* 61, no. 3 (September 1967): 701–16. Kirkpat-rick Sale, *Power Shift*, 159.

[29] Martin Shefter, "Regional Receptivity to Reform: Legacy of the Progressive Era" *Po-litical Science Quarterly* 98, no. 3 (Fall 1983): 459–83. Shefter did not include the south in his essay, thereby omitting two states of what I have termed the Southwest, Oklahoma and Texas. In addition, because of their late admission to the union, Shefter omitted New Mex-ico, Arizona, and Utah.

[30] Immanuel Wallerstein, *The Modern World System* (New York: Academic Press, 1974).

[31] Richard Franklin Bensel, *Sectionalism and American Political Development, 1880–1980* (Madison: University of Wisconsin Press, 1984). Bensel's operationalization has the problem that "regions" are not contiguous, which seems counterintuitive (if intellectually justifiable). Similarly, in *The New Urban America* (Chapel Hill: University of North Caro-lina, 1987), Carl Abbot defined a "sunbelt" of shared developmental characteristics that was not contiguous.

it matters in many ways that this story opens in 1900 rather than, say, 1815, when the cities of Richard Wade's *Urban Frontier* were beginning to thrive. The shape of the national economy, characteristic occupations, the reach of the federal government—all were different than eight decades before. Thus the importance of "history" here is not that a longer view expands the number of cases (as, say, of congressional elections or presidential administrations, or even municipal charter revisions), but rather that the world in 1900 is very different than in 1815, in ways that turn out to be important for city politics. Quite simply, "when" matters. Second, the Southwest was capital-poor. Third, the Southwest (with the exception of Texas) was not so closely tied to the party system as the rest of the nation. Each of these aspects of region had enduring effects on local politics.

In 1900 "strategic location" had obvious concrete referents. More fully explored in Chapters 2 and 3, the effects of strategic location may be anticipated here. The absence of capital was not simply a matter of economic theory. Citizens of southwestern towns had no illusions of living in Adam Smith's universe; here the conscientious pursuit of individual self-interest would not be assisted by the unseen hand. Rather, collective action was required for individual and collective well-being. The early, persistent, and aggressive organization of business leaders gave local politics much of its distinctive character not only in the Progressive Era but also for decades to come.

The absence of strong party organizations paved the way for the adoption of reform city charters, especially nonpartisanship, and for the writing of exclusionary rules. Without party organizations to defend them, the targets of political exclusion were more vulnerable in the Southwest than their counterparts (the eugenically undesirable southern and eastern Europeans) in the Northeast and Midwest. The result was that in the Southwest reformers succeeded in legislating and enforcing more restrictive rules for voting, and reform governments were as a consequence freed from a more equitable distribution of services and collective goods that more, and more partisan, participation might have brought about.

Race

In the preface to the second edition of *Harlem, the Making of a Ghetto*, Gilbert Osofsky wrote, "No perception of the American past is accurate which insists on underemphasizing the special factors of color consciousness, color caste, and racism."[32] The history of municipal reform is no

[32] Gilbert Osofsky, *Harlem, the Making of a Ghetto: Negro New York, 1890–1930* (New York: Harper & Row, 1971), xiii.

exception. Race figured in the motivations of reformers, in the rules they wrote, in the policies they pursued. Race, as variously understood in different generations, was at times a leitmotif and at other times a dominant theme among the motivations of municipal reformers.

The founders of western states and cities were not oblivious to the region's diversity. Race informed both the constitutions of the states and the political rules local leaders wrote for cities. The exclusion of Native Americans from voting was a presupposition of politics everywhere. Almaguer has recently written about the "racial fault lines" structuring California's social and political life in the nineteenth century.[33] California's population was very racially heterogeneous, including Chinese, Japanese, Mexican, African, and Native Americans. Of these, only Mexican-Americans were classed as "white" and so granted political privileges (and these were tenuous). Provisions for the segregation of African-Americans were written into the first Arizona constitution in 1912. In Texas racial segregation was an organizing principle of social life and urban planning; disfranchisement of African-Americans and Mexican-Americans the goal of much legislation limiting access to the ballot; the white primary the foundation of one-party politics.[34]

Racial considerations were also inscribed in local government's structure and activities. Every city policy—hiring of municipal employees, planning and annexation, housing, utilities, and education—reinforced racial division and hierarchy. Although the Texas cities share a great deal with the other cities in this study, consideration of the Texas cities provides evidence that cities in states of the former Confederacy and cities in the Southwest are somewhat different places. It is race that makes the difference. In the Texas cities, with larger populations of color and city governments determined to manage them, political life throughout the century is inescapably charged with conflicts about race. Race relations were at the center of public life and politics in every decade: the arrangements and maintenance of segregation; the appearance of the Ku Klux Klan; the use of the white primary and persistent mobilization against it; issues of police misconduct, public employment, school quality, public libraries, the availability of parks—each of these was on the political agenda and in the press. By contrast, although race is critical to understanding the history and organization of municipal reform, and central to the policies of big-city reform, west of Texas city governments

---

[33] Tomas Almaguer, *Racial Fault Lines: The Historical Origins of White Supremacy in California* (Berkeley: University of California Press, 1994).

[34] See, for example, V. O. Key, Jr., *Southern Politics in State and Nation* (1949; New York: Vintage, 1962), chap. 12, "Texas: A Politics of Economics," and chaps. 27–28 on the poll tax.

spent much less energy in racial management. Moreover, the racial challenges and tensions of southwestern cities were largely obscured from public view. Indeed, for the first half of this century, Anglo, middle-class citizens in Phoenix, San Diego, or even Albuquerque could read the papers, vote, and be active in local civic life almost oblivious to nearby Hispanic and African-American neighborhoods. This was surely not the case for urban leaders, who avoided annexing poor communities of color and were the audience (not to say the targets) of community protests about schools, police, municipal employment, and municipal services. As this list suggests, across regional differences in politics and racial composition, there was a common political agenda for equal services, rights, and respect.

Nothing could be more misleading than the view that the civil rights activism of the 1960s and the lawsuits of the 1970s were, as sometimes presented, a sudden assertiveness of the part of communities long quiescent. Rather, resistance, assertion, and organization are continuous across this century.[35] Whether one listed the many lawsuits in every state claiming constitutional violations or the many letters requesting and demanding better control of local police, or admission to school, or public employment, or a police officer or newspaper reporter of color—any of these is testimony to the tension and agitation in social life that accompanied racism, discrimination, and inequality. Even the purchase of a minority newspaper, like the *Arizona Sun* or the *Houston Defender*, was support of a voice criticizing the established order. In light of the continuous community activity seeking equality, it is not surprising that once the federal government abandoned the great compromise of 1877, race became the means by which reform regimes were undone. Righting racial inequities inscribed in the rules could hardly take place without changing the rules. The federal intervention that required changing the rules was not the intervention of an outside political force, but rather the eventual result of these many small struggles. Race, of course, remains in the rules, and issues of race and its appropriate relation to political institutions remain contentious.

Political Culture

Placing region, institutions, and race at the center of an analysis of municipal reform and southwestern city politics displaces familiar arguments about political culture. Since Richard Hofstadter wrote *The Age of*

---

[35] For a similar argument, see Robin D. G. Kelley, "We Are Not What We Seem: Rethinking Black Working Class Opposition in the Jim Crow South," *Journal of American History* 80, no. 1 (June 1993): 75–112.

Reform, municipal reform has been associated with the middle class and its discontents. Hofstadter wrote that the mugwump, squeezed between the many of enormous immigrant populations and the few of ostentatious wealth, organized to take over municipal government for themselves. "It would be hard to imagine," wrote Hofstadter, "types of political culture more alien to each other than those of the Yankee reformer and the peasant immigrant."[36] Elaborating upon this thought, Edward Banfield and James Q. Wilson offered the "political ethos" theory of local political institutions. "Private-regarding" immigrant/working-class values, they argued, supported the creation of political machines, while "public-regarding" Protestant/middle-class values promoted reform regimes.[37]

Important reservations have been raised about this argument. Students of city politics who compared the ethnic or class composition of cities and towns with their form of government found little of the predicted association. Others suggested the argument was circular: How did we know the values of immigrant or middle-class citizens? By how they cast their votes. Why did they vote that way? Because of their values. Writing well before social historians investigated the values and political sentiments of ordinary citizens, Banfield and Wilson had little empirical or historical evidence for either the private-regarding or the public-regarding ethos. Worse, their characterization of the immigrant/working-class machine ethos seemed pejorative and derogatory, while the characterization of the WASP/middle-class reform ethos seemed simply to take reformers at their flattering and self-serving word.[38]

For all of these reasons, ethos theory does not serve in this book as the analytic key to municipal reform. I do, however, reserve a place for political culture. There are babies in the bath water of ethos theory, and they

---

[36] Richard Hofstadter, *The Age of Reform* (New York, Vintage, 1955), 182. Hofstadter aside, historians have generally argued that business leaders were the most prominent advocates of municipal reform. See Samuel P. Hays, "The Politics of Municipal Reform in the Progressive Era," *Pacific Northwest Quarterly* (October 1961): 157–69; James Weinstein, *The Corporate Ideal in the Liberal State, 1900–1918* (Boston: Beacon, 1968), chap. 4, and Amy Bridges, "Another Look at Plutocracy and Politics in Antebellum New York City," *Political Science Quarterly* 97, no. 1 (1982): 57–71.

[37] Banfield and Wilson, *City Politics*, chaps. 9, 11.

[38] Students of culture might have criticized Hofstadter, Banfield, and Wilson for a naive understanding of the relation between values and behavior. Ann Swidler has argued that such a naive understanding "assumes that culture shapes action by applying ultimate ends or values toward which action is directed, thus making values the central causal element of culture." Yet, Swidler argues, empirical studies consistently refute this idea (as, for example, cross cultural studies of the "protestant ethic" demonstrate). Ann Swidler, "Culture in Action: Symbols and Strategies" *American Sociological Review* 51, no. 2 (April 1986): 273–86, quote is 273; on empirical problems with the protestant ethic, 275–76.

should not be thrown out. Even a passing glance at the personae, policies, and rhetoric of local governments suggests that machine and reform politics are associated with very different values. These values and the practices they name constitute political culture.

Although machine politics and big-city reform are best characterized by their institutional arrangements, neither machine nor reform regimes are wholly understood by looking only at political institutions. Political regimes (as Banfield, Wilson, and Hofstadter emphasized) also exhibit characteristic political cultures. The narrative and argument presented in *Morning Glories* make it possible to clarify the relationships among the middle class, reform values, and political culture of big-city reform.

Values first. Partisan bosses and municipal reformers offered very different views of government and its proper functions. C. K. Yearly describes a confrontation in Baltimore in 1889 that succinctly relates the differences between the major antagonists of city politics:

> Under attack . . . from a taxpayers' association for padded payrolls and "exorbitant" wages in the street-cleaning department . . . Mayor Latrobe reminded his critics that government not only was *not* a business but that the city's hiring policies were a way of helping these men and their families.[39]

As the Baltimore exchange suggests, the argument between bosses and reformers often resembled the argument between New Deal Democrats and Hoover Republicans, the former arguing government should do more and the latter arguing it should do less. In the rhetoric of machine politicians, the working citizen and community diversity played prominent roles; in the rhetoric of the good-government advocate, the "good of the whole" stood in place of diversity or class solidarity. More directly, the list of functions of the governments of big northeastern cities in the middle of the twentieth century (all descendants of political machines) is much longer than the list of functions of big-city reform governments in 1960.

The different values promoted by machine and reform leaders, in conjunction with their very different styles of politics, resulted in quite different political cultures. Ann Swidler has proposed understanding culture as a "tool kit" of traditions, habits, and symbols for organizing behavior, including the "publicly available symbolic forms through which people experience and express meaning." Culture's causal significance lies "not in defining ends of action, but in providing cultural components that are used to construct strategies of action." I propose that *political* culture be understood as the practices, habits, and popular expectations of govern-

---

[39] C. K. Yearly, *The Money Machines* (Albany: State University of New York Press, 1970), 149.

ment and politics, as well as the words, values, and moralities ("publicly
available symbolic forms") generally available for understanding and
evaluating politics.

Municipal reformers not only wrote the rules to win the game of local
politics, they also enjoyed a rhetorical monopoly, a monopoly of public
discourse in southwestern cities. By "public discourse" I mean discourse
"heard" by all citizens. Reformers and their supporters owned the mass
media and, in the absence of well-organized opposition that could force
public debate, the media excluded opposition voices. There were African-
American, Spanish, and labor newspapers in the Southwest, often oppo-
sitional, but their readership was small and surely confined to a target
audience. Thus, although there were alternative voices in local politics,
they were not heard beyond their restricted audiences.

The reader will find the rhetoric of reform throughout the book, chron-
icles of elections and debates over the rules. The function of this public
discourse was didactic, explaining government, politics, and the common
good. As a consequence, public discourse made moral and cognitive contributions to the strength of reform governments. At the same time, the
narrowness of public discourse made it extremely difficult for the most
energetic critics of local government—people of color—to make claims
that majority constituents recognized as legitimate, and so to find allies,
form coalitions, and participate successfully in local politics. Indeed,
until well after the Second World War, most Anglo citizens were likely
ignorant of their complaints. We may look to New York's ethnically balanced tickets or to Chicago for contrary examples. In Chicago the events
surrounding the election of Harold Washington were surely tortuous and
filled with conflict. Nevertheless, African-Americans in Chicago could—
since descriptive representation, majority rule, and ethnic succession
were all understood rules of the game—make the claim, "It's our turn."
Because in reform regimes there were turns neither in principle nor in
fact, reform rhetoric made it difficult to find allies, just as reform rules
made descriptive representation impossible.

As this discussion suggests, the values politicians voiced were given
meaning in the practice of local government. After each electoral victory,
promise is made practice in political institutions, electoral arrangements,
policy processes, and political outcomes of all sorts. This is why political
ethos does not wither away, either in Chicago a generation after the death
of Richard J. Daley or in the Southwest a generation after the organizing
rules of reform regimes were dismantled.

What of class? There is overwhelming evidence about the class difference in sources of support for machine and reform government. Everywhere, machine politicians claimed strong support from working-class
voters, while municipal reformers could count on middle-class voters. In

fights over the adoption of reform charters, labor unions and working-class voters almost always opposed municipal reform,[40] while middle-class and affluent voters usually supported it.

In the Southwest, too, the middle class has been at the center of municipal reform politics. Its role was not to design reform institutions, or organize campaigns to secure them. Rather, the Anglo middle class has been the core constituency of local politics. There were two reasons for this. For one, southwestern cities have been, since the Second World War, somewhat more affluent than the machine descendants of the Northeast and Midwest. No government that alienated affluent Anglo voters (as Daley did their counterparts in Chicago) could survive. Second, the electoral arrangements and political boundaries of reform cities were designed to exclude poor and working-class voters, creating an electorate more middle class than its surrounding community.

From the perspective of the leaders of big-city reform, the middle class was an appealing constituency because its wish list was short. This made it possible to secure their support while pursuing growth and annexation policies that required substantial public subsidy. Reform governments in the suburbs, like Winnetka, were constituted somewhat differently. There high turnout rather than low participation was characteristic.[41] In both suburban and southwestern settings, the preponderantly middle-class electorate was shielded by its homogeneity from demands for redistribution.

Although Hofstadter, Banfield, and Wilson were correct in describing the class character of municipal reform's supporters, there is little evidence they correctly identified the culture and motives of the middle class. The middle-class supporter of reform was imagined to act on "public-regarding" values. *Morning Glories* reveals a certain like-mindedness among the leaders of big-city reform and their middle-class supporters. Opposed to patronage and party politics, supportive of professionalism and allegedly politically neutral scientific approaches to planning and administration, insistent on scrupulously honest administration. Big-city reform governments delivered the goods of urban public life efficiently and well to these constituents. Not the least of these public goods was the assistance to developers who designed communities for

[40] I have discussed elsewhere the relationship between the nineteenth-century working classes and the origins of machine government. *A City in the Republic: Antebellum New York and the Origins of Machine Politics* (New York: Cambridge University Press, 1984), especially chap. 6, and "Becoming American: The Working Classes of the United States before the Civil War," in *Working Class Formation: Patterns in Nineteenth Century United States and Europe*, ed. Aristide Zolberg and Ira Katznelson (Princeton: Princeton University Press, 1986), 157–96.

[41] Robert C. Wood, *Suburbia*, 178.

affluent and middle-class homeowners. There is no evidence of selfless-
ness here. For example, there was opposition everywhere to providing
low-income housing. In the Southwest, affluent and middle-class voters
supported big-city reform when it granted them their wish list and organized to change the rules when it failed to do so.[42]

Growth

Commencing with the publication of Harvey Molotch's "The City as a
Growth Machine" in 1976[43], and reinforced by the appearance of Paul
Peterson's *City Limits*[44], economic growth has been a central focus of the
study of city politics. Growth-centered studies agree that competition
among cities places a premium on the pursuit of economic growth by
local leaders. Peterson argues that, recognizing the requirements of their
situation, the best mayors will work as "able servants" of growth interests (others, less perceptive, will only accede to be "willing slaves"). Ac-
cording to Peterson, because economic growth is a public good, there is a
collective stake in success and widespread popular support for the pursuit of growth strategies.

Molotch argues that the pursuit of growth, even when successful, is
often a mixed bag for cities. Sometimes the costs to government outweigh
the benefit to the local economy; economic development may have negative consequences for the natural environment; growth strategies may
create opportunities for one occupational group at the expense of another. The result is that the pursuit of growth has become increasingly
contentious. The emergence of no growth and slow growth movements
testifies to the decline of uncritical support for economic growth.

[42] For a similar characterization of middle-class political values in California, see Gary J.
Miller, *Cities by Contract: The Politics of Municipal Incorporation* (Cambridge: MIT Press,
1981).

[43] Harvey L. Molotch, "The City as a Growth Machine: Towards a Political Economy of
Place," *American Journal of Sociology* 82 (1976): 309–33, and John R. Logan and Harvey
L. Molotch, *Urban Fortunes: The Political Economy of Place* (Berkeley: University of Cali-
fornia, 1987).

[44] Paul Peterson, *City Limits* (Chicago: University of Chicago Press, 1981). Like many
arguments, Peterson's seems most sensible when stated least ideologically. Thus Peterson
(and others) might have done better to distinguish between *redevelopment*, with its inevitable (in the short run) zero-sum conflicts over space, and development or economic growth
broadly understood. Peterson's argument that urban renewal only appeared conflictual because it coincided with the civil rights movement is just plain silly; Mollenkopf's argument
that urban renewal fueled the civil rights movement in the North is a more sensible reading
of the evidence. John H. Mollenkopf, "The Post-War Politics of Urban Development" in
Marxism and the Metropolis, ed. William Tabb and Larry Sawers (New York: Oxford
University Press, 1978), 117–52.

Molotch also argued that there are specific constituencies that benefit dramatically from growth projects, whether the project in question is refurbishing downtown, recruiting industry, or securing federal contracts. These interests are the most prominent members of urban growth coalitions: businesses with specific stakes in downtown (especially downtown real estate), local media, real estate and transportation interests, construction trades, major employers, and bankers. Despite the costs of their pursuits to some neighborhoods and to local governments, the overwhelming political resources of the "growth machine" assure their ascendancy in policy formation.[45]

The focus on growth has provided key insights to the study of city politics. That competition among cities is a premise of city politics lent substance to the observation that the economic boundaries of cities are permeable; the same premise points to limits both of urban possibilities and of urban autonomy. Yet despite the elaborate theoretical dressing of both *City Limits* and *Urban Fortunes*, the extent to which growth strategies are consensual or provoke conflict, and how well growth serves the common good, or only the interests of the growth machine, are empirical questions. *Morning Glories* provides some evidence in answer to these questions.

Clarence Stone provides a formulation that sidesteps the debate about whether growth strategies are consensual or conflictual by arguing that the private interests of the growth machine have a capacity for civic cooperation that facilitates both policy accomplishments and public support for them. It is less important that their assets give them *power over* than that their resources give them *power to*.[46] In Stone's view, the key to

---

[45] Molotch, "Growth Machine," and John R. Logan and Harvey L. Molotch, *Urban Fortunes: The Political Economy of Place* (Berkeley: University of California, 1987), especially chap. 3.

[46] Clarence Stone, *Regime Politics: Governing Atlanta, 1946–1988* (Lawrence: University Press of Kansas, 1989), for civic cooperation, 5–11; for power over vs. power to, 229. Stone's case study is Atlanta, Georgia. One of Atlanta's retired mayors offers a fine pragmatic description of "civic cooperation." It was, wrote Ivan Allen, the "totally unselfish support of the business community" that "was the secret to Atlanta's success in the sixties": "Banker Mills Lane got the stadium project rolling. Realtor Jack Adair developed the Atlanta Civic Center. Editor Eugene Patterson urged racial understanding, and publisher Jack Tarver gave advice. Banker Ed Smith made it possible for my second bond issue to be understood by the public and, as a result, passed. Robert Woodruff of Coca-Cola endorsed, with anonymous gifts, nearly every critical fund-raising drive to come up. . . . " Allen continues the list to include Atlanta's war on poverty effort; the acquisition of a major league baseball, big league football, and the Hawks to Atlanta; low income housing; and rapid transit. Ivan Allen, *Mayor: Notes on the Sixties* (New York: Simon and Schuster, 1971), 238–50. Compare Peterson: "Those who seem to have 'power' over developmental policies are those who do the most to secure these benefits for all members of the city" (*City Limits*, 147).

understanding local government and policy lies in the informal arrangements between governmental authority on one hand and those who control private resources on the other. It is these informal relations that constitute the urban regime. Elite coalitions are not enough, however, to
describe how growth was managed. In his study of postwar Atlanta,
Stone is also attentive to the effort to create popular endorsements of
regime plans and identifies the distribution of discrete benefits to small
businesses and community leaders as critical to maintaining regime
support.

John Mollenkopf has contrasted northeastern and southwestern styles
of pursuing growth. In northeastern cities, growth interests were con-
strained by the political environment of "contested liberalism." In Southwest, by contrast, growth interests enjoyed an unchecked reign. Elaborating this characterization, Stephen Elkin presented Dallas as a "pure
entrepreneurial" regime, in which organized businessmen were able to
create and foster a political system that was directed at promoting
growth in Dallas in an unusually apolitical environment.[47]

Like Dallas, the other big cities of the Southwest succeeded at the
(mostly) unchallenged pursuit of growth, fueled by competition from the
cities' very beginnings, and unfettered by the political challenges so costly
to local governments elsewhere. The informal relations between government and the growth machine have been close to the surface; that the
business of local government has largely been business has been perfectly
clear.

Morning Glories adds to these sketches of southwestern growth regimes a portrait of the political arrangements that kept them secure. One
consequence of focus on growth by students of city politics has been
attention to elites, with little consideration of popular or electoral politics. Popular support is seen as relatively unproblematic from Peterson's
point of view because he understands the pursuit of growth as rational
and so inherently consensual; Molotch is inattentive to electoral politics
because he understands the pursuit of growth as inevitable given the political power of the growth machine; Elkin presents the key accomplishment of the private sector as placing like-minded politicians in office;
Stone downplays the role of electoral politics to focus on informal arrangements among elites.

The leaders of the model growth machines in *Morning Glories* were
neither so complacent nor so confident. They devoted as much energy to
the design of the political institutions in their cities as to the design of

---

[47] John Mollenkopf, *Contested Cities* (Princeton: Princeton University Press, 1983). Stephen Elkin, *City and Regime in the American Republic* (Chicago: University of Chicago
Press, 1987), 70.

growth strategies. More, they created a "growth community" bound by prosperity, political like-mindedness, and the provision of public amenities. Like them, I see the political arrangements of southwestern cities as the foundation and insurance of their unchallenged pursuit of growth.

The Argument of *Morning Glories*

Early in this century, the strategic location of the Southwest advantaged proponents of municipal reform and provided a disabling environment for reform's antagonists. The result was that almost without exception the small cities and towns of the Southwest adopted reform (that is, commission or city-manager) charters. In the years that followed, reform government proved difficult to bring to life. Nevertheless, reformers could count important accomplishments, of which restriction of the electorate was probably the most important. At midcentury southwestern cities witnessed another wave of charter revision and elite organization; the institutional arrangements of municipal reform were refurbished. As a result, the postwar decades saw the flowering of big-city reform.

Big-city reform was a political system characterized by very low participation and little effective competition. Incumbents could as confidently count on reelection as any machine politician. Popular support was found in affluent Anglo communities, to whom amenities (libraries, better schools, parks) were carefully targeted. The pursuit of growth as conducted by these governments also served their core constituents, as subsidies to developers in effect subsidized middle-class homeowners. The results were a small, contented political community that had good government and knew it was good, and political leaders well insulated from such popular discontent as might exist. The great achievement of big-city reform was the creation of political communities that looked like Winnetka from their sprawling and diverse metropolises.

This accomplishment became, after 1960, a barrier to local government's continuing legitimacy. African-American and Mexican-American communities, long marginalized or excluded, voiced their discontents with increasing insistence, and focused their sights squarely on the institutional arrangements that politically disabled them. Their critique of big-city reform was joined by Anglo, middle-class communities. Wholly committed to growth policies that played the whole against its parts, big-city reform distributed discontents that created pluralities of affluent, Anglo voters who wanted to abandon at-large elections in favor of district representation, and government by civic statesmen in favor of government by politicians. The result was that between 1974 and 1990, the central political institutions of big-city reform were dismantled.

My chapter titles are taken from Richard S. Childs's "The Reformer,"
first published in the *National Municipal Review* in 1927, and presented
at the opening of this chapter. In Childs's presentation the reformer is
successful, but in the wake of victory is jeered by the crowd, "a forlorn
and lonely crank, mustering a pitiful little odd-lot of followers along the
roadside . . ." Neither the reformers I describe here nor Childs himself
were forlorn and lonely cranks. Childs invented the city manager in
1911. Childs's own recollection was that, reading about Galveston's
commission form, he was skeptical of its description as "business-like."
How could it be like a business, he wondered, without a manager? When
Lockport, New York, asked Childs for advice about adopting the commission plan, Childs wrote a manager into the proposed city charter.
Fifty years later Childs was gratified to write that half of U.S. cities over
25,000 population had adopted the plan.

Even if Childs was not as he pictured himself in "The Reformer," a bit
of romanticism about municipal reform is not amiss here. The reality of
urban life and politics in the progressive years was altogether unsavory.
When good-government advocates claimed that amateurs could beat
professionals at the polls with unpaid workers—an idea denounced by
Plunkitt on the low but solid ground that men are best motivated by
financial incentives—it must have seemed as hopeless and laughable as
Plunkitt found it. And when reformers did win, good government must
have seemed to some voters to offer an honest, inspiring, and perhaps
inspired vision of local government. On the other hand, municipal reform, like the progressive movement of which it was a part, was a very
mixed assortment of motivations and goals, of efficiency and elitism,
clean government and racism, the common good and exclusion. As the
place where the municipal reform movement witnessed its greatest triumphs, the Southwest saw not only the best of reform but also its ugliest
impulses realized.

Two

Small but Ambitious

THE CITIES of the Southwest have diverse origins. Some sites date back to ancient native settlements, others to the Spanish empire and Catholic missions. Still others were founded by Anglo homesteaders and speculators. Albuquerque (founded 1706), San Antonio (1718), and San Jose (1777) were outposts and then administrative centers of the Spanish empire. San Diego (1769) was the first California mission of Father Junipero Serra. Dallas (1843), Houston, and Austin were established after Mexico's defeat in 1836. Houston was founded by two speculators from New York City; Austin was identified in 1839 as the most promising site for the capital of the Republic of Texas. Phoenix was settled in 1867 by Anglo homesteaders who, coming across the ruins of Hohokam canals and irrigation systems, recognized the Salt River Valley as a promising site for agricultural development. Oklahoma's future big cities were founded even later, Tulsa in 1882 (at the site of a Creek settlement) and Oklahoma City in 1889, mushrooming in a single day, when the territory was opened.[1]

In 1900 the cities of the Southwest were small, ambitious, and as presented in their own newspapers, blessed with opportunity. The *Austin Daily Tribune* reported in November 1900: "Austin today is more prosperous than ever before. Never in its history probably [sic] has there been such an era of improvement by individual effort and individual money."[2] The *Albuquerque Morning Journal* of February 25, 1912, boasted of Albuquerque as "the Metropolis of New Mexico," "A City of Present Prosperity," and "A City with a Prosperous Future." Perhaps the most spectacular advertising effort was the Panama-California Exposition hosted by San Diego in 1915 to celebrate the opening of the Panama Canal. More than two million visitors attended the exposition, and it left an

---

[1] For Austin, Anthony M. Orum, *Power, Money, and the People; The Making of Modern Austin* (Austin: Texas Monthly Press, 1987), 7; for San Jose, Philip J. Trounstine and Terry Christensen, *Movers and Shakers: The Study of Community Power* (New York: St. Martin's Press, 1982), 80; Bradford Luckingham, *The Urban Southwest: A Profile History of Albuquerque, El Paso, Phoenix, Tucson* (El Paso: Texas Western Press, 1982), for Phoenix, 14; for Albuquerque, 2.

[2] Reported in Sara Lacy, "Austin, 1900–1915" (typescript draft for the Federal Writer's Project Guide to Austin, Texas [never published], September 16, 1938).

elegant legacy in the buildings that still form the heart of San Diego's Balboa Park. Designed by architect Bertram Goodhue, the buildings were praised as a "superb creation . . . with its stately approach, its walls springing from the hillside, its welcoming gateway, its soaring tower, and its resplendent dome."[3] The reality was not so bright. As Goodhue himself said of the exposition buildings, many of which were temporary, their purpose was "illusion rather than reality." Arriving in San Diego at the turn of the century, Oscar Cotton reported, "the consensus . . . in Los Angeles . . . was that San Diego was a 'City of Blighted Hopes.'"[4]

By the standard of 1900, a modern community had well-paved and lighted streets, adequate sewers, electricity and water delivered to households, and street railway systems providing mass transportation. The cities and towns of the Southwest boasted none of these amenities. Many communities worried about adequate supplies of water or feared destructive floods; the least fortunate, like Phoenix and Austin, had worries on both counts. Most desired stronger rail connections to the rest of the country and soon air mail and air travel connections as well. Utility and mass transit corporations were abusive of their contractual obligations, indifferent to consumers, and exorbitant in their charges. The tasks of securing investments, utilities, and transportation absorbed the energies of town leaders, dominated the news, and set the agenda of local politics.

Southwestern towns were also short of people and employers. Austin had a good start with the state capital and the university, although in 1900 it was possible that Austin might try to become an industrial center as well. Houston was locked in intense rivalry with Galveston to the south; Spindletop lay in the future. Phoenix and Albuquerque subsisted on the shipment of products from agricultural surroundings, and Albuquerque boasted the yards of the Atcheson, Topeka, and Santa Fe Railroad, which long remained a major employer. San Diego, without direct rail connections to the East, had actually suffered population decline in the 1890s.

Local governments were not well positioned to solve these problems. Their financial resources were insufficient for the tasks they faced. Municipal debt was increasing as local systems of assessment and taxation fell behind needs for paving, grading, and utilities. Flood control, irrigation, and sometimes water supplies required federal assistance. Most utilities were owned by corporations from other states, and courts were more sympathetic to investor prerogatives than to municipal authorities

[3] Richard F. Pourade, *The History of San Diego* (San Diego: Union-Tribune, 1965), 5:187.
[4] Pourade, *History*, 5:199, 5:32.

when adjudicating disputes between utilities and local governments. Municipal ownership of utilities required resources not immediately at hand, so bonds were sold on the national market.

Finally, these cities and towns were placed in a hostile and sparsely populated natural environment. Warren Leslie's description of Dallas captures this well. "The truth is," Leslie wrote, "there really isn't any reason for Dallas. It sits in the middle of nowhere and nothing. The land around it is dry, black, and unproductive; farmers do battle with it to exist."[5]

To the stark and unpromising settings of southwestern cities and towns, we may contrast the good fortune of the cities of Richard Wade's *Urban Frontier* one hundred years earlier. St. Louis and Pittsburgh were magnificently sited; of Pittsburgh's future as a great city, Wade observes, "nature itself made the suggestion unmistakably." Placed in the path of settlers moving west, the towns of the Ohio Valley were washed repeatedly by waves of settlers who needed supplies, some of whom stayed. Even landlocked Lexington "throve on trade. . . . Streams of overland migrants stopped here, buying everything needed for building a home and for bringing in the first crops." In the heart of the old Northwest Territory, with its fertile, well-watered soil and newly settled homesteads, Pittsburgh, Louisville, and Cincinnati prospered. When street lighting and water were needed, these towns either provided them directly or negotiated hard bargains with small local providers. Of course there were adversities. Native Americans continued to press their own claims to the territory; repeated bouts of smallpox stalled expansion. Nevertheless, growth and prosperity on the older frontier seemed the natural order of things,[6] while in the Southwest a century later all depended on ingenuity at home and collective action, negotiation, and strategy with higher governments and national corporate investors.

In the Southwest, each city-building effort was shaped by the strategic location of the region in the nation's economy and political life. In 1900 the concrete referents of "strategic location" were obvious to southwestern citizens. California, New Mexico, and Arizona suffered from political domination by railroads. The Southern Pacific "machine" and Santa Fe "ring" controlled state, county, and even municipal governments. Efforts to regulate industry in the Progressive Era had a regional

[5] Warren Leslie, *Dallas: Public and Private* (New York: Grossman, 1964), 22. The same might well have been written about San Diego or Phoenix, and with only slight exaggeration suits Albuquerque, Houston, and the Oklahoma cities.

[6] Richard C. Wade, *The Urban Frontier: Pioneer Life in Early Pittsburgh, Cincinnati, Lexington, Louisville, and St. Louis* (Chicago: University of Chicago Press, 1964), chaps. 1 and 2, passim; Pittsburgh, 10; Lexington, 12.

dimension. State and territorial capitals in the West and South rang with denunciations of the depredations of "foreign" corporations. As one historian wrote of the Arizona territory, "Absentee capitalism could not help dominating the [territory's] economic life, and it would have been astonishing if the corporations had not dominated the state's political life as well." Arizona Territory's Governor George Hunt, a tough defender of workers on the railroads and in the mines, termed outside investors "the Beast."[7] In Texas, where insurance premiums greatly outdistanced payments on claims, state legislators demanded the government enact laws forcing insurers to reinvest their profits where they earned them, lest "every dollar in Texas end up in New York."[8] The same debate was held in California, along with an effort to regulate insurance rates and rationalize the banking industry.[9]

Both the capital and the authority needed to create urban growth were at distant locales, in the great cities of the east and the nation's capital. Town leaders recognized that the ordinary operations of national markets offered few good prospects; to transcend the scarce natural endowments of their locations, collective action was required. The creation of energetic and assertive organizations for business leaders gave local politics much of its distinctive character for the most of this century. Local business leaders traveled to Washington to lobby bureaucrats and Congress, bargained with investors, fought utility companies in the courts, mobilized public support for bond issues for capital improvements, and designed new governmental authorities and special districts to bring economic growth to their cities. Their efforts were not without result. By the end of World War I, Austin, Phoenix, Albuquerque, Houston, and San Diego each had grown significantly, and town leaders had formulated strategies for future prosperity.

In this chapter I present the difficulties and prospects of southwestern towns and cities at the turn of this century, focusing on Albuquerque, Austin, Houston, Phoenix, and San Diego. I show how town leaders sought to promote and build their cities, proving by their successes that,

[7] Marjorie Haines Wilson, "Governor Hunt, the 'Beast,' and the Miners," *Journal of Arizona History* 15, no. 2 (Summer 1974): 119.

[8] James A. Tinsley, "The Progressive Movement in Texas" (Ph.D. diss., University of Wisconsin, 1953), 45. For similar struggles in Oklahoma, see Danney Goble, *Progressive Oklahoma: The Making of a New Kind of State* (Norman: University of Oklahoma, 1980), chaps. 6, 7, 8.

[9] Mansel G. Blackford, *The Politics of Business in California, 1890–1920* (Columbus: Ohio State University Press, 1977). Once regulation was established, insurance commissioners were regularly co-opted. The larger issue was overridden by market forces. "By 1911," Blackford writes, "the Pacific Coast led all but two other sections of the country, the Southwest and Northern Plains, in the percentage of insurance reserves derived from the area's premiums being reinvested in the region" (141).

TABLE 2-1
Population of Southwestern Cities, 1890–1920

	1890	1900	1910	1920
Albuquerque	3,785	6,238	11,020	15,157
Austin	14,575	22,258	29,860	34,876
Dallas	38,067	42,638	92,104	158,976
Houston	27,557	44,633	78,800	138,276
Phoenix	3,152	5,544	11,134	29,053
San Antonio	37,673	53,321	96,614	161,379
San Diego	16,159	17,700	39,578	74,683
San Jose	18,060	21,500	28,946	39,642

Sources: U.S. Bureau of Census, *Census of Population, 1890* (Washington, D.C.: Government Printing Office, 1895), tables 5, 6.

U.S. Bureau of Census, *Census of Population, 1900: Population* (Washington, D.C.: Government Printing Office, 1902), part I, table 23.

U.S. Bureau of Census, *Census of Population, 1910: Population* (Washington, D.C.: Government Printing Office, 1912), part II, table II.

U.S. Bureau of Census, *Census of Population, 1920: Population* (Washington, D.C.: Government Printing Office, 1922), part I, vol. III, table 10.

as Char Miller and David Johnson observed of Texas cities, geography was not destiny.[10]

Advertising

In 1900 the cities and towns of the Southwest were small but ambitious. Of the group studied here, the largest, Houston, had a population of 44,633, while the smallest, Phoenix, had only 5,544 inhabitants. As their towns were lacking population and money, the first task for local leaders was to advertise for settlers and investors. Everywhere newspapers provided generous accounts of opportunity and growth, promoting the local economy for an audience of potential investors, consumers, and settlers. A special edition of the *Albuquerque Morning Journal* for February 25, 1912, presented New Mexico's many opportunities. Albuquerque was featured as a "modern city with well-graded streets, concrete sidewalks, electric lights, a street railway system, important mercantile and manufacturing establishments, two daily newspapers, and other evidences of great and growing prosperity." Grounding that claim to growing pros-

[10] Char Miller and David R. Johnson, "The Rise of Urban Texas," in *Urban Texas, Politics and Development*, ed. Char Miller and Heywood T. Sanders (College Station: Texas A & M University Press, 1990), 29.

perity was Albuquerque's status as a hub of the Santa Fe Railroad, with direct connections to Topeka, Chicago, and El Paso. San Diego boosters boasted (mendaciously) that the city "claims as its true backcountry the entire southwestern region."[11] Phoenix too advertised agricultural prosperity. In 1913 the *Arizona Gazette* announced a "World of possibilities and Wealth in Alfalfa; Great Profits in Egyptian Cotton and Sugar Cane." The Santa Fe helped Phoenix advertise. In August 1908 a special edition of the railroad's magazine, *The Earth*, was devoted entirely to the Salt River Valley, and more than 130,000 copies were distributed.[12]

In the same years "San Diego Business establishments that want Arizona Trade" advertised regularly in the *Arizona Gazette*. "Del-Mar, The Newport of the Pacific" claimed that "a visit to this terrestial [sic] paradise" will result in a "departure with regrets or . . . immediate arrangements for your permanent home." Other San Diego advertisers offered merchandising advice for the Mexican market, investment opportunities, legal assistance, life insurance, and accommodations at "Arizona's Seaport."[13] Austin's Chamber of Commerce published and distributed a pamphlet, "Progressive Austin Has It," "to place before you a list of Austin manufacturers, with a message from each of them." This was important because "Pride in her beautiful location and institutions of learning has caused Austin to advertise these to the neglect of her manufacturing and marketing interests."[14]

If the written word were inadequate, organized celebration might entice outsiders to come and look. Albuquerque hosted an annual Territorial Fair in the 1890s. From 1899 to 1915 Houston's No-Tsu-Oh (Houston spelled backwards) Festival, modeled on New Orleans's Mardi Gras, mobilized the city to attract autumn buyers. Segregated but not quiescent, the city's black community organized its own De-Ro-Loc carnival.[15] In 1915, to celebrate the opening of the Panama Canal and advertise its own port, San Diego hosted the Panama-California Exposition.[16] To finance the exposition, the city issued a million dollar bond

[11] Pourade, *History*, 5:9.

[12] The Southern Pacific also distributed a pamphlet about the valley. Geoffey Padraic Mawn, "Phoenix, Arizona: Central City of the Southwest, 1870–1920" (Ph. D. diss., Arizona State University, 1979), 290.

[13] *Arizona Gazette*, January 2, 1913, 2.

[14] Austin Chamber of Commerce, "Progressive Austin Has It" (Austin: Chamber of Commerce, ca. 1920).

[15] Sibley, Marilyn McAdams, *The Port of Houston: A History* (Austin: University of Texas Press, 1968), 142, and David G. McComb, *Houston: A History* (Austin: University of Texas Press, 1981), 108.

[16] The *Arizona Gazette* saw the exposition as "a great opportunity . . . offered to Arizona to advertise her resources" and urged the state to "show the possibilities of her soil" by presenting an exhibit (January 7, 1913, 4).

offering, and a similar amount was raised through private subscription. The exposition's contribution was not only a transient one of tourist dollars and national visibility. At the exposition Joseph Pendleton, a battalion commander of the Marine Corps, convinced Marine Commandant George Barnett to support his vision of a marine advance base on the California coast. San Diego also won the support of the assistant secretary of the navy, Franklin D. Roosevelt, who attended the exposition and placed a navy dirigible base in San Diego.[17]

Lobbying Higher Governments, Building a Local State

The paucity of local resources for solving local problems provoked organization to pursue investment and expertise from elsewhere. Early economic footholds were gained by competing successfully in state or territorial legislatures for institutions like universities, prisons, and asylums, as well as for designation as county seat or state capital. In 1885 Phoenix's representatives in the Arizona territorial legislature secured an insane asylum (and its $100,000 appropriation), Tempe won a normal school, Yuma retained its prison, and Florence was awarded $15,000 for a bridge[18] (while Tucson was sorely disappointed to receive only the university).[19] In the Arizona Territory, the site of the capital was in contention from 1864, when it was first placed at Prescott, until it finally moved to Phoenix more than twenty years later. Tucson mounted campaigns for the capital in 1881 and 1885; Phoenix in 1879, 1883, 1887, and 1889, and the capital moved several times. In addition to insisting on the virtues of their respective home towns, lobbyists had material inducements for legislators. In 1885 a proponent of Tucson complained:

> We are doing all we can. . . . Prescott wines, dines, and "sees" the members of both houses with liberal prodigality and profusion. We have never had a cent to give a supper or treat to a drink. You can readily imagine the great disadvantage under which we labor.

---

[17] Pourade, *History*, 5:194–95.

[18] Karen Lynn Ehrlich, "Arizona's Territorial Capital Moves to Phoenix," *Arizona and the West* 23, no. 2 (1984): 236. Similar events took place in New Mexico. An enterprising representative to the territorial legislature secured a university for Albuquerque in 1889, in part by arranging for the distribution of benefits to other cities. A School of Mines was given to Socorro, and a College of Agriculture to Las Cruces, while Las Vegas was granted an insane asylum. Albuquerque had been awarded a prison in 1885. Not satisfied, Albuquerque citizens lobbied to have the capital moved from Santa Fe for most of the 1890s, without success. Marc Simmons, *Albuquerque: A Narrative History* (Albuquerque: University of New Mexico Press, 1982), 311, 231.

[19] Luckingham, *Urban Southwest*, 25.

One thousand dollars economically and properly disbursed would have infallibly put the capital at Tucson. . . . Now you can see what is the matter.

Armed with a war chest estimated at $10,000, Phoenix won decisively in 1889.[20] Earlier, San Jose citizens voiced similar complaints. The first state legislature of California convened in San Jose in 1849, but the city's "honor was short-lived, for she was soon out-bid and out-bribed by other communities desirous of . . . the capital." As late as the 1930s, the desire to recapture the capital remained "a sort of indigenous folklore" in San Jose. The desire was understandable: San Jose's economy was dominated by the seasonal fluctuations of harvesting, transporting, and canning the produce of the surrounding Santa Clara Valley. Government employment would have been an important stabilizing force.[21]

More often than the state capital, the nation's capital was a site of urban competition and lobbying. Both San Diego and Houston requested federal assistance to develop port facilities; Phoenix, Austin, and Albuquerque could not solve their flooding and water supply problems without enormous federal investments in dams. In each case securing assistance followed an elaborate pattern of leadership organization, persuasion of relevant federal bureaucracies, lobbying Congress, public mobilization, and local state-building. Efforts to secure the Roosevelt Dam for Phoenix and harbor improvements for Houston illustrate these processes well.

Albuquerque, Phoenix, San Diego, and Austin all had serious water problems. In Phoenix flooding and droughts were of concern primarily because the city staked its growth on shipping the agricultural production of its surrounding area, the Salt River Valley. The valley suffered drought in 1898–99 and 1901, and floods in 1891, 1900, and 1908. Organized residents were worried about water problems and active in seeking solutions. The Maricopa County Board of Supervisors and the County Board of Water Storage Commissioners, the Phoenix Chamber of Commerce, and the Phoenix and Maricopa Country Board of Trade all concerned themselves with water problems.

There was some hope that private means might be found to construct a dam both to prevent floods and to provide for water storage. The Hudson Reservoir and Canal Company purchased a site for a dam, but could not raise sufficient capital to build it. Similarly Behring Brothers (Britain) discovered the project to be economically unfeasible. The city and county's poverty, relative to the cost of solving local problems, was revealed when leaders sought support for the dam from local sources. In-

[20] Ehrlich, "Territorial Capital," 237–38, 140.
[21] Robert Thorpe, "Council-Manager Government in San Jose, California" (M.A. thesis, Stanford University, 1938), 1–2, 3.

vestigation quickly revealed that the capital required to build a dam exceeded *the entire assessed valuation of Maricopa County*, making funding a project with local bonds impossible.[22] After efforts to secure private sector construction of a dam failed, the reclamation efforts of the federal government (in which Arizona citizens had naturally taken an interest all along) became the sole target of lobbying activity.[23]

The federal government and in particular the U.S. Geological Survey had been concerned about water reclamation projects for some time. In 1888 Congress appropriated $100,000 for an irrigation survey, and in the next year the USGS surveyed the Salt and Gila River Valleys. The Agriculture and Interior Departments were also interested in irrigating the Salt River Valley. Phoenix sent Benjamin Fowler to Washington to lobby for the territory's interests and, in concert with George Maxwell (a Californian who had organized the National Irrigation Association), Fowler began campaigning at the Department of Interior and the USGS. On behalf of the Salt River Valley Water Storage Committee, Fowler offered the USGS $1,500 to extend its irrigation surveys, an offer that was accepted. Equally important, Maxwell and his colleagues lobbied Congress successfully for an amendment to the 1902 Reclamation Act providing that private lands could be included in federal projects.[24] In addition to Fowler and Maxwell, Dwight Heard, Lloyd Christy, and Joseph Kibbey were active in Washington and Phoenix in support of Salt River Valley interests.

At home in Arizona, the next task was to mobilize landowners and to create a new quasi-governmental agency in support of the effort to secure the dam. The Water Storage Commission drew up a plan for the Salt River Water Users Association, whose purpose was to persuade landowners to pledge their lands as collateral to repay the federal government for constructing a dam under the Reclamation Act. By July of 1903 more than two hundred thousand acres had been pledged, and a contract for the Tonto Basin Storage Reservoir (later the Roosevelt Dam) was signed in February 1904.[25] Not only did the Roosevelt Dam create the possibilities for prosperity in the valley, its construction was an enormous public works project involving construction of roads, a saw mill, office buildings, a camp, blacksmith and carpenter shops, and a steam power plant;

[22] John H. Krenkel, "The Founding of the Salt River Water Users Association," *Arizona and the West* 23, no. 1 (1984): 85.

[23] Krenkel, "Founding," 82–90.

[24] Karen L. Smith, "The Campaign for Water in Central Arizona, 1890–1903," *Arizona and the West* 23, no. 1 (1984): 127–48.

[25] Krenkel, "Founding," 88–89. Similarly, Albuquerque supported the creation of the Bernalillo County (Rio Grande) River Commission, which was empowered to tax residents to provide funds for dikes and dams to protect city and crops from repeated floods.

making bricks; burning lime; and so on. When the dam was completed eight years later, Theodore Roosevelt himself traveled to the site to participate in the festivities.[26] Roosevelt, Fowler, Christy, Heard, and Kibbey all became local heroes for this accomplishment.

Houston's efforts to create a harbor followed the same pattern of leadership organization, attention to bureaucrats, lobbying Congress, popular mobilization, and local state-building. Houston is located on the Buffalo Bayou, about fifty miles inland from the port of Galveston on the Gulf of Mexico. That Houston's ambitions were not nature's intent may be inferred from one visitor's remark that "I yearned to see that seaport, even if I had to employ a detective to hunt it up." Not surprisingly, solving Houston's harbor problems required years of effort. While Phoenix wooed the USGS, Houston's audience was the Army Corps of Engineers, which doubted the feasibility of Houston's plans. The Rivers and Harbors Committee actually visited Houston in 1897, were feted, and, thanks to a providentially large rainfall, appropriately impressed. Representative Joseph C. Hutcheson later recalled, "This little bayou of ours, that was usually only a few feet deep in the city was, at that time by the grace of God, five feet above every bank from here to Galveston!"[27]

In the wake of the hurricane that destroyed Galveston, Congress was inclined to look favorably on Houston. In 1902 Congress appropriated $1 million for the bayou, which was dredged to a depth of 18½ feet; a turning basin was added by 1908. This left the channel still inadequate to accommodate the ships commonly plying Gulf waters, while the federal monies were exhausted.

Local leaders then turned from lobbying Washington to local mobilization. They proposed creating the Harris County Houston Ship Channel Navigation District to continue the work, and voters approved both the creation of the district and a $1.25 million bond issue to provide matching funds for further federal assistance. In 1909 the mayor proposed a $2 million bond issue to deepen the Bayou. The *Houston Chronicle* was quick to editorialize on the stake of the average resident in the success of this effort. Applauding the Houston Labor Council's support for the bond issue, the editors wrote, "in a growing town like Houston the wage-earner's best chance to get ahead financially is to buy a home and reap the benefit of advanced land values"; deepening the bayou meant "Houston's great future growth will be absolutely guaranteed."[28] The Chamber of Commerce left neither creation of the navigation district nor bond pas-

---

[26] Editors of the *Journal of Arizona History*, "Water for Phoenix: Building the Roosevelt Dam," *Journal of Arizona History*" 18, no. 3 (1977): 286.

[27] Sibley, *Port of Houston*, 113, 116.

[28] *Houston Chronicle* January 7, 1909, 4.

sage to chance, organizing meetings to persuade the public and campaigning in each district.[29]

Finally, Houston created a new authority to manage its port. In 1913 the city created a Harbor Board and issued $3 million in bonds to support it.[30] The next year the project was complete, and Houston finally celebrated deep water. The No-Tsu-Oh king, formerly King Nottoc, was rechristened King Retaw. Not to be outdone by fictional rulers, Houston's Mayor Campbell, Governor-elect James Ferguson, and President Woodrow Wilson also participated in the celebration.[31] As the conclusion of the channel's construction was the beginning of a new era of expanded commerce, young men from the city's leading families chose the celebration to introduce the Red Roosters, an organization dedicated to selling Houston to its environs.[32]

The same story of organization, persuasion, lobbying, mobilization, and state-building might be told over and over again. San Diego applied for help from the Army Corps of Engineers to dredge the entrance to her harbor as early as the 1850s (although congressional approval was not gained until 1890). The Chamber of Commerce also sent H. P. Wood to Washington in 1900 to lobby for, among other things, the construction of the Panama Canal. San Diego leaders sought investments from the armed forces and repeatedly persuaded the Army Corps of Engineers and the navy of the city's need for harbor improvements; its representative in Congress, William Kettner, was sure to secure a place on the Rivers and Harbors Committee; and the city sought ever stronger ties to the armed forces. So skilled did San Diego's representatives become in lobbying Washington that when Fort Rosecrans required further appropriations, its commandant applied to the Chamber for help in his appeals to Congress. Public subscriptions as well as bond campaigns provided funds for harbor improvements, for bridges, roads, and railroads, and for the California-Panama Exposition.[33]

Austin's water problems plagued it for decades, and the Colorado River was not effectively controlled until 1942. There was activity to dam the river beginning in 1888. Austin, like Houston, watched hopefully as the Army Corps of Engineers surveyed the river and the flood damage it wreaked, lobbied Congress, and railed against federal refusal

---

[29] Sibley, *Port of Houston*, 136.

[30] McComb, *Houston*, 65–67.

[31] Sibley, *Port of Houston*, 144. Wilson was not present, but fired a cannon in Houston by pressing a pearl-topped button in Washington.

[32] Sibley, *Port of Houston*, 142–43.

[33] Pourade, *History*, 5:196, 199–200, Abraham Shragge, "Boosters and Bluejackets: The Civic Culture of Militarism in San Diego, California" (Ph.D. diss., University of Cliafornia, San Diego, in progress), chap. 2.

to supply adequate funds. In 1915 the Chamber of Commerce formed the Colorado River Improvement Association, and the next year the association received a $25,000 appropriation from the federal government. This was hardly a down payment, as solutions to the flooding problems of Austin lay decades ahead.[34]

Negotiating with "the Beast"

Since local capital was in short supply, representatives of cities and towns courted private investors. For their part, banks, utilities, insurers, street railway companies, and land developers were looking for likely sites. A pamphlet advertising the Austin National Bank boasted that "A group of Pennsylvania financiers . . . made a survey of the entire southwest before selecting Austin as the best location for the bank they desired to organize."[35] When representatives of New York's Chamber of Commerce, bankers, and merchants' associations visited the city, the *Austin-American Statesmen* likened the city to "a blushing maiden . . . here to be won by he who is chivalrous and brave enough to try."[36]

Even larger in scale and more important for urban prospects were railroads. Securing adequate rail connections was for the most part accomplished late in the nineteenth century. Houston, Phoenix, and Albuquerque all staked their growth on the shipment of commodities from surrounding areas. Phoenix secured spur lines from the Southern Pacific and the Santa Fe before 1900; Houston was a railroad hub by 1910. Albuquerque's very important relation to the Atcheson, Topeka, and Santa Fe Railroad was largely fortuitous. When Santa Fe owners planned to cross the New Mexico territory in the 1870s, the most direct route fell across the land grant of Jose Leandro Perea. Perea, however, allegedly still resentful of the U.S. conquest of northern Mexico, refused to sell his land at a reasonable price. Albuquerque then won the railroad by default.[37]

Although San Diego's advertisements claimed the entire Southwest as her hinterland, this was hardly the case. For one thing few San Diego business leaders were aggressive in developing commercial agriculture in

[34] Anthony Orum, *Power, Money, and the People*, chap. 4.

[35] Gideon, Samuel Edward, *Austin and the Austin National Bank, 1890–1940* (Austin: n.p. 1940), 4, and see *supra*, n. 6.

[36] *Austin-American Statesman*, April 27, 1901, 1, quoted in Frank Staniszewski, "Ideology and Practice in Municipal Government Reform: A Case Study of Austin" (University of Texas at Austin, Studies in Politics, 1977), 60.

[37] Simmons, *Albuquerque*, 215.

the Imperial Valley east of the city, allowing Los Angeles to take the lead there. More damaging, despite many campaigns, subscriptions, and railroad recruitment committees, San Diego was unable to secure a direct rail connection to Arizona until 1919. Even then, the line was controlled by the Southern Pacific, and so threatened to slight San Diego in favor of Los Angeles. The impact on the city of the prospect of this connection was dramatic: when plans for the railroad were announced "real estate prices immediately advanced twenty five per cent."[38]

The urban communities of the Southwest also required utilities and mass transit. Initially these were provided by local firms. San Diego represents the extreme case: in 1900 John D. Spreckels owned a water supply company and the streetcar franchise, promised a railroad east to Yuma, Arizona and, no doubt to applaud his own city-building efforts, published two of San Diego's three newspapers.[39] Undercapitalized and enjoying monopoly franchises in most places, locally owned utilities provided inadequate service to some customers and, unable to keep up with urban expansion, no service at all to others.

Albuquerque's 1914 mayoralty election was waged over whether public or private ownership of the water supply company was preferable, and the sewer system was also troublesome.[40] Three years later the city was still attempting to buy the water supply company as well as to force the street car company to meet its contractual obligations.[41]

In the 1890s Houston's locally owned water company exemplified the inadequacies of small-scale utilities. Unwilling to pay for the installation of meters, the company provided no incentives for customers to conserve water or fix leaks. As a result water pressure fell dangerously low, and when a local hospital caught fire, fire fighters could not save it. The city's residents were at risk, and its structures declared uninsurable.[42]

As a national market in local utilities appeared, street railways, electricity, gas, sewers, water supply systems, and telephones were more likely to be provided by national firms than local investors. General Electric, for example, organized a holding company for local utilities in order to create a market for its own generating equipment. Pacific Gas and Electric served Arizona as well as California, and Pacific Light and

[38] Pourade, *History*, 5:86, 92; Shragge, "Boosters and Bluejackets," chap. 2.

[39] Pourade, *History*, 5:15.

[40] Michael J. Schingle, "Albuquerque Urban Politics, 1891–1955, Aldermanic vs. Commission Government" (senior thesis, University of New Mexico, August 1976), 12.

[41] Dorothy I. Cline, *Albuquerque and the City Manager Plan* (Albuquerque: University of New Mexico 1951), 7.

[42] Harold F. Platt, *City Building in the New South* (Philadelphia: Temple University Press, 1983), 137, 141–44; for National Board of Fire Insurance Underwriters, 173.

Power, based in Los Angeles, considered acquiring water rights enabling them to control San Diego's water supplies. Utilities in small cities were commonly owned by firms in Chicago, Boston, New York, or as in the cases of Phoenix and San Diego, Los Angeles.

Local consumers and local governments alike felt that these firms delivered precious little service at too high a price. In his annual message to the city council in 1900, Mayor Samuel Brashear described these problems in Houston:

> If any improvement be noticed in the pressure furnished by the water company, it is far from being in compliance with the contract. The same may be said of the power furnished by the electric light company. For these reasons the mayor and finance committee continue to withhold 50 per cent of the amount of all bills rendered by these companies . . . the contract price . . . is . . . unsatisfactory, and the rates exorbitant.
>
> The spirit manifested by the street railway company in resisting the enforcement of the transfer ticket ordinance, and declaring that it will oppose the collection of the assessments against it for its share of the cost of the recent street paving, is certainly cause for dissatisfaction.[43]

Worse, cities had little reliable legal recourse in their efforts at regulation. For example, in 1890 the Texas Supreme Court found that transit companies had vested rights in the streets over which their lines ran. Municipal governments could not exercise their police powers in any way that impaired the company's "right of occupancy."[44] Not surprisingly, the Public Utilities Committee of the Texas League of Municipalities found "the legal situation governing and controlling the right of various cities . . . to exercise the power of rate regulation is in a tangled and dubious condition." For their part utility owners viewed urban and county administrations as "as pitiless a pack of howling destroyers, as . . . the gaunt and hungry wolves" of "the Siberian steppes." In addition to being unreasonable, mercenary, and corrupt, local officials posed the threat of the "demon and destroyer, Municipal Ownership."[45]

For Houston's Mayor Brashear, Albuquerque's Mayor Henry Westerfeld, and others, municipal ownership seemed the only sensible alternative. Brashear claimed, "That municipal ownership of public necessities is a cure for the usual troubles arising with private corporations which

[43] S. H. Brashear, "Mayor's Message, February 1900" (Houston: City of Houston, February 5, 1900), 2.

[44] Platt, *City Building*, 142.

[45] "Proceedings on Public Utilities," *Texas Municipalities* 9, no. 4 (July 1922): 65. Owner's sentiments are John Britton, vice president of Pacific Gas and Electric Company, in 1909, advocating state regulation. Quoted in Blackford, *Politics of Business*, 87–88.

furnish these commodities to our people, as well as a financial saving to the city, cannot longer be questioned by reasonable, disinterested persons."[46] In 1903 Democrats in San Diego advocated public ownership of gas, electricity, and water supply.[47] Austin purchased its water and light systems;[48] both the Phoenix Sewer and Drainage Company and the Phoenix Water Company were bought by the city government. There was little resistance, largely because the firms were unprofitable; later some were reprivatized.[49]

Where franchises appeared profitable, however, there was strong opposition to their municipalization. Municipal ownership was especially difficult in the territories, where issuing bonds for the purchase of utilities (or any other purpose) required congressional approval. Congress supported Phoenix's purchase of her water system from a Boston-owned company but disapproved purchase of the sewer system. Shortly afterwards, the sewer system collapsed (literally), and as a result, congressional approval was forthcoming. Acquiring the electric company proved impossible. Pacific Gas and Electric supplied electricity to Phoenix residents, although not satisfactorily. Municipal ownership was proposed and a referendum brought to the electorate. Pacific Gas and Electric stepped up services and mounted an intense public relations campaign in Phoenix; despite this, the measure passed with majority support. Pacific Gas and Electric also campaigned in Washington, effectively keeping approval for another bond issue off the congressional agenda.[50]

Differences between local governments and utilities were not only disputed in the courts or through negotiation. Small guerrilla wars were also waged in the streets. Houston suffered the indignity of having the community's lights turned off when the city government threatened Houston Electric Power and Light with competition. Houston also tried to encourage efficient service delivery by creating competition among street railway companies. Although this had some advantages, competing street railway firms literally tore up the streets in their efforts to establish rights on promising routes.[51] Most often, however, one company simply

[46] Brashear, "Mayor's Message," 2.

[47] William E. Smythe, *History of San Diego, 1542–1907* (San Diego: History Co., 1908), 477. Earlier competing water companies supported competing mayoral candidates (476).

[48] Sara Lacy, "Contemporary Scene" (draft ms. for the Federal Writers' Project, *Austin History and Guide*, Barker Texas History Collection, University of Texas at Austin, August 10, 1937), 7.

[49] Karen Lynn Smith, "From Town to City: A History of Phoenix, 1870–1912" (M.A. thesis, University of California at Santa Barbara, 1978), 170–72.

[50] Mawn, "Phoenix," 327–41, and Smith, "Town to City," 171–73.

[51] Platt, *City Building*, 136, 132–33.

bought the other's franchise, or a third company bought them both. In Albuquerque too, efforts to create competition among street railway firms collapsed as the erstwhile competitors merged operations.[52] Although even brief periods of competition improved service delivery, franchise holders understandably preferred monopoly. Charles B. Holmes, the owner of a Chicago street railway syndicate, argued forcibly that Houston would be boycotted by northern capitalists if her government failed to see the virtues of natural monopolies in public services, and urged citizens to "unite with us in developing the interests of the city."[53]

The conflictual relations between cities and utilities tended toward the resolution Holmes suggested. This happened both because firms could create monopolies through the market and because firms could refuse, as Holmes did, to invest if threatened with competition. Although municipal ownership was the answer in some places, and although there were repeated efforts by local authorities to create competition, monopoly franchises and negotiation were the more common result, if for no other reason than that cities could not finance their own utilities and mass transit.

Even more than securing harbors, dams, or railroads, providing utilities placed local government at the center of managing growth. Continuing the metaphor of the *Austin-American Statesman*, we might say that if southwestern cities were blushing maidens, city fathers endeavored to insure that, if they were to lose their daughters, the young ladies would at least be taken honorably by their out-of-town suitors. This put politicians in the most delicate of positions: if political leaders were too aggressive in their negotiations with outside investors, their cities were threatened with refusal to invest or worse. Houston's progressive mayor Samuel Brashear, for example, was forced from office largely because of his very aggressive stance toward utility investors.[54] If, on the other hand, city government conceded too much to utility owners, voters were likely to reject officeholders as tools of eastern investors. As late as 1933 a handbill circulated in Phoenix denounced "the power and gas barons" who let consumers' money be "shipped to Wall Street Power Barons." "Call each candidate for city commission," the author advised, "and ask how they stand on present light and gas rates."[55] In this setting negotiating a good franchise contract was both an achievement with direct benefits for residents and a political triumph.

[52] Simmons, *Albuquerque*, 333.
[53] Platt, *City Building*, 128–29.
[54] Platt, *City Building*, 178.
[55] Clippings file, library of the Arizona Capitol, copy in author's possession.

"Cooperation between City Officials and Chambers of Commerce in City-Building"

Without adequate economic resources or political authority, the cities and towns of the Southwest faced formidable survival problems at the turn of the century. Local businessmen and political leaders organized to aggressively seek investment and assistance from higher governments and national economic interests. Phoenix's Commercial Club and Civic Federation were founded before 1890; Albuquerque had a Commerce Club, later the Chamber of Commerce, which began campaigning for investors and residents in the 1890s. There was also a Boosters' Association and its journal, the *Albuquerque Booster*.[56] In San Diego the Civic Association organized business leaders concerned with waterfront development, and the San Diego–California Club devoted itself to advertising and promoting the city.[57] Houston boasted a Board of Trade, a Commercial League, Business League, Manufacturers Association, Merchants' and Business Men's Association, Industrial Club, Bankers', Jobbers' and Manufacturers' Association, the 200,000 Club, Young Men's Business League, and a Junior Chamber of Commerce, as well as the Red Roosters.[58]

The role of these organizations expanded as they sought outside investments and tackled problems of city-building. In 1917 *Texas Municipalities* published articles on "The Commercial Secretary" (that is, the secretary of the Chamber of Commerce) and "Cooperation between City Officials and Chambers of Commerce in City Building." The commercial secretary was in earlier times a post for "the merchant who was 'busted,' who was a good fellow, and his friends put him in office to keep him from starving." Now, however, the job was a career, and one for which universities and colleges were beginning to provide training. No doubt this was because the agenda of the Chamber of Commerce was changing. "Only ten or fifteen years back the whole and sole duty of the commercial club was . . . factory getting. Every commercial club . . . had as its slogan, 'More Smoke.' " By 1917 the scope of its activities properly included "better living conditions, better housing, better sanitation, and better ed-

---

[56] Simmons, *Albuquerque*, 327.

[57] Mary Gilman Marston, *George White Marston: A Family Chronicle* (San Diego: Ward Ritchie Press, 1956), 1:84, Pourade, *History*, 6:9.

[58] McComb, *Houston*, 83–84. Char Miller and David R. Johnson discuss the aggressive entrepreneurship of Houston and Dallas business leaders in "The Rise of Urban Texas," in *Urban Texas: Politics and Development*, ed. Char Miller and Heywood T. Sanders (College Station: Texas A & M University Press, 1990), 3–29. "San Antonio," the same authors observe, "is another story altogether, for it has displayed a remarkable lack of entrepreneurial aggressiveness. . . . At the outset of the twentieth century . . . local wisdom in San Antonio denied any important place to collective effort or risk taking" (12, 15).

ucational facilities." The task of the chamber of commerce was "to create
. . . sentiment" in favor of appropriate remedies, while the city official's
responsibility was "to execute the plan as a result of this sentiment."
Leaders of the Austin, Houston, and San Diego Chambers of Commerce
saw their role, and their relations with city officials, in just that way.[59]

Austin's businessmen organized a Board of Trade in the 1880s (later
the Commercial Club), a Merchants Association in 1901, and a Business
League as well. There the Chamber of Commerce engaged in a very wide
range of activities. In addition to working on Colorado River flooding
problems, the Chamber commissioned a health survey of the city, worked
for creation of a paid fire department, negotiated the merger of the city's
competing telephone companies, acquired Barton Springs for the provision of water to the city, and began, in 1917, "educational work for the
council-manager form of government." These efforts and others constituted "its active program for the growth of Austin."[60]

The *National Municipal Review* praised the broad range of activities
of the Houston Chamber of Commerce. "Without an aggressive business
organization," the *Review* editorialized, "a city may be likened to a ship
without a rudder." Among other things, Houston's Chamber worked for
the ship channel and campaigned for more rapid street paving. The
Chamber reached the public by organizing "a corps of public speakers"
in the wards, by "hiring three cartoonists" to supply the newspapers with
free cartoons, and by paying movie theaters to show slides advocating
Chamber proposals at "every moving picture show in the city."[61]

As the activities of the Austin and Houston chambers suggests, chambers of commerce and like organizations were concerned not only with
particular projects, like harbor improvements, but also with city building
most broadly understood. One indication of this commitment was investment in city plans. National planning consultants were hired in Austin,
San Diego, and Dallas, while Houston created a City Planning Commission. In Austin the Chamber of Commerce "first began the agitation for a
City Plan . . . in 1915." The desire was some time in coming to fruition,

[59] Ed H. McCuiston, "The Commercial Secretary," and J. E. Surrat, "Cooperation between City Officials and Chambers of Commerce in City Building," *Texas Municipalities* 4,
no. 4 (July 1917): 141–43, 138–40. Surrat, secretary of the Sherman Texas Chamber of
Commerce, saw little room for conflict between the Chamber and city government: "My
plan has been to let the other fellow handle any job that he wants to handle, unless his
handling it is in clear conflict with some pronounced policy of the chamber of commerce.
This seldom, if ever, happens, and by working on this principle [of amicable division of
labor] the chamber of commerce and city officials can avoid all conflict."

[60] Lacy, "Austin," 4, 7; Walter E. Long, *Something Made Austin Grow* (Austin: Chamber of Commerce, 1948).

[61] Jerome H. Farbar, "The Houston Chamber of Commerce," *National Municipal Review* 2, no. 1 (January 1913): quotes are from 104, 105.

but Austin's downtown still bears the imprint of Koch and Fowler's *City Plan* of 1928. Koch and Fowler did not confine themselves to the physical development of the city, but also were concerned with the sources of its growth. "While Austin has some industrial development" the planners observed,

> industrial development will not be the controlling element that will build future Austin and develop its future character. On account of the location of the numerous state institutions, schools, and the State University, . . . Austin, with the natural beauty of its topography and the unusual climate making it an ideal residential city, it is only natural that the chief characteristic of greater Austin will continue . . . essentially a cultural and education center.[62]

Similarly, John Nolen's report to San Diego's Chamber of Commerce (1908) charted streets, parks, and public plazas, and also recognized both Balboa Park (which Nolen thought was a mistake) and the Bay as key to the city's development of commerce, recreation, and tourism. Little came of the first plan, but Nolen remained in correspondence with local planning advocates and in 1924 was again hired, this time by a coalition of private organizations and the city council, to draft a plan for the city. Lack of support for both the first and the second plans revealed local disagreement on competing claims to the waterfront, some favoring development for recreation and tourism, others commercial development, and still others more accommodation of the navy.[63]

In Dallas the adoption of a city plan in 1910 was one of several progressive steps "forced" on the government by "voluntarily organized groups of businessmen interested in the larger development" of the city. The *Dallas Morning News* joined the Civic Improvement League in advocating planning, and "in one year printed over eight hundred columns" explaining the uses of planning. Thus "public opinion forced the commission to hire" George Kessler, a planning engineer from Kansas City, who provided a plan in 1919. Like the plans of Nolen in San Diego and Koch and Fowler in Austin, Kessler's plan not only provided a map,

[62] Koch and Fowler, "A City Plan for Austin, Texas" (Koch and Fowler, consulting engineers, mimeograph, 1928), 3. On initial Chamber interest in planning, Walter E. Long to W. T. Mather, November 9, 1926 (Walter E. Long Papers, Austin History Center, Box 1). Long was secretary of the Chamber of Commerce. Long's papers also include a clipping from the *Dallas Morning News*, August 8, 1926, discussing the importance of racial segregation. Similarly, the Houston City Planning Commission wrote in 1929: "These negroes are a necessary and useful element in the population and suitable areas with proper living and recreation facilities should be set aside for them. Because of long established racial prejudices, it is best for both races that living areas be segregated" by mutual agreement, since segregation by law was unconstitutional. Report of the City Planning Commission, 1929, p. 25. Oscar Holcombe Papers, box 3.

[63] Pourade, *History*, 5:97–101, Marston, *George White Marston*, 89–92.

but also embodied an economic growth strategy for Dallas. With that on paper, the "Kessler Plan Association . . . carried on a concerted campaign, directed from Chamber of Commerce headquarters, for further public works."[64]

The efforts of organized elites had widespread salience because failure meant community tragedy and successes meant possibilities for prosperity and growth. In the first decades of the twentieth century, these towns experienced significant successes. Each city made progress developing a growth strategy and securing its fundamentals. Galveston's tragedy, the discovery of oil, and the creation of a superior harbor all promoted Houston's role as a port city. Houston also had industrial ambitions, and these were well under way not only with oil-related industries but also with even greater employment by the railroads. Albuquerque relied heavily on the Santa Fe yards and was also beginning to promote herself as a health site. Austin and San Diego were greatly discouraged in the pursuit of industry. Austin's flooding problems caused some to despair of industrial prospects. Later, elites decided against the pursuit of industry and favored instead the creation of a white-collar city employed at the university and in the state bureaucracy. San Diego was by the end of the First World War wed to the armed forces, and aspired to a stronger position attracting tourists. San Jose and Phoenix continued to stake growth prospects on shipping the produce of their agricultural surroundings; Phoenix looked as well to attracting health seekers from less hospitable climates.

Small wonder that authors of local histories lauded urban elites for their collective entrepreneurial achievements. Karen Lynn Smith wrote that Phoenix was distinguished by the selfless dedication of turn of the century leaders; G. Wesley Johnson concurred that the national orientation of Phoenix leaders "suggests why Phoenix may have taken off economically, compared to neighboring towns such as Wickenburg or Florence, where purely local interest and perspectives predominated—and where little growth occurred after the 1880s."[65] Anthony Orum praised the "orchard planters" of Austin without whose devotion "the commu-

[64] Harold A. Stone, "City Manager Government in Dallas," in *City Manager Government in Nine Cities*, ed. Harold A. Stone, Don K. Price, and Kathryn H. Stone (Chicago: Public Administration Service, 1950), 271–72. Surrat may have thought of Dallas when he wrote "Cooperation between City Officials and Chambers of Commerce in City Building" for *Texas Municipalities* in 1917. By 1926 Surrat was secretary to the Kessler Plan Association in Sherman (letter to W. E. Long, September 7, 1926, Long Papers, box 50).

[65] Karen Lynn Smith, "Town to City," 210, G. Wesley Johnson, "Generations of Elites and Social Change in Phoenix" in *Community Development in the American West: Past and Present Nineteenth and Twentieth Century Frontiers*, ed. Jessie L. Embry and Howard A. Christy (Provo: Brigham Young University, 1985), 79–109.

nity itself" might never have taken form, leaders of vision who succeeded at "symbolizing the people."[66] Historians of San Diego credit "father" Alonzo Horton and John D. Spreckels for vision and generosity.

Further progress for southwestern cities required not only continued success with outsiders, but also more efficient and powerful local governments. Local governments had already been augmented by the creation of Harbor Boards, Navigation Districts, and like authorities. These administrative inventions exercised governmental powers in pursuit of growth objectives. City governments also needed regular revenues adequate for paving, grading, and schools, as well as increased borrowing capacity for larger capital investments. In addition to augmenting their taxing powers, local governments needed to monitor expenses more carefully and tailor spending to growth strategies. Existing institutional arrangements seemed to contemporaries inadequate to these tasks, and town leaders mobilized to recast them. Like Childs's Reformer, town leaders set forth cheerfully toward sure defeat.

[66] Anthony Orum, *Power, Money, and the People*, 51–52.

Three

Setting Forth Cheerfully

IN 1917 the *National Municipal Review* asked, "Why should business men be concerned with city government?" The answer was "the purpose of enlightened municipal government is to make a city a safe place in which to do business":

> No farsighted executive cares or dares risk his concern . . . to the attention of an indifferent and mismanaged city administration. [Local government] has so intimate a relationship to the prosperity of the community . . . that the modern executive has been compelled . . . to take a vigorous stand on urban problems.

The same farsighted executive would, in the author's view, embrace municipal reform. A "new" city government would place the city "on a sound financial basis"; require efficiency of municipal employees, provide "enough water at low cost"; "motorize" the fire department to lower insurance rates; employ "adequate police for strikes [*sic*], disasters, and fires"; organize metropolitan transportation, regulate housing and sanitation, and insure low taxes.[1]

These claims spoke directly to the concerns of southwestern city builders. Houston's problems, summarized by the *Chronicle* in 1913, fairly represent the difficulties of local governments in these years:

> The city owes a large public debt with very little improvements to show for the vast sums of money that have already been spent. Only a small percentage of our streets are improved, the sewerage and drainage systems are sadly inadequate, while our school facilities are not sufficient to take care of the children should compulsory education be established.[2]

San Jose's situation was much the same. On one hand the city suffered a poor level of services, exemplified by "a capricious policy of street improvement." On the other:

> Everybody knew the city was in debt but beyond that there was no accurate information available, since every department kept separate accounts. . . . As for the city's status, if the present rate of expenditures were to continue for the

---

[1] Harry A. Toulmin, Jr., "Your Chamber of Commerce and Your City Government," *National Municipal Review* 6, no. 5 (September 1917): 614–15.

[2] *Houston Chronicle*, October 16, 1913, 4.

remaining five months of the fiscal year San Jose would face [a] . . . deficit of
. . . $30,000. Half the streetlights were discontinued and by measures of this
sort the city was steered through the crisis.[3]

Some citizen activists in the Southwest had long been organized in pursuit of better government. Middle-class residents of Houston formed a
Good Government League in 1895; in Austin and San Jose, there were
attempts at reform in 1890s; in Phoenix, the city council itself wrote to
the National Municipal League for advice about local government
reform.

To solve the financial and management problems of local government,
leaders of southwestern cities looked to the municipal reform movement.
The cities themselves were prominent in the movement for municipal
reform. National Municipal League meetings were held in Los Angeles in
1911; Dallas, Fresno, Los Angeles, and Austin were represented among
the league's officers in 1916.[4] Urban leaders in California organized the
California Municipal League in November of 1913; their counterparts in
Texas organized the Texas League of Municipalities in the same year.
Alongside the eastern intellectuals associated with the National Municipal League—William Bennett Munro of Harvard, Charles Beard of Columbia, and Clinton Rogers Woodruff, secretary of the league, among
them—were academics from the Southwest, equally active in municipal
reform: Thomas H. Reed of the University of California, Edwin Cottrell
of Stanford, Arthur G. Peterson of San Diego City College, and Herman
G. James of the University of Texas at Austin.

The regional setting structured the stage for municipal reform as it did
for community efforts at economic development. The tensions that per-
meated the struggle for economic growth also animated politics. As
Dewey Grantham wrote of Texas, "The problem [of controlling outside
corporations, especially the railroads] was exacerbated by the pervasive
yearning for economic growth, on the one hand, and the colonial character of capital investment and the enormous influence of the corporations
on the other."[5] The national parties were suspect because of their ties to
large corporate interests; the West, like the South, was fertile ground for
populism, free silver sentiment, radical unionism (in the Western Federation of Miners and the International Workers of the World), and social-
ism. The same issues galvanized western progressivism and played a role

[3] Robert Thorpe, "Council-Manager Government in San Jose, California" (M.A. thesis,
Stanford University, 1938), 9, 12–13.
[4] "Twenty-first Annual Meeting of the National Municipal League," *National Municipal Review* 5, no. 1 (1916): 168–94.
[5] Dewey Grantham, *Southern Progressivism: The Reconciliation of Progress and Tradition* (Knoxville: University of Tennessee Press, 1983), 100.

in municipal reform. Municipal reform was tied to local desires for growth and fears of economic subordination; in southwestern cities, municipal reformers were men who hoped to tie their communities more closely to national investors. Their claims to leadership rested in part on their successes negotiating with outside investors and higher governments. While reformers in New York or Boston tended to be "the interests," reformers in the Southwest were—or at least claimed to be—regional patriots fighting to secure better things for their towns without compromising with "the Beast." And because these communities really were in need of outside assistance, it was rational for voters to support municipal reform.

The Regional Setting of Municipal Reform

Just as southwesterners were latecomers to economic development, they were also latecomers to national politics. The well organized and well disciplined parties of the east, resting securely on the emphatic partisanship of their supporters, were absent from the Southwest. Here the major parties were not so well positioned either in the cities or in the countryside. Regional concerns about outside control made the major parties suspect from a popular point of view. Republicans and Democrats competed with one another but also suffered challenges of populists, socialists, and soon, progressive insurgents. (It is worth noting that these recent popular insurgencies belie any suggestion that a conservative political culture "naturally" gave rise to reform governments shortly after the turn of the century.) In the territories of New Mexico and Arizona, party organization was a product of national patronage. Territorial governors were appointed by the president and in turn appointed territorial officials. This added to the burdens of parties seeking popular support: not only were the parties suspect for their ties to railroads, mines, and other large investors, but they were also regarded as carpetbaggers because of their roots in the nation's capital. In Texas Democratic partisanship was a given (once the Populist threat receded), although unquestioned party preference did not mean strong local or precinct organizations. Similarly, Republicans had an overwhelming lead in California, although local, much less precinct, organization was scarce.

The local political setting for reform campaigns was altogether different than in the older, big cities, which first fostered the reform movement. In the Northeast in the progressive years, urban politics was characterized by strong party organizations on one hand and their opponents in the municipal reform movement on the other. This was the period of "militant" party organization, strong machines, and well-heeled structural and social reformers. The cities and towns of the Southwest present a quite different picture. Parties were not rooted in neighborhoods and communities but "hung like marionettes" on weak strings of elite partisanship.[6] Thus the provocation to reform campaigns was hardly domination of local government by well-organized partisan machines. Although reformers might denounce incumbents as "bosses," most of these cities had neither strong enough political organizations, nor strong enough partisan attachments, to merit the term "machine." As will be shown below, reformers spent much more energy denouncing contemporary governmental arrangements than incumbent politicians. And although reformers emphasized the good character of their candidates, they staked their claims for reform government on the new institutions proposed for city charters rather than on the men who would run those governments.

The weakness of party organizations in southwestern cities advantaged reformers in several ways. First, the opposition to reform was weaker. The strong party organizations of the Northeast that claimed the allegiance of many citizens and successfully defended themselves against the attacks of municipal reformers were not present in southwestern cities. Second, as state governments moved to restrict suffrage with poll taxes, literacy tests, and like devices, neither party regarded the disfranchised as potential constituents whom they had a stake in defending. The result was that campaigns for municipal reform were waged before a limited audience of potential voters, while those disfranchised were most likely to have been opponents. Third, Martin Shefter has argued that weak parties meant the West had a greater "regional receptivity to reform." Because the third party system was not well established in the west, and the issues dividing the Democrats and the Republicans did not have much salience for western voters,[7] the electorate was more easily drawn to voting for the Progressives and to supporting nonpartisanship, initiative, referendum, and recall. Shefter's analysis of California showed, moreover, that Progressives brought new voters into the electorate.[8] Just as voting

[6] This is a paraphrase of Philip J. Ethington's comment that in San Francisco in the 1890s "the urban party 'machine' did not rest on a base of support in the neighborhoods so much as it was suspended like a marionette from above." *The Public City* (New York: Cambridge University Press, 1995), 342.

[7] My own reading is that voter antipathy to the major parties was more relevant than voter apathy about third-party system issues. Animosity toward the Republicans and their strong ties to the "Octopus" surely motivated the leaders of the Lincoln-Roosevelt League and dominated their appeals to voters.

[8] Martin Shefter, "Regional Receptivity to Reform: Legacy of the Progressive Era," in his *Political Parties and the State* (Princeton: Princeton University Press, 1994), 459–83. Of the states considered here, Shefter considers only California. Shefter points out that although California joined the union before the Civil War, the state lacked the traditional party organization of the East and Midwest. Shefter excluded Oklahoma and Texas because

for the Progressive party and the antiparty measures it supported may have come more easily in the west because Democratic and Republican party attachments were weaker, so the region was more hospitable to municipal reform.

Region also adds a new dimension to another line of argument about municipal reform. While political scientists have focused on middle-class values, historians since Hofstadter have generally argued that business leaders were the most prominent advocates of municipal reform. Martin Shefter and I have argued for the nineteenth century, and Samuel Hays and James Weinstein for the Progressive Era, that businessmen organized and campaigned for municipal reform to curb the extravagance of machine governments and centralize political control.[9] Weinstein, for example, titles his chapter on municipal reform "The Small Businessman as Big Businessman," capturing his argument that in the city smaller entrepreneurs could play the creative and directing role that executives of major corporations played in national politics. "Chambers of commerce and other organized business groups," Weinstein argued, "were the decisive element . . . which made the movement a sweeping success."[10]

The account provided here alters this picture by recognizing the dependence of southwestern cities on resources secured elsewhere. In this context, the success of businessmen as reformers was not simply a consequence of the greater resources they brought to political conflict, but also of their capacity to win from outsiders, including state and national governments, the investments their communities required. Thus they provide an excellent example of Clarence Stone's "power to." Not only did this distinguish them from competing local elites, it also provided voters with good reasons to support them, despite the antidemocratic features of reform charters. The account here differs from prior accounts, then, by recognizing that the regional setting empowered and legitimated those business leaders whose "power to" seemed best linked to collective advance.[11]

---

of their allegiance to the Confederacy, and New Mexico and Arizona because they did not become states until 1912.

[9] Amy Bridges, "Another Look at Plutocracy and Politics in Antebellum New York City," *Political Science Quarterly* 97, no. 1 (1982); Martin Shefter, *Political Crisis, Fiscal Crisis: The Collapse and Revival of New York City* (New York: Basic Books, 1985); Samuel P. Hays, "The Politics of Municipal Reform in the Progressive Era," *Pacific Northwest Quarterly* (1964): 157–69; James Weinstein, *The Corporate Ideal in the Liberal State* (Boston: Beacon, 1968), chap. 4.

[10] Weinstein, *Corporate Ideal*, 99.

[11] In addition, Hays and Weinstein provide only cursory accounts of local campaigns for municipal reform and the attendant political struggles. I offer a more complete account of reform rhetoric and opposition arguments, revealing what contemporaries thought was at stake in the adoption of reform charters.

For all of these reasons, in the Progressive Era Albuquerque, Houston, Austin, San Diego, Phoenix, and dozens of other cities refashioned local government to be more powerful and efficient, creating new institutional arrangements that shaped local politics for decades to come.

Campaigning for Municipal Reform

After Galveston adopted commission government in 1901, there was a presumption that any change in local government arrangements would follow Galveston's lead.[12] Galveston was devastated by a hurricane in 1901, and prominent citizens in the Deep Water Committee took the opportunity this created to draft a plan for a new and businesslike administration. Under the auspices of the commission government the state legislature created, these men rebuilt the city. The achievements of Galveston's commission government were trumpeted at the National Municipal League meetings in 1906, in *Harper's Weekly*, *McClure's*, and elsewhere. As Bradley Rice explained, "Galveston's contribution to municipal reform . . . temporarily became the core of urban progressivism."[13]

Galveston was a portent of urban political futures not only for the charter it was given, but also for the kinds of opposition the proposed commission government aroused. Some who opposed the Galveston plan voiced apprehension about "rich man's government." In fact the men of the Deep Water Committee did own a controlling interest in the city's banks and corporations, and much of the city's real estate as well. More emphatically, the plan was opposed as undemocratic. As proposed—and as initially implemented—the commissioners in Galveston's new government were appointed by the governor. This provoked one politician to claim the plan "disfranchises free citizens of Texas, destroys the right of local self-government, violates the Constitution of the States, holds in derision the Declaration of Independence, [and] tramples underfoot the fundamental principles of a free republic." More succinctly, the plan was denounced as "receivership in disguise." These objections hardly mattered since the citizens of Galveston did not vote on the plan, which was authorized by the state government.[14]

[12] Galveston was not the first city to adopt a commission government charter; there were precedents in New Orleans, Mobile, Memphis, and Selma. Galveston, however, because of the spectacular circumstances in which reform was adopted and implemented, served as the national exemplar of the benefits of commission government. Bradley Robert Rice, *Progressive Cities: The Commission Government Movement in America, 1901–1920* (Austin: University of Texas Press, 1977) 17–18.

[13] Bradley R. Rice, "The Galveston Plan of City Government by Commission: The Birth of Progressive Idea," *Southwestern Historical Quarterly* 78, no. 4 (April 1975): 366–408.

[14] Rice, "Galveston Plan," 401, 388.

Despite these objections (which were not given nearly the press Galveston's "success" was), participants in the National Municipal League were unanimous in their support of commission government, nonpartisanship, citywide elections, and civil service reform. Commissioners were to be elected to serve both as heads of departments and as members of the city council. The thought was that these arrangements would centralize administration and simplify lines of authority.

Citywide elections and nonpartisanship[15] were in their initial conception as much offensive weapons aimed at machine and party organization as constructive elements for the new scheme. Each was aimed at breaking the ties of voter to officeholder that kept machine politics alive. Later the addition of a city manager was proposed. Under the city-manager plan, the city council (composed ordinarily of aldermen without administrative responsibilities but in some cases of commissioners) was meant to vote on matters of policy, while the city manager executed policy and administered the departments of local government.

Everywhere, proposals for municipal reform provoked heated debate. The dominant themes of reformers' arguments were the substitution of business for politics, government by virtuous men, and the promise that reformed local government would be more conducive to municipal growth. Opponents of reform saw in commissions and city managers autocratic arrogations of power and argued for representation and democracy in local government.

Reformers campaigned for commission government by promising "the substitution of business for politics."[16] That phrase summarized both the purported virtues of the commission and manager forms and the alleged vices of the arrangements they were meant to replace. "Business" signified simplicity, clear lines of responsibility, and efficiency in administration. Efficient administration would put an end to fiscal mismanagement, enable government to retire its debt, and so lower taxes.

The removal of "politics" from local government meant an end to corruption and "bossism."[17] San Diego was considered "a concrete case of despotism," a part of California's system of "government *of* the machine, *by* the bosses, *for* the public utility corporations."[18] Indeed, argued an

---

[15] Texas presents a different case, but with similar results for reformers. There cities considering nonpartisanship risked abandoning the Democratic white primary, and although cities were quick in their adoption of municipal reform, often they retained partisan (really one-party) elections.

[16] *Arizona Gazette*, January 22, 1913.

[17] *Austin Daily Statesman*, December 24, 1908.

[18] William E. Smythe, "Responsible Government for California," *Out West* 26, no. 5 (May 1907): 456–61.

Arizona editorial, "many cities had been compelled to adopt [commission government] as a matter of self defense of its citizens against corrupt political machines and grafting politicians. . . . Business and politics will not mix to the advantage of the taxpayer in any municipality. . . . commission government [will] divorce politics from municipal management, and . . . install business in its stead".[19]

Both the installation of businesslike government and the removal of politics from local administration argued for nonpartisan elections. Parties were hardly the safeguard of democracy that they had once claimed to be. If citizens were dissatisfied with local government under party rule, "there was nothing they could do about it before the succeeding municipal election, and the chances were that even then they could not prevail against the machine. If the machine happened to be overthrown that would be accomplished by an opposing machine and one party machine is as bad as another and as wasteful and disregardful of the interests of the people. Under the proposed charter there can be no party machine because there can be no parties."[20] Theodore Roosevelt had argued that "the worst evils that affect our local government arise from and are the inevitable result of the mixing up of city affairs with the party politics of the nation and state."[21] Nonpartisanship was appropriate for local government because party politics was irrelevant to urban administration. "What had tariff revision or bank guarantees," asked an Austin reformer, "to do with the condition of Austin streets?"[22] The *Arizona Republican* agreed: "No city can flourish as luxuriantly in the shadow of politics as in the sunshine of nonpartisan cooperation. There is apt to be no civic spirit in politics. When men divide their loyalty between city and party, the former gets a meager share of it."[23]

Nonpartisanship promised to unite all those desiring reform in its pursuit. "There can be no harmony without sacrifice of principle. If there be sacrifice . . . let it be of partisanship rather than patriotism."[24] In place of self-serving career politicians, commissions would provide "virtuous government by virtuous men." The commission plan would provide "for

[19] *Arizona Gazette*, October 7, 1913. See also *Arizona Gazette*, October 9 and 13, 1913, and the *Arizona Republican*, November 7, 1912. The *Albuquerque Morning Journal* denounced the opponents of reform as politicians, September 16, 1917. Reformer George Marston argued, "The city of San Diego is simply a public corporation and the rules applying to the business management of any corporate interests ought to apply to the management of the city's affairs" (*San Diego Sun*, December 20, 1908, 1).

[20] *Arizona Republican*, August 20, 1913, 4.
[21] Smythe, "Responsible Government," 461.
[22] *Austin Daily Statesman*, December 29, 1908.
[23] *Arizona Republican*, August 2, 1913, 4.
[24] *San Diego Union*, January 3, 1909, 10.

the employment of the best men we can hire to run this large business, men of capacity and honesty."[25] Freed from party domination, "The people, on the alert, will always be standing together against the politicians, for good government."[26]

These noble sentiments sometimes masked more instrumental partisan motives. In Albuquerque and Phoenix, Democrats threw their support to nonpartisanship as the suburbanization of their constituents eroded the likelihood of victory in municipal elections.[27] In Albuquerque, Democrats "while affirming our allegiance to the time-honored doctrines of the party in national affairs, believe that partisan politics have no place in the administration of local affairs and should be eliminated . . . in the election of city officers."[28] In Phoenix nonpartisan slates allowed Republicans and Democrats to unite against Socialists, who at times polled a respectable portion of the vote.[29] In San Diego nonpartisanship seemed a good vehicle for Progressive Republican leaders who wished to wean voters from old guard Republicans and their local organization.[30]

In San Diego and Albuquerque, local administrations were attacked. In Albuquerque the *Morning Journal* complained:

> The democratic organization, one of the most perfect organizations ever put to work . . . here, was liberally supplied with money which was expended lavishly. At every polling place democratic "workers," the majority of them on the payroll of the organization, were lined up. The big lines of men employed on the sewer construction work were brought by the wagon load, dumped out and voted for the democratic ticket, and hauled back to the sewer again.[31]

More often care was taken to distinguish between honorable local politicians and objectionable charter arrangements. A. C. Baldwin, advocating a new charter for Austin in 1908, insisted, "It is not the men we complain of, but the system." Similarly, the *Arizona Gazette* editorialized, "There is little doubt that [Phoenix] is better governed than most cities. . . . it is no disparagement to those who have governed it in

[25] *Arizona Republican*, November 8, 1912, 4.

[26] Ibid., August 20, 1913, 4.

[27] Michael J. Schingle, "Albuquerque Urban Politics, 1891–1955: Aldermanic vs. Commission Government" (senior thesis, University of New Mexico, August 1976), 10–13.

[28] *Albuquerque Morning Journal*, March 26, 1912, 3.

[29] Joseph. C. Smith, "The Phoenix Drive for Municipal Reform and Charter Government, 1911–1915" (Arizona Historical Foundation Manuscript Collection, Arizona State University, Tempe, April 1975), 7–9.

[30] Grace Louise Miller, "The San Diego Progressive Movement, 1900–1920" (Ph.D. dissertation, University of California, Santa Barbara, 1976), chap. 3.

[31] For San Diego see *supra*; for Albuquerque, Schingle "Albuquerque Urban Politics"; quotes the *Journal* of April 6, 1910.

the past to say that they have not been in a position to give it the best in their power."[32]

Among the systemic causes of inefficiency and disregard for the general good was the election of city council members from wards. Wards were pernicious because "a local alderman will work for his ward against the general welfare of the city."[33] "The typical alderman," argued an Austin professor, "always was, always is, and always will be more anxious to please his little crowd of ward voices and supporters than a commissioner elected at large."[34] Even more condemning was the argument that "so long as the town is divided by wards and controlled by politics the growth of the town will be retarded."[35] At-large elections would "tend to the best interests of the whole city, and do away with sectional interests."[36] To those who saw in the wards a commitment to democracy, reformers proposed initiative, referendum, and recall.[37]

Taken together these changes promised to create an environment conducive to growth. "Business administration," promised reformers in the Texas capital, "would make Austin grow."[38] In 1913 Houston's voters were urged to adopt amendments to the city charter, as "the present charter . . . is behind the times," and "the proposed amendments are necessary to give Houston what is needed to build for the future."[39] In 1912 and 1913, the *Arizona Republican* also linked its arguments for commission and nonpartisan government to growth:

---

[32] *Austin Daily Statesman*, December 24, 1908, 2; *Arizona Gazette*, October 7, 1913, 4.

[33] *Austin Daily Statesman*, December 29, 1908.

[34] *Ibid.*, December 29, 1908, 5.

[35] Shipe quoted in Frank Staniszewski, "Ideology and Practice in Municipal Government Reform: A Case Study of Austin" (University of Texas at Austin Studies in Politics Series I : Studies in Urban Political Economy, paper no. 8, 1977), 27.

[36] The chairman of the Publicity Committee on Charter Amendments in the *San Diego Union*, January 10, 1909, 14. And similarly, "An official is the servant of his constituents: if his obligation is to all the people then he will serve all the people; if it is to only a portion of the people . . . then he will serve that portion, even to the injustice of the whole;—that is but human nature the world over" (*San Diego Union*, January 3, 1909, 10.) Smythe, "Responsible Government," makes the same argument.

[37] "Above all, the [Arizona] *Gazette* believes in direct government by the people. It believes in the initiative, referendum, and the recall. It does not fear to trust the people" (October 10, 1913, 4); and see also November 7, 1912, 1. Houston's Mayor Campbell saw in an initiative, referendum, and recall "the power [the people] should have of initiating any legislation they want or recalling any officer . . . who is careless of his trust. . . . With the initiative, recall, and referendum in our charter the people would have a club in their own hands that would be calculated to secure for them the best possible service." (*Houston Chronicle*, October 13, 1913, 12).

[38] *Austin Statesman*, December 29, 1908.

[39] *Houston Chronicle*, October 14, 1913, 8.

A very patent thing is that this will be the charter of Phoenix or the present antiquated awkward charter will obtain indefinitely. The city now struggling forward and moving in spite of the charter will continue to be handicapped at a stage of its existence when its form of government ought to be made to encourage and stimulate its growth.[40]

A new charter would "unloose the bonds of the city which have so retarded the growth of Phoenix."[41]

Opponents of commission government found fault with each of these arguments and proposals. Some opposition was purely practical: local politicians objected to changes that would likely throw them out of office. In San Diego, the *Sun* reported: " 'The push'—or in other words, Boss Hardy's local Republican machine—has got the word to vote against the proposed charter amendments. This means that the word has gone out to faithful to vote the charter changes down . . . and keep the city government just as it is now."[42]

The dominant theme of opposition was the desire for democracy and representation, beginning with the process of reform itself. New charters were often drafted by boards of freeholders or specially appointed commissions that were not themselves representative.[43]

Commission government was opposed as too centralized, a criticism leveled at the small number of commissioners, citywide elections, and the concentration of responsibilities in the council. Centralization of administration was held to be an autocratic arrogation of power, and the man who drafted Austin's proposed commission charter was charged with "seeking to become the boss of [a local] Tammany."[44] Similarly, in Albuquerque one ward meeting resolved to oppose the commission charter, believing "it unwise and imprudent to entrust the affairs of the city to the unrestrained control of three men. . . . there is no limitation upon the power of the all powerful commission and . . . the proposed form . . . is unrepresentative."[45]

[40] November 5, 1912, 4

[41] *Arizona Republican*, November 6, 1912, 4. The positive experience of other cities that adopted commission government was also brought to the attention of voters. For example, the *San Diego Union* reported on Des Moines (January 10, 1909, 9) and El Paso (January 7, 1909, 8).

[42] *San Diego Sun*, January 11, 1909, l.

[43] In Phoenix there were protests that (despite claims that it represented all the citizens of Phoenix) the committee to draft the charter included no labor representative. The Phoenix Trades Council demanded "as citizens of the community that the working class be represented in the forming of this charter, and that the working class have representation on the commission," a demand that met with no response. By contrast, representation of the elite women's clubs was agreed to (*Arizona Republican*, April 17, 1913).

[44] *Austin Daily Statesman*, December 24, 1908.

[45] *Albuquerque Morning Journal*, September 22, 1917, 2.

There was opposition everywhere to abolishing wards for electing city councilmen. In Albuquerque the *Morning Journal* argued that under the mayor-council system the working man could "go to his alderman and secure anything in reason for his ward," while under the proposed commission plan worker and neighborhood would not be represented. For this and other reasons, the *Journal* opposed the commission plan, fearing domination by the "'silk stocking' fourth ward." Hispanic politicians in Albuquerque also cautioned their constituents that the influence of Spanish-speaking voters would likely decline under commission government.[46] In Austin it was argued that "under the aldermanic system the citizens are assured direct representation in the affairs of the municipality, and direct control over ward improvements. Ward representation is in line with the democratic doctrine of local self-government. Commission government destroys this principle and establishes a centralization in municipal affairs."[47] Austin's Alderman Cuneo defended himself as "a man who did his duty to his ward every day."[48]

Parties were also defended (although infrequently). In San Diego Republicans asked: "Who is speaking? A political demagogue worse than a political boss, because the former is responsible to no one but a boss is responsible to the party."[49] In Texas the Democratic party was of course a bulwark of white supremacy, and nonpartisanship was suspect on those grounds. Alderman Harry Haynes in Austin defended "politics" against reform as the heart of democratic self-government:

> The boosters of this so-called reform government frantically claim that all ward lines and all politics must be eliminated. No my friends, we of the east side— especially the old Eighth Ward—we remember a time when we were represented in the council by mugwumps and negroes and the terrible struggle we had to wrest the city government from them, and I do not think we are ready to disorganize or eliminate politics at the demand of a few men.[50]

One year after Austin adopted commission government, local Democrats announced their intention "to continue city organization and . . . seek amendment to [the] city charter cutting out non-partisan primaries."[51]

More broadly, there were objections to the substitution of business for politics. The *Houston Labor Journal* editorialized against "hired mayors" in October of 1917:

[46] Schingle, "Albuquerque Urban Politics," 18.

[47] *Austin Daily Statesman*, December 27, 1908, 2.

[48] *Austin Daily Statesman*, December 24, 1908, 3.

[49] *San Diego Union*, August 31, 1911. Clipping in the Meyer Lissner Collection, Stanford University.

[50] November 12, 1908, quoted in *Austin American*, August 4, 1924.

[51] *Austin Daily Statesman*, April 6, 1909, 1.

Let us get back to real representative government and clear the issue of all this "business" buncombe and running municipalities on the "per cent" groove as private corporations are run. Corruption never springs from the gutter. You may find some "thing" in the gutter willing to be tempted, but the source of temptation comes from above—from the so-called business element and the pubic utility corporations and municipal contractors who have waxed fat off municipal corruption for a half century and longer. And the idea of turning a city government over to this element to reform it is not only preposterous, but absolutely silly. . . . "Per cent" is what they are after; and commission government will never be a success because you can't keep the Big Rich from grafting.[52]

Although those who proposed new charters claimed to be for business administration in place of politics, it was more likely, opponents argued, that one machine would simply replace another. Commission government in Austin would be "an office holding trust, and . . . enable the trust to so establish itself in power that the people would become powerless to free themselves from the octopus."[53] Albuquerque's commissioners would be better labeled "kaiser number one, kaiser number two, and kaiser number three."[54] San Diego's proposed manager was denounced as a potential czar.[55]

Although the language of these debates was extravagant, the goals of reformers and fears of opponents were not fanciful. The centralization of authority provided by commission charters facilitated bypassing neighborhood desires and interests. Changes in taxing authority equally threatened neighborhood interests. In the nineteenth century, and in some places well into the twentieth, street paving and other amenities were financed by special assessments. Property owners were assessed for their contribution to improvements immediately affecting them. When cities abandoned this in favor of more general systems of taxation, the means was provided to tax the periphery, as it were, to finance improvements at the center (or deemed by the center as good growth investments). In Albuquerque the proposed increased taxing power was seen as a direct threat to working class homeowners. Opposing their limited incomes to the situation of two of the proposed charter's well known supporters, the *Albuquerque Morning Journal* editorialized:

Mr. Metcalf can pay for any kind of paving in front of his home, and so can Mr. Coors. But what does it mean to the man of small income who has been

[52] *Houston Labor Journal*, October 5, 1917.
[53] Incumbent Mayor Maddox in *Austin Daily Statesman* December 24, 1908, 3.
[54] *Albuquerque Morning Journal*, September 22, 1917, 6.
[55] Harold A. Stone, Don K. Price, and Kathryn H. Stone, *City Manager Government in Nine Cities* (Chicago: Public Administration Service, 1950), 179.

able to secure title to a humble home for which he probably still is paying on the installment plan?

It would mean ruin.

But Mr. Metcalf and his friends will say that no commission would do such a thing.

Do you want to take that risk? . . .

The ratification of this charter with that provision in it would be the most disastrous thing that could occur to Albuquerque.[56]

In addition to denying neighborhoods direct representation by abolishing wards, reform charters also proposed making it more difficult to vote and hold office. While supporters of commission government did not draw attention to the antidemocratic features of their proposals, opponents of commission government were quick to point them out. In Phoenix a 1912 charter restricted suffrage to taxpayers. (This was held unconstitutional by the state/territorial government.)[57] In Austin only property holders were to vote in recall elections, and officials were to post $10,000 bond before taking office.[58] Proposals to cut the pay of public officials were equally likely to discourage any but the affluent from seeking municipal posts.[59] For each of these reasons opponents of municipal reform argued that although new charters were seductive in their promise of efficient administration, it was nevertheless to be hoped that "our people will not be beguiled into sacrificing their political rights."[60]

Victory

Beguiled they were. Houston approved commission government in 1905, and Austin and San Diego followed suit four years later. Phoenix adopted a commission-manager charter in 1913, and Albuquerque in 1917. They were part of a long string of triumphs for municipal reform across the country. Between 1900 and 1922 San Diego, Pasadena, and twenty other cities in California; Albuquerque and Las Vegas in New Mexico; Tulsa, Oklahoma City, and twenty-two other cities in Oklahoma; Phoenix and Douglas in Arizona; and Galveston, Houston, Dallas, Forth Worth, El Paso, Austin, San Antonio, and seventy other cites in Texas adopted reform charters.[61]

[56] *Albuquerque Morning Journal*, September 22, 1917, 6.
[57] Smith, "Phoenix," 12, 13.
[58] *Austin Daily Statesman*, December 29, 1908, 2.
[59] For Phoenix, for example, see Smith, "Phoenix," 10, 21.
[60] *Austin Daily Statesman*, December 24, 1908, 3.
[61] Rice, *Progressive Cities*, 113–25.

How may we account for the many triumphs of municipal reform? First, suffrage restriction enacted by state legislatures paved the way for successful municipal reform campaigns. Since opposition to municipal reform came generally from organized labor and working-class voters[62] suffrage restriction, generally hampering the have-nots, was bound to enhance reform's chances of success. Texas provides the most persuasive evidence. In Texas the poll tax dramatically decreased the eligible electorate; in Houston almost two-thirds of the electorate was disfranchised in 1903, and Houston enacted its own city poll tax as well.[63] The same laws disfranchised many in Austin and throughout Texas. Aside from Galveston—which did not vote on its commission charter but was given the charter by the state legislature—there were no successful reform campaigns before the Terrell Election Law passed.[64] Although African-Americans were the most prominent targets of the Terrell Law, the constitution of urban electorates was also one objective of disfranchising legislation. In 1891 the *Dallas Morning News* endorsed not only disfranchisement of Negroes, but also the "agrarian agitators of the large cities."[65]

Elsewhere suffrage restriction was not as dramatic but is suggestive nevertheless. In Albuquerque protests in the wake of the adoption of the city-manager plan claimed that there were "many disfranchised" by faulty registration lists. The charter was endorsed by a vote of 553 to 397. Since the majority for the charter was 156, and there were reports that as many as two hundred may have been disfranchised by errors in the registration lists, there was room for doubt even though the *Morning Journal* declared the election "cleanly and honestly won."[66] As San Diego considered its series of charter changes, California suffered generally declining turnout, spurred in the city by nonpartisanship (required by the state legislature).[67] In addition, only "freeholders" could vote on charter

---

[62] That is the evidence of these cases and those reviewed by Rice in ibid.

[63] Harold F. Platt, "City-Building and Progressive Reform" in *The Age of Urban Reform: New Perspectives on the Progressive Era*, ed. Michael H. Ebner and Eugene M. Tobin (Port Washington: Kennikat Press, 1977).

[64] Rice, *Progressive Cities*, lists all commission government adoptions in Texas. There are none between Galveston in 1901 and Houston in 1905. Beaumont provides a good example of a city in which there were several campaigns for reform, none successful until after 1903 (Paul E. Isaac, "Municipal Reform in Beaumont, Texas, 1902–1909," *Southwestern Historical Quarterly* 78, no. 4 [April 1975]: 409–30).

[65] Quoted in Morgan Kousser, *The Shaping of Southern Politics* (New Haven: Yale University Press, 1974), 203, n. 30.

[66] *Albuquerque Morning Journal*, September 26, 1917, 2.

[67] Michael Paul Rogin and John L. Shover, *Political Change in California* (Westport: Greenwood, 1970), 28.

changes.[68] California and Arizona each had both literacy tests and registration requirements.

Second, municipal reform was favored by well-organized and popular local elites. Opposing political leaders were often wealthy and well organized too. In the Southwest reformers were not the "old elite" of their towns, but were distinguished from their elite opponents by their youth, later arrival in the West, financial connections to the East, opposition to municipal ownership, and successful negotiations with outsiders. In Phoenix municipal reform was an accomplishment of the same men who had secured Washington's commitment for the Roosevelt Dam and brought the Southern Pacific and Santa Fe Railroads to Phoenix, Lloyd Christy, Joseph Kibbey, Benjamin Fowler, and Dwight Heard. Heard, for example, brought his inheritance to Phoenix from Chicago (while maintaining financial ties to the East), developed residential communities on the outskirts of Phoenix, bought the *Arizona Republican*, and became a prominent progressive leader.[69]

In San Diego Edward Fletcher, William Smythe, Edgar Luce, and George Marston pressed the cause of reform. Their effort was part of (and subordinate to) a statewide struggle against the Republican party and the Southern Pacific machine. In the city this meant conflict with old guard Republicans, who were led by political boss Hardy and San Diego magnate John D. Spreckels. Marston was a member of San Diego's older business elite, an owner of a large retail establishment and prominent member of the Chamber of Commerce. Ed Fletcher and William Smythe came to San Diego from the East and Midwest and competed with Spreckels in land and water development efforts. Smythe was also active early in the National Irrigation Congress, working with Benjamin Fowler and others to lobby in Washington for the National Reclamation Act.[70]

The Texas cities reveal the same pattern. In Houston the case for reform was pressed by those who organized the navigation district and the harbor board. The author of Austin's new charter was M. M. Shipe, who

[68] *San Diego Union*, January 3, 1909, 9.

[69] G. Wesley Johnson, "Generations of Elites and Social Change in Phoenix," in *Community Development in the American West: Past and Present Nineteenth and Twentieth Century Frontiers*, ed. Jessie L. Embry and Howard A. Christy, (Provo: Brigham Young University, 1985), 87; George S. Hunter, "The Bull Moose Movement in Arizona," *Arizona and the West* 10, no. 4 (1968): 343–62, 355, 359; Karen Lynn Smith, "Town to City: A History of Phoenix, 1870–1912" (M.A. thesis, University of California, Santa Barbara, 1978), 177; newspaper coverage of reform campaign.

[70] Lawrence B. Lee, "William E. Smythe and San Diego, 1901–1908," *Journal of San Diego History* 19, no. 2 (Spring 1973): 10–24; Miller, "San Diego Progressive Movement"; correspondence between Meyer Lissner and E. A. Luce, Lissner papers, box 20, Stanford University.

moved to Austin as a representative of "Kansas City capitalists" and was granted a franchise for an electric street railway. Shipe was an early participant in efforts to construct a dam, and later built the suburb of Hyde Park and financed construction of a road from the town center to the development. (Shipe christened the road "the speedway.")[71] In the same city, Alexander Penn Wooldridge, model civic leader, advocated reform and became mayor under the new charter. Wooldridge championed the establishment of a free public school system and a public library, began organizing for a system of dams fifty years before they became a reality, owned one of the city's first street railways, and was a leader among the city's bankers.[72]

In Houston municipal reform was championed by Oran T. Holt, a retired attorney for the Southern Pacific; John Kirby, an east Texas lumber magnate and owner of newspapers in both Austin and Houston (who paid to have Haskins and Sells audit Houston's books); and Horace Baldwin Rice, "one of Houston's major intermediators with national corporations." Their victory marked "the first time . . . local brokers of outside information, capital, and technology were offered unprecedented, almost irresistible, weight in the political balance of power."[73]

Third, there is some evidence of the preferences of outside investors. Researching the activities of the Boston firm Stone and Webster (which eventually owned Houston's street railways) Walter Campbell found they were impressed with Galveston's commission government. Campbell reports that George Johnson Baldwin, Stone & Webster's most important executive in the South, visited Galveston in October 1901 and sent back a long memo praising the commission form. Campbell comments:

> Standing alone this [judgement] . . . means little but it is extremely important within the context of Stone & Webster's acquisition and consolidation of street railway and electric companies throughout the nation and the South [between 1898 and 1904]. S&W sought allies among the local men often mentioned as the promoters of the commission form of government: businessmen with city-wide interests.[74]

[71] Louis Robert Pietzsch et al., *The Austin Electric Railway System* (Austin: University of Texas, 1906), 4; *American Biography* 48 (American Historical Society, 1931): 233–34; *Austin Magazine* 27, no. 7 (July 1985): 91; *Austin American Statesman*, July 3, 1990, C-1, 2.

[72] Anthony M. Orum, *Power, Money, and the People: The Making of Modern Austin* (Austin: Texas Monthly Press, 1987), chap. 2; Frank Staniszewski, "Ideology and Practice," 11.

[73] Platt, "City Building," 29; on Rice, Harold L. Platt, *City Building in the New South: The Growth of Public Services in Houston, Texas, 1830–1910* (Philadelphia: Temple University Press, 1983), 208. For Kirby, Mary Lasswell, *John Henry Kirby Prince of the Pines* (Austin: Encino Press, 1967), and on Haskins and Sells, Platt, "Progressive Reform," 38.

[74] Walter E. Campbell (University of North Carolina, Chapel Hill), letter to this author,

From their point of view, a system that insulated city government from neighborhood demands while increasing government's authority and taxing powers was bound to be a more responsive partner in franchise negotiations as well as a more fiscally sound investment for bankers. Without investment, federal assistance, public utilities, and a market for bonds, prospects for urban survival were slim. As some utility owners recognized, municipal reform promised to facilitate all of these goals.

Finally, aggressive promotion of reform charters by the National Municipal League, and the testimony of satisfied local public officials and investors increased the visibility and appeal of the commission and later, the city-manager form of government. Supporters of municipal reform quoted liberally from articles in the *National Municipal Review* to make their case in local newspapers; the National Municipal League supplied speakers and consultants as well.

At the moment reformers celebrated triumph after triumph in the Southwest, they lamented their repeated losses in the Northeast. The *National Municipal Review* reported in 1922:

> As everyone knows, Mayor Hylan was re-elected in New York for a four-year term. The combination of Hearst and Tammany proved invincible. *The opposition was unable to strike a popular issue, to discredit Tammany, or to convince people that they had no designs on the five-cent fare.* Hylan talked the old patter about the interests, the traction trust, etc., and got away with it. Tammany won every place on the board of estimate and every contest for borough office.[75]

There municipal reformers could not prevail against the partisan loyalties of machine supporters. Neither could they, as they did in the Southwest, steal from the city's political leadership the mantle of protecting the people from the trusts and interests and protecting the five-cent fare (since so often reformers *were* the interests). Across the country, voters had very good reasons for the quite different choices they made.

Appropriately enough for the Southwest, the approval of a new charter by Austin voters was not sufficient to change the charter, for the charter required approval by the state legislature as well. So local elites mounted

---

July 28, 1991. Campbell shared a memo written by Baldwin from Galveston. Baldwin found the city "(. . . rebuilt to an astonishing extent) city commission in charge excellent business men . . . for 2 yrs & best element now in control and will remain so until city in good shape again" (George Johnson Baldwin, memo, October 2, 1901, George Johnson Baldwin Papers, Southern Historical Collection, University of North Carolina at Chapel Hill). Campbell also believes that Baldwin suggested Stone and Webster push for commission government in Houston.

[75] *National Municipal Review* 11, no. 1 (January 1922): 34, emphasis added.

a final campaign, to insure the legislature's assent. The Austin Business League gave the legislators, their wives, and their families a banquet costing "not less than $1500." M. M. Shipe and A. P. Wooldridge explained their support of the charter; the legislators promised quick approval.[76]

Early returns on municipal reform encouraged those who had campaigned for it. In San Diego, Edgar Luce crowed over the disabling effect of nonpartisanship on the Republican machine:

> The machine was powerless to whip their followers into line for the "ticket." They tried every method but failed. They could not trade, could not center their strength. . . . They did not have the old cry of "regular Republican" to aid them. In fact the new system left the machine helpless and without its old weapons with which to "lineup" its forces. The new system therefore is a great boon to independent good government politics.[77]

Houston's mayor, Ben Campbell, speaking to the second annual convention of the League of Texas Municipalities in 1914, expressed his satisfaction with commission government:

> Our experience is that it brings good results. I do not know that we are any exception to the rule, but I want to tell you now that there is not a business organization in Texas, managed by its president and board of directors, in which there is any more concert of action, uniformity of opinion, solid, strong, undivided effort, for the upbuilding of the whole city, than exists today in the city council of Houston. I believe that the reason for that is . . . our present form of city government.[78]

In San Jose, newly installed manager Thomas Reed implemented improved public health measures, designed more careful procedures for recruitment of fire fighters and police officers, and modernized municipal administration from better bookkeeping to the appointment of a civil engineer to tackle flood control, sewage disposal, paving, and street cleaning. These initiatives were reported by the *National Municipal Review* as the "stirring record of five months' work."[79]

Not only did cities and towns boast new forms of city government but also an array of special districts, commissions, authorities, and quasi-governmental bodies to market bonds, provide infrastructure, and facili-

[76] *Austin Daily Statesman*, January 5, 1909, 2.
[77] Edgar Luce notes, Meyer Lissner Papers, Stanford University Archives, quoted in Grace Miller, "San Diego Progressive," 61.
[78] Ben Campbell, "The Commission Form of Government," *Texas Municipalities* 2, no. 2 (April 1915): 36.
[79] Robert Brooks, "Commission Manager Government in San Jose, Cal." *National Municipal Review* 6, no. 2 (March 1917): 238–41, 240.

tate growth. Like their counterparts in the great cities of the Northeast, city builders in the Southwest used these administrative inventions of the Progressive Era to further their economic and political goals. And with more success than municipal reformers in those great cities, leaders in southwestern cities and towns built new local states to meet the challenges of the next generation.

Four

Sure Defeat

THE BUSINESSMEN who organized reform government, the citizens who supported it, and the intellectuals who propagandized for it shared a vision of reform governance. In this vision, the abolition of ward representation and partisanship broke the link between particularistic citizen demands and municipal government. The reduction of the mayor to a ceremonial role (where the office of mayor continued to exist at all) did away with opportunities for demagoguery. City managers, appointed rather than elected, were to be "removed as far as possible from the immediate effects of public opinion,"[1] while civil service segregated municipal employment from the foibles of partisan appointments. The city council, as a group of commissioners, would draft broad policies and execute them with businesslike practices. Local governments were to be "frugal and sparing,"[2] services adequate and administered professionally, and utilities reined in from their efforts to rob the public.

Although municipal reformers succeeded at having new charters enacted and the initial experience of commission government in some cities made leaders optimistic, in the years before the Second World War, the arrangements reformers imagined were not institutionalized. Commission governments gave way to a series of disappointments; city manager government was equally difficult to bring to life.

Reformers' work nevertheless had profound effects on local politics. Reformers aimed to disable party leaders by enacting civil service legislation and creating nonpartisan elections. Reform charters created environments that made building political organizations difficult and so pro-

---

[1] This was the philosophy of Thomas Reed, who drafted San Jose's city-manager charter in 1915 and served as the first city manager. Quoted in Valerie Ellsworth and Andres J. Garbely, "Centralization and Efficiency: The Reformers Shape Modern San Jose Government, 1910–1916," in *Businessmen and Municipal Reform: A Study of Ideals and Practice in San Jose and Santa Cruz, 1896–1916*, ed. David W. Eakins (San Jose: San Jose State University, 1976), 15.

[2] James H. French, mayor of San Antonio in the 1870s, encouraged government officials to be "frugal and sparing," "to use every effort to keep down and even reduce taxation." Quoted in David R. Johnson, "Frugal and Sparing: Interest Groups, Politics, and City Building in San Antonio, 1870–1885," in *Urban Texas, Politics and Development*, ed. Char Miller and Heywood T. Sanders (College Station: Texas A & M University Press, 1990), 33–57, quote is 53.

moted political disorder. The elimination of a strong mayor and the move to nonpartisanship did, as reformers intended, make the construction of a centralized and dominating political machine nearly impossible. Nonpartisanship created an environment in which unity among politicians was very difficult to achieve; in both the commission form and under city manager charters, the tendency to disorganization and factionalism was very strong. The result was the most common form of local politics in the Southwest: a bewildering array of factions and personalities, transient alliances and "rings" governing with little consistency, and few notable politicians—strongly resembling in these characteristics V. O. Key's *Southern Politics*.

At the same time, there continued to be opportunities for petty corruption, for collusion among city officials and real estate or utility interests, for the political use of municipal employment, and for courting the disadvantaged. So the occasional talented politician might, like Boss Tweed, triumph over institutional adversity to create political order. This was the second pattern of local politics, leadership by *sunbelt centralizers*. By the trust other politicians put in his good word, he constructed a "ring"; by his use of municipal employment, he built an organization; by his solicitous concern for the outcast, he organized intense popular support.

Although reformers in the Southwest did not succeed at creating the businesslike governments they imagined, the institutional arrangements they created shaped local politics in the Southwest for generations. The foundations of big city reform—low participation, low tax rates, absence of corruption, minimal social provision, and government in the service of growth—were all in place from the Progressive Era through the 1940s. Thus if reformers did not secure maximum gains, they did succeed at minimizing their regrets.

Impacts of Reform Charters

From its beginnings in the nineteenth century, the municipal reform movement aimed to sever the ties of popular groups and local politicians. There were a variety of motives for this—distrust of the lower classes (as when one New Yorker argued, "We should be governed by mind instead of muscle"), ethnic and racial hostility (as when an Austin citizen complained, "Never before in the history of the city has the Negro played such a prominent part in politics . . ."), and party animosity. Like their counterparts elsewhere in the country, municipal reformers in the Southwest sought to loosen the ties of popular will and government action. Both suffrage restriction enacted by state governments and the institutional arrangements of municipal reform promoted that goal.

In Austin business leaders dissatisfied with city government were sensitive to the effects of rule changes and asked the state legislature to adapt the city charter accordingly. In 1901 the city adopted citywide elections, and quickly amended the charter again to provide one alderman from each ward elected citywide and one elected in the ward. Historian Frank Staniszewski summarized the effects of these changes:

> Through these provisions, candidates of the newly formed Business League of prominent merchants was able to elect nearly half the council in at-large elections and at least two ward candidates in their strongest wards. Aldermen were increasingly from the ranks of attorneys, bankers, Business League leaders and owners of the larger dry goods, liquor, and building material establishments.[3]

More generally in Texas, the immediate effects of suffrage restriction and municipal reform in the first decade of the century were dramatic. The abolition of ward representation and restricted suffrage, taken together, changed the composition of city councils. In Galveston, at-large election of councilmen after 1895 "effectively ended Negro participation in Galveston's city government" and returned three men who carried the city but not the ward in which they resided.[4] More profoundly, new charters altered the balance of political power. Before 1900 in both Galveston and Houston, citywide labor organizations were influential and important in city politics. Moreover, these white organizations were allied with African-American labor organizations. Even a generation after reform government was established, labor had not regained its political influence.[5]

Citywide elections also changed both representation and rewards. In Houston it was claimed that at-large elections not only resulted in different officials than wards would have elected, but also skewed policy outcomes. Testifying before the Houston Charter Commission in 1938, one commissioner argued that while residents on the south side of town supplied four-fifths of the city's tax revenue, a like amount or more of the city's expenditures were lavished on the neighborhoods of the north and east.[6]

---

[3] Frank Staniszewski, "Ideology and Practice in Municipal Government Reform: A Case Study of Austin" (University of Texas at Austin Studies in Politics, series I, paper no. 8, 1977), 22–23.

[4] Bradley R. Rice, *Progressive Cities: The Commission Government Movement in America, 1901–1920* (Austin: University of Texas Press, 1977), 372.

[5] Harold Platt, "City-Building and Progressive Reform: The Modernization of an Urban Polity, Houston, 1892–1903," in *The Age of Urban Reform: New Perspectives on the Progressive Era*, ed. Michael H. Ebner and Eugene M. Tobin (Port Washington, N.Y.: Kennikat Press, 1977), 28–42, 41.

[6] Minutes of the Houston Charter Commission, March 24, 1938. Houston Municipal Research Center.

The institutional arrangements and suffrage restrictions of the prewar period created regimes of low participation. The most general indication of low participation is turnout in municipal elections. As shown in table 4-1, compared to cities in the Northeast with strong party organizations, the southwestern cities studied here had very low turnout in municipal elections. This is so even though the generous denominator—all adults over twenty-one—disadvantages New York, Chicago, and New Haven, with their considerably larger foreign-born populations (see table 4-2).

In 1933, Roscoe Martin wrote an analysis of Austin's municipal election (which selected five city council members). Martin was interested in "the composition and voting habits of . . . the electorate,"[7] and his findings demonstrated that reformers succeeded at shaping the electorate. Martin was blessed by the careful record keeping of the poll tax list, which recorded each elector's name, race, occupation, birthplace, age, and years of residence in the city. There was also the poll list, which recorded who actually voted. Martin's first discovery was that of all adults aged twenty-one and over, 63 percent did not qualify to vote. Of the 37 percent who did qualify, 52 percent voted. With one in five (19.2 percent) adults voting, 10.9 percent elected the winning ticket. More affluent neighborhoods displayed higher turnout than poorer ones; by much greater margins, whites were more likely to vote than African Americans. "Neither Negroes nor Mexicans, therefore," Martin concluded, "achieve the position of importance as electoral groups to which their numbers entitle them."[8]

Everywhere in the Southwest, political communities were selective, constituted of more financially comfortable, more Anglo adults than formed the urban community as a whole. Whatever the claims of politicians about pursuing the good of the whole or friendship for workers or people of color, low participation restricted the constituencies to which they were attentive. Both the somewhat chaotic, faction-ridden politics of cities like Phoenix and San Diego, and the better organized politics of Austin, Houston, and Albuquerque, rested on this relatively narrow base of participation. Succeeding sections present accounts of these most common patterns of local politics in the Southwest before World War II.

V. O. Key in the Sunbelt

In the immediate aftermath of the adoption of reform charters, even a casual observer of local politics might have recognized many politicians

---

[7] Roscoe C. Martin, "The Municipal Electorate: A Case Study" *Southwestern Social Science Quarterly*, 14, no. 3 (December 1933): 193–237.

[8] Martin, "Municipal Electorate," 230.

TABLE 4-1
Turnout in Municipal Elections in Selected Cities, 1920–1945

	Reform Cities							Machine Descendants		
	Houston	San Jose	Phoenix	San Diego	Austin	Albuquerque	Dallas	New York	New Haven	Chicago
1920	NA	26.1	NA	—	—	—	—	—	—	—
1921	—	—	16.0	28.9	20.6	—	13.2	32.7	37.8	—
1922	NA	26.1	NA	—	—	42.0	—	—	—	38.9
1923	—	—	NA	17.2	28.0	33.3	16.0	—	35.6	—
1924	NA	33.8	NA	—	—	—	NA	—	—	—
1925	—	—	NA	30.3	—	—	—	28.5	37.8	—
1926	15.1	37.8	NA	—	16.0	NA	—	—	—	—
1927	—	—	NA	32.1	14.9	17.5	15.2	—	41.2	48.6
1928	22.3	37.1	NA	—	—	—	—	32.3	—	—
1929	—	23.8	15.9	29.0	4.2	—	12.6	—	47.7	—
1930	18.9	31.8	25.1	—	—	55.4	—	—	—	—
1931	—	—	11.9	29.9	24.9	26.9	5.9	—	53.8	51.5
1932	17.9	40.7	NA	34.9	—	—	—	44.1	—	—
1933	—	20.0	NA	—	20.4	—	11.9	—	53.0	—

Year										
1934	19.1	27.8	NA	—	—	33.8	—	—	—	—
1935	16.3	—	NA	32.5	2.8	39.1	11.9	—	58.5	45.8
1936	—	35.0	NA	—	2.1	—	7.3	44.4	55.4	—
1937	14.8	20.9	NA	19.1	—	47.3	—	44.4	55.4	—
1938	—	37.5	NA	—	17.3	48.4	9.8	—	58.4	62.3
1939	26.4	—	NA	30.1	—	—	—	49.0	52.2	—
1940	—	39.2	13.1	—	5.1	—	4.9	—	—	—
1941	10.0	—	25.9	24.6	—	—	—	—	—	—
1942	—	35.8	NA	—	4.3	—	1.2	—	44.0	51.9
1943	21.9	—	NA	22.1	—	—	—	—	—	—
1944	—	37.7	NA	—	4.2	—	1.9	35.9	55.2	—
1945	—	22.4	NA	—	—	—	—	—	—	—
Median	18.4	34.4	15.9	29.9	10.0	39.1	11.9	35.9	55.2	48.6
Average	18.3	31.4	18.0	27.8	16.6	38.2	10.2	38.1	52.2	49.8

Sources: Elections returns for Albuquerque and Dallas through 1929 and for Phoenix, San Diego, San Jose, and Chicago are from their respective Offices of the City Clerk. For New Haven, files of Robert Dahl. For Dallas, 1931–45, Carolyn Jenkins Barta, "The *Dallas News* and Council-Manager Government" (M.A. thesis, University of Texas at Austin, 1970), 147–55. For Austin, "Elections, 1924–1979," (City of Austin, Public Information Office, 1979). For Houston, Kenneth E. Gray, "A Report on the Politics of Houston" (mimeograph, Harvard-MIT Joint Center for Urban Studies, 1960), II-21–22. For New York, *World Almanac, 1938* (New York: World Telegram, 1938), 796, *World Almanac, 1946* (New York: World Telegram, 1946), 30.

TABLE 4-2
Percentage of Population Foreign-born
in Selected Cities, 1930

Albuquerque	4.6
Austin	0.3
Dallas	2.5
Houston	3.8
Phoenix	4.6
San Antonio	3.5
San Diego	17.8
San Jose	16.7
Chicago	24.9
New Haven	35.8
New York	33.1

Sources: U.S. Bureau of the Census, *Census of the Population, 1930: Population* (Washington, D.C.: Government Printing Office, 1932), table 23.

from the old regimes. In Albuquerque Clyde Tingley, first active in Democratic party politics as the territory was granted statehood, was elected to the city council in 1916, when the city enjoyed partisan mayor-council government. An opponent of municipal reform, Tingley was reelected to the council after commission-manager government was adopted, and soon became the city's leading politician. In Austin aldermen Haynes and Cuneo served under three different city charters.

San Diego looked different. After charter revision in 1905, municipal reformer John Sehon was elected mayor, and after commission government was adopted in 1909, not only did reformers sweep the offices at stake in the municipal election, but reforming Republicans appeared to dominate the local party organization. Nevertheless, the efforts of reformers were undermined as former stalwart progressives became allies of John Spreckels and the Hardy machine. John Sehon ran as a Progressive reformer for San Diego's mayoralty in 1905 and won. Yet "old guard Republicans won seats on the City Council and Sehon found himself . . . stranded amidst the hostility of the organization Republican city council."[9] Whether because he was discouraged by this experience or because his principles were malleable, by 1913 Sehon was an organization Republican himself.[10] In 1909 Grant Conard, earlier a candidate of the

[9] Grace Louise Miller, "The San Diego Progressive Movement, 1900–1920" (Ph.D. diss., University of California, Santa Barbara, 1976), 45.
[10] Miller, "San Diego Progressive Movement," 147.

Nonpartisan League, won as municipal reformers swept the local election. Two years later, however, the *Sun* claimed Conard had "lost sight of the flag quickly." "When [Conard] had a chance to proceed along constructive lines . . . he failed sadly," and rather than stand by those who supported his election, "he turned the other way. . . . Conard is bidding for 'push' support."[11]

In San Diego reform victories were transient and superficial; Republican dominance soon returned and with it the centrality of John Spreckels to local politics. Spreckels delivered water, street railways, and eventually a direct line from the East to San Diego. He was a staunch Old Guard Republican who opposed reform in every guise. In Los Angeles, Progressive Meyer Lissner lamented: "San Diego is a one-man town. . . . That is the whole trouble." Former congressman W. W. Bowers defended San Diego's choice: "I know that all of us were very glad to get the railroad, and with all its extortions we had rather do with it than without. I had rather have water with monopoly than no water and no monopoly." In 1915 all pretense to reform was given up as the commission charter was abandoned and the city reverted to mayor-council government.[12]

Most frequently, the commission form of government was subject to straightforward politicization. In the pure commission form citizens elected, citywide, the heads of city departments. Citizens in Austin, for example, elected five commissioners, who headed the departments of parks and public property, streets and improvements, police and public safety, finance, and public affairs, this last also serving as mayor.[13] Commissioners inevitably became closely associated with their service-providing bureaucracy. In San Diego, each commissioner "was more concerned with his department's obtaining the items requested in the budget than he was in trying to determine what was best for the total operation of the city."[14] Services provided won friends among citizens and among the firms most closely concerned with departmental work. Employment opportunities provided the material for construction of personal machines.

This was the situation in Dallas, which had nonpartisan commission

[11] Miller, "San Diego Progressive Movement"; for Conard's career: 51, 63, 90–91. Miller reports that while the San Diego *Union* (a Spreckels/old guard Republican newspaper) did not print editorials favoring Conard, the paper "backed Conard in its news columns" (91).

[12] Lissner quoted in Miller, "San Diego Progressive Movement," 129; Bowers quoted in Richard F. Pourade *History of San Diego* (San Diego: Union-Tribune, 1965), 5:36.

[13] Harold A. Stone, "City Manager Government in Austin," in *City Manager Government in Nine Cities*, ed. Harold A. Stone, Don K. Price, and Kathryn H. Stone (Chicago: Public Administration Service, 1940), 414.

[14] Daniel Edward Stone, "The Evolution of Municipal Budgeting in the City of San Diego, California" (M.A. thesis, San Diego State University, 1967), 71.

government from 1907 to 1931. In the genteel language of a proreform observer, "It was common practice for [each commissioner] to depend for political support on his departmental subordinates." Similarly, he went on, the commissioner was bound to court the favor of "those pressure groups that had a direct interest, usually a selfish one, in his work."[15] In Houston commissioners became so closely associated with the services they administered that even when the city abandoned this form of government, councilmen persisted in playing their old roles. As one explained to the Houston Charter Commission in 1938, if citizens continued to expect council members to help them with their utility or paving or sewer problems, the hapless politician could only—as a responsible public servant—respond. That this built his personal following among the people was simply the side-effect, an unintended consequence, of his desire to do good.[16]

Failing to halt the collusion of city officials and interest groups, the courting of constituent interests, or patronage employment, the commission form also failed to provide for centralization or leadership, encouraging instead entrepreneurship among the commissioners. There was conflict among commissioners for budget shares and over the boundaries of departments. Worse, elections hardly secured competent administrators, since voters were not able to judge managerial ability. Had municipal reformers known more of their own history, they might have anticipated this. A similar set of charter revisions were enacted for New York City in 1849. Throughout the 1850s citizens in New York elected seven "little mayors": the comptroller; the street commissioner; the commissioners of repairs and supplies, streets and lamps, and the almshouse; the counsel to the corporation; and the city inspector (whose province was public health). Each little mayor controlled the budget, hiring, and policies of his own department. (In the case of the almshouse, for example, the commissioner determined who received public assistance.) Each campaigned for election independently, boasting their generosity or Americanness, and accused opponents of tightfistedness or bigotry. These arrangements made coherent public policy, efficient administration, and budgetary control impossible.[17]

In southwestern cities before World War II, at best collusion among commissioners might create a "ring" that governed coherently; more often competing cliques and individuals worked (as their predecessors in

---

[15] Stone, "Municipal Budgeting," 273–74.

[16] Houston Charter Commission Minutes, Houston Municipal Research Library, March 3, 1938.

[17] Amy Bridges, *A City in the Republic: Antebellum New York and the Origins of Machine Politics* (New York: Cambridge University Press, 1984), 136–37.

New York had) to keep themselves in office.[18] Austin's Alexander Wooldridge, a champion of the commission form in 1909, had reservations by 1913. "In the commission form of government I have realized the need for a little more concentration of power in some one person," he reported to the League of Texas Municipalities; ". . . there is a tiny bit of the autocrat needed somewhere in efficient municipal government."[19]

City-manager government, if not subject to the same forms of politicization as commission government, was nevertheless equally difficult to institutionalize. City councils were loathe to give up the prerogatives to which they were accustomed. In Phoenix commission-manager government was a "cruel disappointment."[20] There the *Arizona Republican* editorialized that local government "is hardly distinguishable at this hour from the old political regime from which the charter was supposed to deliver us."[21] Local government resumed a familiar patronage style, with the city manager's position "simply the choicest plum of the patronage game."[22] In April 1915 the city council proposed charter amendments to the electorate to decrease the manager's powers, and these were passed.[23] Rapid turnover of city managers was one result: Phoenix had twenty-three managers between 1920 and 1940.[24] And local government was corrupt. "Bootlegging, narcotics trafficking, prostitution, and gambling prospered with police protection," not incidentally providing an ample source of municipal revenue. Gambling establishments contributed through fines; prostitutes and madams were required to post bonds monthly, and these were "recorded as the fine payment for a 'vagrancy'

[18] Rice, *Progressive Cities*, 91–93. In Denver these and other problems converted the city's businessmen from procommission reformers to advocates of the old strong-mayor form in just three years. The *Denver Times* summarized their judgment: "The return of [the boss] may mean 'one man' power, but that is better than no-man power" (ibid., 91). See also J. Paul Mitchell, "Boss Speer and the City Functional: Boosters and Businessmen versus Commission Government in Denver," *Pacific Northwest Quarterly* (October 1979): 155–64.

[19] Alexander Penn Wooldridge, remarks reported in *Proceedings of the First Annual Convention of the League of Texas Municipalities* (Austin: University of Texas, 1914), 7–8.

[20] G. Wesley Johnson, "Generations of Elites and Social Change in Phoenix," in *Community Development in the American West: Past and Present Nineteenth and Twentieth Century Frontiers*, ed. Jessie L. Embry and Howard A. Christy (Provo: Brigham Young University, 1985): 92.

[21] *Arizona Republican*, June 8, 1922, quoted in Michael Kotlanger, "Phoenix, Arizona, 1920–1940" (Ph.D. diss., Arizona State University, 1983), 483.

[22] Kotlanger, "Phoenix," 483. "Choicest plum" is a quote from Stephen Rockstroh, "An Analysis of Phoenix Municipal Administration, 1881–1952" (M.A. thesis, Arizona State University, 1952).

[23] Geoffrey Padraic Mawn, "Phoenix, Arizona: Central City of the Southwest, 1870–1920" (Ph.D. diss., Arizona State University, 1979), 446–47.

[24] Kotlanger, "Phoenix," 483.

arrest."[25] In the 1940s the proceeds of these payments for protection were simply divided among the members of the city council.[26]

In Albuquerque the commission-manager plan fared no better. The city council insisted on interfering with municipal administration. At times council resistance to manager government was manifested by its refusal to search for a qualified manager, appointing local men who might not be qualified but could be expected to be cooperative. On other occasions the council did appoint qualified men who quickly quit in disgust.[27] Similarly, Oklahoma City had fifteen managers in thirty-nine years.[28] San Diego adopted council-manager government in 1931. There too the city council showed little disposition to bring the charter to life, alienating those managers who hoped to take their executive responsibilities seriously. As the *San Diego Union* commented, the city council functioned as "a group of co-equal and rival city managers, each eager to have a finger in every pie." City council members were elected citywide but nominated by districts. As under the mayor-council government, San Diego's city-manager government made decisions by referring them to the council member whose district was concerned. Here too there were rumors of municipally sanctioned vice and organized crime. San Diego had four unhappy city managers in three years.[29] Similarly, an observer of San Jose complained, "Numerous contacts between department heads and councilmen which by-pass the manager's desk entirely detract from the respect due that office."[30] Local politics in San Jose in the 1930s was a struggle between the manager's office and local politicians who opposed his prerogatives; over the course of the decade the manager seemed to gain the winning hand.[31]

In Phoenix "a curious combination of big city bossism and Old West frontierism"[32] characterized city government for decades. In San Diego

[25] Kotlanger, "Phoenix," 531, 525.

[26] Harry Rosenzweig interview, Arizona Historical Society, Phoenix Oral History collection.

[27] Dorothy I. Cline, *Albuquerque and the City Manager Plan, 1917–1948* (Albuquerque: University of New Mexico Press, 1951), 16–26.

[28] Leonard E. Goodall, "Phoenix: Reformers at Work," in *Urban Politics in the Southwest*, ed. Leonard E. Goodall (Tempe: Arizona State University Institute of Public Administration, 1967), 114; George J. Mauer, "Oklahoma City: In Transition to Maturity and Professionalization," in ibid., 89.

[29] Harold A. Stone, "City Manager Government in San Diego," in *City Manager Government in Nine Cities*, ed. Harold A. Stone, Don K. Price, and Kathryn H. Stone (Chicago: Public Administration Service, 1940), 169.

[30] Robert Thorpe, "Council-Manager Government in San Jose, California" (M.A. thesis, Stanford University, 1938), 80–81.

[31] Thorpe, "San Jose," chaps. 3, 4, and 6.

[32] Goodall, "Phoenix," 114.

"each election was a free-for-all, with independent candidates enlisting as much personal support as possible."[33] In Albuquerque "the uproar and confusion of factionalism engulfed" the early years of the city manager plan.[34] Hastily constructed alliances were offered to citizens as the "independent ticket," the "people's ticket," the "citizens' ticket," the "charter ticket," the "progressive ticket," the "nonpartisan ticket," or, on a more boosterish note, tickets like "Greater Albuquerque," "Forward Dallas," and "Onward Austin."

Reform charters disorganized politicians without effectively inhibiting some of their most grievous practices. Thus, the most frequent pattern of reform politics was an array of factions, personal followings, and hastily assembled and equally short-lived alliances. This most common pattern of politics under reform charters has much in common with the political life presented by V. O. Key in *Southern Politics*. Key argued that "technically the description of the politics of the [one-party] south amounts to the problem of analyzing the political struggle under a system of nonpartisan elections."[35] Absent parties, southern politics lacked consistent lines of popular division, campaigns were issueless, leadership mediocre at best. On the whole such governments could be neither responsive nor efficient, and despite occasional populist rhetoric, their tendencies were conservative.[36] Likewise the factionalized politics of postreform cities boasted few notable politicians or ambitious policies, and, absent parties, little connection between popular desire and political will.

Boss Tweed Heads West

Municipal reform charters created environments with strong barriers to organization building, yet there continued to be opportunities for petty corruption, for collusion among city officials and real estate or utility interests, for the political use of municipal employment, and for courting the disadvantaged. In this way the political disarray that followed municipal reform efforts created opportunities for able politicians. These *sunbelt centralizers* overcame institutional adversity to create political order and successful careers for themselves. In Dallas, briefly, J. Waddy Tate provided leadership under the commission form, as did Maury Maverick in San Antonio. Most impressively, in Albuquerque Clyde Tingley, in Houston Oscar Holcombe, and in Austin Andrew Zilker coordinated governance despite a series of charter changes. Later, Zilker's protégé

---

[33] Harold Stone, "San Diego," 143.
[34] Cline, *Albuquerque*, 12.
[35] V. O. Key, Jr., *Southern Politics in State and Nation* (New York: Vintage, 1962), 16.
[36] V. O. Key, Jr., *Southern Politics*, chaps 1, 14.

Tom Miller dominated city government in Austin for decades despite charters that created environments hostile to centralization.

Tingley, Holcombe, and Miller were far and away the most successful urban politicians in the prewar sunbelt. Each dominated his city for nearly three decades by organizing massive popular support and conducting administrations efficient enough to stave off for a generation another round of reforming zeal. Oscar Holcombe first took office as mayor of Houston in 1921 and left that office for the last time in 1957, having served as mayor for twenty-two of the intervening thirty-six years. Clyde Tingley migrated to Albuquerque in 1911, and the next year became a Democratic precinct organizer in Albuquerque's Second Ward. First elected to city commission in 1916, by 1923 Tingley, along with two allies on the five-member commission, dominated city government. A year later the *Albuquerque Herald* editorialized that in place of commission government there was "one man government" in Albuquerque.[37] Tingley was Albuquerque's leading politician from that time until 1946 (except for the years 1934–38, when he was governor of New Mexico) and served on Albuquerque's city council until 1955. Tom Miller first campaigned for the city council in 1933, and after winning a seat, was elected mayor by the city council. Miller was Austin's mayor from 1933 until 1949, and again from 1955 to 1961.

Political longevity distinguishes Holcombe, Miller, and Tingley from the other sunbelt centralizers. The character and personal history of each of these men is distinctive, but their public personae and political roles have critical elements in common. All were opposed to commission and then manager government. Each of these politicians presented a populist image, campaigning as a friend to organized labor and people of color. Each was a party builder, well aware of the political uses of public employment, and each increased the reach, organization, and order of local parties. In both New Mexico and Texas, state party organizations, recognizing municipal employees as an important organizational resource, resisted the advent of civil service. Similarly, state parties were loathe to allow local organizations to disintegrate even where city charters were nominally nonpartisan. All Democrats, the centralizers profited mightily from Democratic ascendancy in Washington in the 1930s.[38] Holcombe, Tingley, and Miller insured their dominance of city politics by pursuing growth strategies that found support not only among the kind of small businessman always dependent on city government (like tavern owners)

---

[37] *Albuquerque Herald*, May 27, 1924.

[38] Roger Lotchin, "Power and Policy: American City Politics between the Two World Wars," in *Ethnics, Machines, and the American Urban Future*, ed. Scott Greer (Cambridge, Mass.: Schenkman, 1981), 21.

but also among the sort of far-seeing and wealthier businessman whose economic stake was in planning, real estate, and growth. Despite their claims of friendship for ordinary voters, benefits to organized labor and people of color were minimal. And although sunbelt centralizers campaigned as opponents of municipal reform, they made crucial rhetorical, symbolic, and material concessions to reform and its supporters.

Albuquerque's Clyde Tingley was an exemplary sunbelt centralizer. Tingley fought the change from mayor-alderman to commission government in 1917. In 1922 the *Albuquerque Morning Journal* described Tingley's campaign as a battle against the "blighting influence of big business domination . . ."[39] Both Tingley's blue-collar past and his lack of education were prominent in his political style. Tingley carried his union card well into his old age (although, having married well, he had enough money to do without paid employment after he moved to Albuquerque).[40] In 1912, the year New Mexico was admitted to the union, Tingley became a Democratic precinct organizer in Albuquerque's Second Ward, which embraced Hispanic and Anglo working-class neighborhoods. There Tingley forged enduring links with the Spanish-speaking community. As an alderman, as "mayor," and later as governor of New Mexico, Tingley was solicitous of organized labor and of disadvantaged citizens. Tingley the alderman had an open door to citizen complaints; Tingley the mayor toured the city searching for problems to solve; Tingley the governor intervened to settle a strike of timber and sawmill workers and also threatened to send the national guard to stop a lockout by the El Paso Electric Company. In the last case, Tingley sent WPA trucks with food for the striking workers and then, over a bottle of scotch and a steak dinner, persuaded employers to grant the strikers a raise. His comment was that the employers were "just trying to starve them out, and I wasn't going to let them."[41]

How Tingley might reconcile this populist stance with retaining the support of Albuquerque's aggressive developers is suggested by the following anecdote. In the early 1950s the developer of an outlying community wanted water and sewer connections provided by the city. In the commission meeting, Tingley declared, "I could never support sewer ex-

[39] *Albuquerque Morning Journal*, April 2, 1922.

[40] There are many stories about his lack of education. Among them, the following: Tingley called a friend to ask for the return of a gun. When the friend complained he couldn't hear, Tingley shouted: "GUN. G as in gonorrhea, U as in onion, and N as in pneumonia." "Remembering Clyde Tingley," *Albuquerque Journal Magazine*, January 4, 1983, 12.

[41] E. Ferguson to Joseph L. Dailey, May 20, 1955. Ferguson Papers, Coronado Room, University of New Mexico Library. The library also has the very useful manuscript of Ferguson's biography of Tingley.

tensions that far out when in the shadow of City Hall, people don't have water and sewer." The motion was tabled. Later in the meeting, when most of the audience had dispersed, the motion was brought up again; this time Tingley voted yes.[42]

Tingley was also skilled at building political organization. In 1923 the *Albuquerque Morning Journal* editorialized, "We have in effect abandoned the commission form of city government, retaining the form only, and . . . for the most part the city is being administered by a small ring of politicians whose aim seems to be the holding up of a local political machine."[43] The *Journal* was right. Tingley had learned the rudiments of party organizing in his Second Ward days. One former policeman testified that he and his fellows were required to contribute $50 for local campaigns. Whether that story is true or apocryphal, it is surely true that Tingley expected those with political appointments to do political work.[44] Papers from his years in the governor's office list state employees and rate their willingness to work in elections. In the state highway department, for example, S. Walker, a voucher clerk, "voted democratic and worked hard," and Gene Baca, another clerk, "worked hard and voted right." Others "voted democratic but failed to work" or worse, like R. W. Bennett (an engineer), "absolutely refused to help the Democrats in any form."[45] Writing in 1939, Thomas Donnelly reported that state employees were required to return 2 percent of their salaries to the Democratic party.[46] Small wonder that while Tingley was in Albuquerque municipal politics boasted "precinct organizations, campaign headquarters, fund-raising drives, and citywide electioneering." The same organization was important for state partisan efforts; from a statewide point of view, the municipal employees of Albuquerque were too valuable a resource to be left to nonpartisan disorganization.[47] Conversely when, years later, Tingley lost the gubernatorial primary (and with it,

[42] I am indebted for this anecdote to Marion Cottrell. Interview, May 18, 1994.

[43] *Albuquerque Morning Journal*, March 7, 1923.

[44] Michael J. Schingle, "Albuquerque Urban Politics, 1891–1955: Aldermanic vs. Commission Government" (senior thesis, University of New Mexico, August 1976), 71. A political ally of Tingley told Ferguson the following story. When Tingley ran for governor in 1936, the highway department opposed his candidacy. When Tingley won, department representatives said they hoped Tingley would not take punitive measures. Tingley's response: "I'm not going to do anything puny—I'm going to fire those damn bastards." Ferguson papers, University of New Mexico, 1936 file.

[45] Tingley Papers, 1935, State Records Center, Santa Fe, New Mexico, 185.

[46] Thomas C. Donnelly, "New Mexico: An Area of Conflicting Cultures," in *Rocky Mountain Politics*, ed. Thomas C. Donnelly (Albuquerque: University of New Mexico Press, 1940), 240.

[47] Cline, *Albuquerque*, 12–13.

control of the Democratic Party in New Mexico), he lost partisan support in Albuquerque.[48]

Tingley was also exemplary for his commitment to Albuquerque's growth. In the 1939 campaign for the city commission, Tingley's Greater Albuquerque Ticket promoted him as "Albuquerque's Number One City Builder." Tingley could claim credit then and later for utilities and infrastructure that kept pace with growing population, a park system, a zoo, an expanded school system, a beach (along a trickle of the Colorado River), a civic auditorium, and an airport.[49] As governor, Tingley was a link to the Roosevelt administration, and secured substantial WPA and other grants for New Mexico. These not only enhanced his reputation for concern with popular welfare but also increased the number of government employees both in the state government and in Albuquerque.

In Houston, Oscar Holcombe's career paralleled Clyde Tingley's. Holcombe was relentless in his opposition to the manager charter proposed for Houston in the 1940s. Echoing labor's claims that the city-manager form was undemocratic, Holcombe campaigned in 1946 that "Tammany Hall has never had a more subservient and obedient 'puppet government' than this inner circle of the Charter Committee machine has inflicted on Houston during the last four years." The hand picked candidates of the Charter Committee, he continued, "will . . . owe their allegiance, not to you, the people, but to their . . . master minds, the inner circle of the Charter Committee political machine."[50] Elected mayor in 1947, Holcombe declared he had received "a mandate . . . to no longer be governed by all of the cumbersome and impractical limitations and restrictions of the city manager system," and pledged to ignore the charter to the extent he legally could. Houston, Holcombe insisted, was too large to be governed "by the city manager part time remote control system."[51] Unlike his opponents, Holcombe rejoiced in being a politician and defended the choice of a political career: "Politicians run this country, and if there were not more good politicians than bad ones, this country would be in very bad shape."[52]

Holcombe had strong ties to organized labor and to Houston's

[48] Schingle, "Albuquerque," 84.

[49] *Albuquerque Journal*, March 31, 1946.

[50] Speech over KTRH radio, October 18, 1946; transcript in Holcombe Papers, Houston Municipal Research Center, box 4.

[51] Campaign speech, KTHT radio, July 21, 1947, Holcombe Papers, box 4, folder 4, Houston Municipal Research Center.

[52] Campaign speech, October 5, 1948, Holcombe Papers, box 4, folder 4, Houston Municipal Research Center.

African-American community.[53] Holcombe's most important act in winning these constituencies was his opposition to the Ku Klux Klan in the 1920s. The Klan presence in Texas was so threatening to labor and to people of color that this stance was sufficient to label a politician their friend. In the 1920s Holcombe had endorsements from a long list of unions.[54] In addition to his opposition to the Klan and to city-manager government, Holcombe could point to the amicable relation between Houston city government and organized municipal employees during his tenure. The City-County Employees Union, Local 1347 of the International Hod Carriers, Building, and Common Laborers' Union of America, was organized in Houston in 1919 as a racially integrated union with seventy-five members. By 1933, not only did the union discuss compensation, civil service reform, and pensions with city officials, but also was allowed a payroll checkoff for union dues. The union was not officially a bargaining agent, but it informally represented sanitation, water works, street maintenance, sewer, zoo, and humane department employees, city mechanics and janitors. It claimed to indirectly represent all city employees.[55]

Holcombe's record with unions in the private sector was not so good. In 1937 longshoremen waged a bitter strike. CIO official John Crossland recalled the men "were practically on a starvations basis. . . . they were having to scrounge groceries any place they could get them, and we were helping them. Oscar Holcombe was mayor at that time . . . and it was the order of the day to give a guy a dollar a year and make him a deputy, and then the companies would pay him a fat salary for being a strikebreaker." Worse, "Houston police and special officers ('scabherders') beat the seamen and longshoremen . . . unmercifully. They went in homes and beer joints and everything else . . . and just beat the hell out of them."[56] Thus Holcombe administrations seem not to have provided relief from the generally brutal relationship between local police and union workers.

Holcombe was also solicitous of the African-American community, supporting the United Negro College Fund and promoting Texas State University for Negroes; in 1933 the Colored Carnegie Library was formally opened. African-Americans were included in Holcombe's efforts to

[53] On at least one occasion, Holcombe won the endorsement of the city's Spanish press. Holcombe Papers, box 1. *La Tribuna*, November 13, 1924.

[54] For Union endorsements, see Holcombe Papers, box 1, folders 1 and 2. Holcombe had endorsements in the early 1920s from the Culinary Workers, the United Brotherhood of Carpenters and Joiners, and various railroad workers' unions.

[55] Marilyn D. Rhinehart, "A Lesson in Unity: The Houston Municipal Workers' Strike of 1946," *Houston Municipal Review* 4, no. 3 (Fall 1982): 140.

[56] John Crossland interview, Oral History Collection, Labor History Archives, University of Texas at Arlington.

provide services for Houston. There was persistent demand in the African American community for vocational schools, and although one was not founded for young men, in 1938 the city boasted a public school for training young African-American women to be "perfect" domestic servants, the Houston Vocational School of Household Service.[57] In his 1946 campaign, Holcombe boasted that he had built or obtained as gifts to the city Jefferson Davis Hospital, Tuberculosis Hospital, the Children's Tubercular Hospital, and Houston Negro.[58] The next year Holcombe testified before Congress in favor of expanded funding for public housing to solve the "daily growing . . . problem—our slums and the great number of people forced to live in them."[59] Attentive to the African-American middle class as well as the less fortunate, in 1948 Holcombe made a public appeal for an appropriate site for a Negro golf course to be donated to the city.[60]

The *Houston Press* headlined a report on the city's African-American community in 1931: "Houston's Little Harlem Thrives on Laughter," but African-American leaders presented a more sober picture. In 1937 Rev. Bertron M. Jacson wrote to Mayor Fonville for relief from the terrible conditions in African-American neighborhoods, which lacked sewerage, and newspapers reported the death rate at 19 per 1,000, while the white death rate was 11 per 1,000. At about the same time, a report of the Houston Community Chest observed that although state legislation was more permissive, in Harris County mothers' pensions were only granted to white widows.[61] In 1939 the *Mirror*, reporting on the Texas Negro People's Congress meeting in Austin, reported "Houston and Beaumont are the only two major cities in Texas which still operate under the 'white man's primary' system, which deprives thousands of citizens or residents from having a voice in the selecting and actually electing city officials."[62] A decade earlier J. B. Harris had sought an injunction to prevent the Harris County Democratic party from enforcing a state party rule restricting primary elections to white voters; his suit was unsuccessful.[63]

[57] The school's instructor, Nellie Dillon, held degrees from the Tuskegee Institute, Prairie View State College, and the Universities of Wisconsin and Southern California. Applicants with high-school degrees were preferred; graduates could expect "a thorough health exam, including a Wasserman test," and several job opportunities. After a year's successful service in one of these, her degree was awarded. *Houston Chronicle*, January 23, 1938, 14.

[58] Holcombe Papers, box 4, KTRH speech November 1, 1946.

[59] Holcombe Papers, box 4, testimony dated October 30, 1947, 67.

[60] *Houston Press*, July 27, 1948.

[61] Houston Community Chest and Councils, "The Program for Family Welfare and Relief: Summary of Findings and Recommendations" (mimeograph, Houston Municipal Research Center, ca. 1937), 11.

[62] *Houston Press*, April 15, 1931; (Houston) *Mirror*, March 4, 1939.

[63] *Houston Post*, July 20 and 24, 1928.

The lack of access to the polls was not without consequence. Two years later the *Negro Labor News* cautioned Houston's newly appointed police chief that he would "perhaps find a different situation among Negroes in Houston than in other sections for the reason that Negroes do not vote and none can claim particular 'pull' at City Hall." The result was that "too often . . . the law abiding Negro has been subjected to the same treatment of police brutality dealt the worst element of criminal."[64]

Holcombe was extremely attentive to building political organization in Houston. Holcombe carefully surveyed municipal employees, offering pledge cards (with union labels!) which they might "just sign and return."[65] Holcombe's papers include lists of women's organizations, African-American neighborhood organizations, and union leaders. Each precinct had a woman and a man serving as cocaptains.

Holcombe was a skillful booster for his city, traveling to St. Louis and Rocky Mountain cities to promote Houston's virtues as a port. More, Holcombe was a city-building pioneer in appointing a planning commission for Houston as early as the 1920s. Holcombe's campaigns consistently stressed public improvements to accommodate growth: roads, bridges, water plants, a new farmers' market, sewers, expanded fire protection. Houston's "magnificent projects," Holcombe boasted, "are the results of dreaming and planning by Oscar Holcombe." Campaigning again in 1950 Holcombe argued:

> I have served as Mayor of Houston for 18 of the past 29 years. . . . Practically all of the major municipal improvements which you see and enjoy each day, such as the Civic Center, the broad and beautiful freeways, the paved, widened, and improved streets . . . were either originated and planned, or designed and constructed during Holcombe administrations.[66]

Holcombe was as comfortable with reformers' rhetoric as any member of the Charter Committee, claiming in one reelection campaign, "By your votes you . . . employed me as manager of this great business institution; now comes the time for the biannual meeting of the stockholders of the corporation of Houston." Similarly, Holcombe took credit for "getting the politics out" of the public schools, separating the school board from city government.[67]

---

[64] *Negro Labor News*, February 15, 1941.

[65] Political Campaign Collection, Houston Municipal Research Center, box 1. There are pledge cards for 1926, 1946, and 1948. The letter is from 1948. See also Holcombe Papers, box 1, for a 1924 survey of municipal employees and the report of the police superintendent on his pledge-card campaign in the department.

[66] Campaign speech, October 3, 1950, Holcombe Papers, box 4, folder 9, Houston Municipal Research Center.

[67] Campaign speech, 1924, Holcombe Papers, box 1; KTHT speech, October 25, 1946, Holcombe Papers, box 4.

In Austin Andrew Zilker played a role comparable to Holcombe and Tingley. Austin changed from mayor-council government to commission government in 1909 and adopted city manager provisions in 1924–26. Zilker exercised influence in all three regimes, holding office under the first, important to the Yett administration (1919–26) in the second, and organizing the election of his protégé Tom Miller to the mayoralty during the third. Like Holcombe and Tingley, Zilker and later Miller opposed municipal reform. Miller resided in a neighborhood that felt unrepresented in the manager plan; both he and Zilker allied themselves with those antagonistic to it.[68]

Like the other sunbelt centralizers, Zilker and Miller presented themselves as friends to organized labor and people of color. Miller, himself from a lower-class family, was both prolabor and pro–New Deal.[69] Successful at creating a mostly white-collar community, Austin did not have the strong labor movement of either Albuquerque or Houston. There were labor organizations, however, and Zilker and Miller solicited their support. Zilker and Miller were also consistently supported by Austin's African-American community. The contrast to the first city manager could hardly be more pronounced. "Shocked by the [politicians'] practice of speaking at Negro churches," the manager "resentfully" compared their electoral support for Miller et al. "with that of the rats to the Pied Piper." This was in contrast to the Mexicans, who, a "veteran campaigner" explained, "listen, accept favors, and then vote independently."[70] With nonpartisan elections, African-Americans had a stronger presence in the electorate than in other Texas cities (even if, as Roscoe Martin observed, their voting strength was far below their presence in the adult population).[71] Miller delivered enough to African-American constituents to make African-American support more rational than the city manager's

[68] Harold A. Stone, "City Manager Government in Austin," provides an account of Zilker and the transitions in Austin government (in *City Manager Government in Nine Cities*, ed. Harold A. Stone, Don K. Price, and Kathryn H. Stone [Chicago: Public Administration Service, 1940], 428, 434. For Zilker, also Joe O'Neal, interview with Harry Warren Nolen, June 26, 1974, Austin History Center; for Zilker's sponsorship of Tom Miller, A. Orum interview with Emmett Shelton, Sr., May 5, 1983, Austin History Center.

[69] Labor support was not without its contradictions. Labor divided in the 1931 election, with the result that in 1933 the Zilker group excluded union candidates from its ticket. Moreover, the ticket was "conspicuously supported by the head of the open-shop committee of Austin builders and real estate developers" (Stone, "City Manager Government in Austin," 438). If Miller and his fellows nevertheless received labor support, it is tribute to Key's assertion that contradictory coalitions were more easily maintained in the absence of parties (Key, *Southern Politics*, 117).

[70] Stone, "Austin," 436, 437.

[71] Ralph J. Bunche, *The Political Status of the Negro in the Age of FDR* (Chicago: University of Chicago Press, 1973) estimated that African-Americans cast 1,200 to 1,500 of 8,000 votes cast in municipal elections in the mid 1930s (467). Roscoe Martin's study of the 1933 election put the number much lower: fewer than 800 votes of 7,511 cast.

account suggested. Streets in African-American neighborhoods were paved; a branch of the public library was provided.[72] There was also a park for African-American residents, with a swimming pool, football field, and baseball diamond. African-Americans were counted among municipal employees, including garbage men, trash collectors, and janitors. Four were police officers.[73]

Zilker and Miller built political organizations with municipal employees. The centrality of municipal employees was evidenced by Roscoe Martin's investigation of Austin voters. Municipal employees took their political obligations quite seriously: 87.6 percent of the men voted (compared to 58.1 percent in the electorate as a whole) and 71 percent of the women voted (while 44.7 percent of women in the general electorate voted).[74] Miller and Zilker also maintained political organizations predating manager government. Under the mayor-council government, Zilker's own ward and political stronghold was the Tenth. One anecdotal index both of popular attachment to the old mayor-council government and of the persistence of political organization is that the recreation department's boys' club was still called the Tenth Ward Club twenty years after the Tenth Ward was done away with. More generally, "ward and neighborhood patriotism" persisted well beyond the time when wards functioned as political territories.[75]

Austin's Tom Miller was also a strong supporter of Roosevelt's administration, and the city was rewarded accordingly. Miller drove to Washington to petition the Public Works Administration for funds to support a list of projects the mayor, council, and city manager planned for Austin that would provide more than three hundred thousand man-days of work. Miller's next task was to campaign for a bond issue so Austin could raise the matching funds required for federal assistance. Successful at persuading both bureaucratic and popular audiences, Miller and his administration received funds not only from the PWA, but also from other New Deal agencies.[76] Miller, the Chamber of Commerce, and Congressmen James Buchanan and Lyndon Johnson also worked to secure funds for dams on the Colorado River.[77]

[72] African-Americans also demanded sewers, African-American police officers, and African-American nurses in the public hospital. I have not determined if Miller responded to these demands. See Floylee Hunter Hemphill, "Mayor Tom Miller and the First Year of the New Deal in Austin, Texas" (M.A. thesis, University of Texas, 1976), 89–97.

[73] Bunche, *Political Status*, 467.

[74] Martin, "Municipal Electorate," 234–35.

[75] Stone, "City Manager Government in Austin," 421, 434; for the persistence of African-American community organizations, see Hemphill, "Mayor Tom Miller," 37, 47.

[76] Hemphill, "Mayor Tom Miller," 72–85.

[77] Austin Chamber of Commerce, *Something Made Austin Grow* (Austin: Chamber of Commerce, 1948), 30.

Austin realized reform government to a greater extent than either Houston or Albuquerque before World War II. It might be said that Albuquerque, Houston, and those cities that suffered from disorder and factionalism created—from a reformer's point of view—pathological institutionalizations of reform politics. By contrast, Austin, by accommodating those social forces whom reformers usually antagonized, created a government that came closer to reformers' hopes. After the adoption of the manager charter in 1924–26, political campaigns predictably were contests between a Zilker ticket and a proreform ticket. Quite quickly local politics became less competitive and remarkably stable. The same four men served on the city council from 1933 to 1946; the fifth, also first elected in 1933, died in office and was succeeded by his son.[78] Stability reflected political learning on both sides. On one hand, politicians reconciled themselves to a political system with fewer opportunities for patronage appointments (although municipal employees remained politically important), gaining in exchange command of a government with a much larger budget for municipal improvements. On the other hand, the city's most ardent reformers and boosters learned to broaden their appeals. For example, to secure a majority for a large bond issue, reformers promised (and delivered) streets and sewers to Austin's African-American neighborhoods. More, once the city council worked out a settled division of labor with the city manager, businessmen and reformers were content to retire from campaigning and allow politicians to govern, secure that "their interests [were] not threatened."[79]

Sunbelt centralizers were the Boss Tweeds of the sunbelt. Tweed created order out of New York's political disorder in the 1860s. One one hand, he worked in the city and the state legislature to amend the city's charter to strengthen home rule and centralize control. On the other, Tweed arranged for government donations to denominational schools, orphanages, hospitals, and the like. Of this money, nearly three quarters went to Catholic institutions at a time of widespread anti-Catholic feeling.[80] Spending for city services and capital improvements provided patronage opportunities both in employment and in awarding contracts, and these were used by Tweed and his colleagues to build political organization.

Like Tweed, sunbelt centralizers formed strong alliances with other politicians, put government employees to good organizational use, and styled themselves the benefactors of laboring men and those of low sta-

---

[78] The men were Charles Alford, Tom Miller, Simon Gillis, C. M. Bartholomew, and Oswald Wolf. Bartholomew died in 1940 and was succeeded by his son. Gillis resigned in March of 1946. City of Austin, "Elections, 1924–1979," Public Information Office, 1979.

[79] Stone, "City Manager Government in Austin," 430–32.

[80] John W. Pratt, "Boss Tweed's Public Welfare Program," *New York Historical Society Quarterly* 45 (1961): 196–211.

tus. If the benefits awarded those constituencies were small, they were important in the regional political context of harsh attitudes toward working people and people of color. Moreover, sunbelt centralizers benefited from those institutional arrangements meant to distance politicians from constituents. The antidemocratic features of reform charters gave politicians latitude in the concessions they granted, while the legal environment of the region was hostile to disadvantaged constituencies. With or without de jure nonpartisanship in local elections, sunbelt centralizers in Texas and New Mexico were prominent both for their local accomplishments and for their national party connections. Tom Miller laid it on the line: "I'm a yellow dog Democrat. I'd vote for a yellow dog if he's on the Democratic ticket."[81]

Outside the Southwest, sunbelt centralizers had a contemporary counterpart in Kansas City's Tom Pendergast. Pendergast constructed a formidable machine despite Kansas City's city-manager charter. In 1938, when would-be reformers met as the Houston Charter Commission to draft charter changes (which were not successful at the polls), Pendergast was the subject of some discussion. One member of the commission had this to say about Pendergast:

> I respect a good politician. I respect Tom Pendergast. I would accept his word as quickly as I would accept the word of anyone. . . . This is the part they played. They control the popular vote. . . . It is a pleasure to go to Kansas City and to see the constitution of the streets and see the good judgment and care that has been exercised in their public buildings. It is a pleasure to read of the structures which have been built making it one of the most attractive cities to live in this country. That has come from the city manager form of government.[82]

If that reformer's analysis was correct, Pendergast governed because he and his colleagues accepted a division of labor between themselves and the city manager. The politicians organized consent while the city manager saw to it that the city's infrastructure kept pace with growth (and, one presumes, that the city was fiscally sound). Similarly, it may be that those in Austin, Albuquerque, and Houston who valued growth came to value the services of politicians who could "control the popular vote" and who themselves put growth at the top of municipal government's agenda.

Minimum Regrets

Although the reform regimes of the interwar years were not what reformers imagined, the defeat of municipal reform was not absolute. Everywhere, reform regimes secured central elements of the reform agenda:

[81] Shelton interview.
[82] Houston Charter Commission, box 2, minutes of June 20, 1938.

restricted participation, low tax rates, absence of corruption (except in Phoenix), minimal social service provision, government in the service of growth and, in Arizona and California, continued erosion of party organizations. Southwestern city governments in the interwar years also had more amicable relations with public utilities than in the Progressive Era. Key's description of one-party politics in the states of the South describes as well the nonpartisan politics of municipal reform. Local elections seemed to reflect an "issueless consensus" in which the goal was simply to elect the best men, whose concerns set the agenda of local government.[83] For all of these reasons, it may be said that municipal reformers were entitled only to minimum regrets.

The low participation regimes of the Southwest offered government that was "frugal and sparing." The governments elected in the Southwest— even the governments of sunbelt centralizers ostentatious in their affection for labor and people of color—spent considerably less than their northeastern counterparts on schools, hospitals, and charity. While Boss Frank Hague's Jersey City spent $26.15 per capita on health, charity, and schools, Houston (with the same population) spent $14.93. Similarly, while New Haven spent $24.23 on health, charity, and schools, same-size San Diego spent $19.21. (Figures are for 1936.)[84]

Local government efforts during the New Deal reflect not only a limited commitment to alleviating distress, but also the political status of selected constituents. African-Americans fared worst. Holcombe and Miller solicited the support of African-American voters and made much of their provision for the African-American community, yet these provisions remained minimal. The African-American community fared better in Austin than in Houston, perhaps because of its ability to participate in Austin elections. Nevertheless, in both Houston and Austin, African-Americans were ineligible for relief during the Great Depression, although in Austin a cannery was built to provide employment.[85]

The distribution of what little assistance there was tied local government more closely to its middle-class constituents. In Albuquerque, for example, public works projects funded by New Deal programs improved middle-class neighborhoods, not the communities of the working classes or the poor.[86] This too echoes Key's analysis of southern politics. "If there is a single grand issue" in the contest of haves and have-nots, Key

---

[83] Key writes, for example: "Within this framework of a limited suffrage . . . The issue becomes one of who is the 'best man' or the 'most competent' man to carry out what everyone is agreed upon" (*Southern Politics*, 308).

[84] See note 89 below.

[85] Shelton interview; the cannery is also mentioned in Hemphill, "Mayor Tom Miller."

[86] This is the finding of Charles Beibel, "Making the Most of It: Public Works in Albuquerque during the Great Depression, 1929–1942" (typescript, Albuquerque Museum, 1986).

wrote, "it is that of public expenditure." Absent parties, the have-nots
were without sustained representation; in an environment of low participation "the scales in the have–have-not conflict [were] tipped by the exclusion of a substantial sector of the have-not population. . . . professional politicians often have no incentive to appeal to the have-nots."[87]

Frugality showed up in the bottom line. While financing the infrastructure demanded by rapid population and industrial growth, local governments kept tax rates and debt low.[88] In San Diego the property tax burden (measured by property taxes per capita) was lower in 1936 than
1923; in Houston property taxes per capita increased by merely 10 percent between 1921 and 1938; in Austin the property tax burden remained nearly constant from the early 1920s through the early 1930s.
The frugality of southwestern city governments is more impressive when
compared to their same-size northeastern counterparts. New Haven's tax
rate in the 1930s averaged 188 percent of San Diego's; Boss Hague's
Jersey City imposed 175 percent the tax burden of Oscar Holcombe's
Houston.[89]

[87] Key, *Southern Politics*, 307.

[88] This argument contradicts the findings of the most careful comparative study of expenditures by machine and reform governments, "Bosses, Reform, and the Socioeconomic
Bases of Urban Expenditure, 1890–1940" by M. Craig Brown and Charles N. Halaby, in
The Politics of Urban Fiscal Policy, ed. Terrence J. McDonald and Sally K. Ward (Beverly
Hills: Sage, 1984), chap. 3. The authors examine general expenditures for thirty cities and
conclude, "Neither machines nor structural reform has a strong net influence on fiscal
policy, at least as presented by the level of general expenditures in cities" (90–91). Los
Angeles, San Francisco, and Denver are the only southwestern cities in their sample. Not
surprisingly, the authors have trouble finding reform regimes, and they report: "We originally intended to assess urban reform movements in the same way that we approached
machine politics [i.e., winning successive elections]. It soon became apparent, however, that
reformers consolidated city power so seldom and so briefly that another approach would
have to be taken" (77). Halaby and Brown measure reform influence not by the election of
good government advocates to office but by the acceptance of structural reforms. They
think the most significant effects of political style are in those cases where machines battle
reform competitors, hardly a likely scenario in the Southwest. A study comparable to theirs,
for southwestern cities, would be difficult because some of these cities were too small for
data on their budgets to be collected by the census bureau. Ideally, a study of the effects of
"machine" and "reform" on expenditures would compare same-size cities with dominant
machines to counterparts with reformers securely in political control. I do not present data
to claim that reform structures generally meant modest budgets. Rather, I claim that in the
cities for which I have information, reformers had good reason to feel their city budgets
were "frugal and sparing" compared to same-size machine cities.

[89] These calculations are from Bureau of the Census, *Financial Statistics of Cities*.
(Washington, D.C.: GPO, 1931) and *Financial Statistics of Cities Having a Population over
100,000* (Washington, D.C.: GPO, various years). New Haven/San Diego average is for are
1932–36; Jersey City's property taxes per capita averaged 174.5 percent of Houston's for
1930–36. Unfortunately Phoenix and Albuquerque were too small to be included in the

TABLE 4-3
Population of Southwestern Cities, 1920–1950

	1920	1930	1940	1950
Albuquerque	9,138	16,223	22,969	60,726
Austin	21,972	33,811	57,969	85,954
Dallas	158,976	260,475	294,734	434,462
Houston	88,528	190,150	264,418	397,823
Phoenix	19,005	31,301	43,666	73,047
San Antonio	161,379	231,342	253,854	408,442
San Diego	53,706	103,133	145,052	225,923
San Jose	39,642	57,654	68,457	95,280

Sources: U.S. Bureau of Census, Census of Population, 1920: Population (Washington, D.C.: Government Printing Office, 1922), part I, vol. III, table 10.

U.S. Bureau of the Census, Census of the Population, 1930. (Washington, D.C.: Government Printing Office, 1932), table 23.

U.S. Bureau of the Census, Census of the Population, 1940. (Washington, D.C.: Government Printing Office, 1943), vol. II, part 4, (New Mexico), table 32; part 6 (Texas), table 31; part 1 (Arizona), table 31; part 1 (California), table E-35.

U.S. Bureau of the Census, Census of the Population, 1950. (Washington, D.C.: Government Printing Office, 1952), vol. II, part 31 (New Mexico), table 34; part 43 (Texas), table 34; part 3 (Arizona), table 34; part 5 (California), table 34.

Local governments and their partners in the business community continued the aggressive pursuit of growth that dominated the agenda of earlier generations. They surely succeeded at population growth (table 4-3). Progress was also made in economic growth. As in the Progressive Era, in the interwar years the requisites of growth were often in the financial and industrial centers of the East and in Washington; as a result, growth required the aggressive collective action of local economic and political leaders. Sunbelt centralizers were active purveyors of growth strategies for their cities; everywhere too private sector organizations—the Chamber of Commerce and its relatives—continued their collective pursuit of growth. In Phoenix and San Diego, with weaker governments, private-sector organizations were more obviously in the lead, but in Austin, Houston, and Albuquerque as well their role was important. Austin continued its aversion to industry, growing as a white-collar city. Phoenix diversified its efforts as an entrepôt. Albuquerque and Houston continued with strong industrial bases, Albuquerque with the Santa Fe railroad yards, Houston boasting the oil industry and its port, and San Diego wed to the armed forces.

fiscal census in this period; after 1931 (when the census included all cities of 100,000 population rather than 30,000, as earlier), Austin was too small.

Those who fought for municipal reform desired orderly growth and efficient administration. To those ends they sought to loosen, if not to sever, the ties of politicians to popular groups, and to institute businesslike management practices. In the Southwest the weakness of parties and restrictions on voting assisted the enactment of reform charters. The same process meant that municipal reform was not obviously or enthusiastically the popular will. Broadly speaking, since reform government was not the clear choice of the majority (although it was a choice of some voter majorities) and since reform charters inadequately provided for representation, reform was institutionalized in ways heavily dependent on "extra-constitutional" devices to organize consent and popular support.

Belying reformers' success at enacting manager and commission charters, reform governments in the first half of the twentieth century did not create apolitical, businesslike administrations. Reform governments before World War II succumbed to two patterns that may be understood as pathological institutionalizations of reform. The first pattern was disorder and factionalism, or perhaps "rings" of commissioners. Political life in Phoenix or San Diego, for example, bore strong resemblances to the regimes described by Key in *Southern Politics*, lacking consistent lines of popular division and boasting few notable politicians or ambitious public policies. The second pattern was government by sunbelt centralizers. These leaders all claimed to be opponents of municipal reform, appealed to working people and citizens of color, built political organizations, and were skillful in the pursuit of ambitious growth strategies for their cities. Despite these unanticipated outcomes, reform regimes secured central elements of the reform agenda: restricted participation, the erosion of partisan organizations, and local governments that were "frugal and sparing." Whatever the unanticipated consequences of reform, reformers were entitled only to minimum regrets.

Nevertheless, reformers were neither cheerful nor secure that their interests were safe. A leitmotif of local politics in the interwar years was the call for reform, usually with little effect. As defense spending increased in the 1940s and new economic dangers and opportunities loomed on the postwar horizon, businessmen became increasingly concerned that local economies were not well positioned for postwar growth and local government was ill-equipped to manage postwar challenges. In addition, migrants from the North and Midwest added new constituencies receptive to reform. As a result, in the 1940s and 1950s there was another round of reform campaigning and charter revision.

Five

The Little Movement Becomes Respectable

IN THE LATE 1930s and through the 1940s, the cities of the southwest became home to more people and industry as a part of the country's effort in the Second World War. The magnitude of wartime changes was intimidating. In San Diego, for example, the resident population doubled in four years. In an effort to accommodate these residents, more housing was built between 1940 and 1943 than in the preceding thirty years, and still the city had a terrible housing shortage! Everywhere newly created defense industries mushroomed to become major components of local economies.[1]

Urban leaders looked over infrastructure and economy with great concern. Where wartime industry had prospered, cities were crowded and ill-equipped to accommodate rapidly swelling populations. The prospect of war's end brought worries about keeping wartime industries operating and triggered aggressive recruitment of new industries. These two concerns dominated local politics for a generation after the end of the war.

Sustaining newer economies required mobilizing longstanding skills of city promotion and recruitment. Just as many southwestern cities did in the Progressive Era, in the 1940s the San Jose the city council appropriated funds for a national publicity campaign, to be conducted by the Chamber of Commerce. Over the course of the next decade, IBM, General Electric, Pittsburgh Steel, Owens Corning, and Kaiser each established outposts in San Jose, joining two young Stanford engineers, William Hewlett and David Packard, who came to the city in 1938.[2]

---

[1] For San Diego, Gerald Nash, *The American West Transformed: The Impact of the Second World War* (Bloomington: Indiana University Press, 1985), 58–59. For Phoenix, Bradford Luckingham, *The Urban Southwest: A Profile History of Albuquerque, El Paso, Phoenix, and Tucson* (El Paso: University of Texas Press, 1982), 78. Changes in the West during the war have been chronicled well by historians: Nash, *American West Transformed*, Carl Abbott, *The Metropolitan Frontier: Cities in the Modern American West* (Tucson: University of Arizona Press, 1985), chap. 1. Chap. 2 provides an excellent overview of political changes subsequent to the war. Roger Lotchin, *Fortress California, 1910–1961: From Warfare to Welfare* (New York: Oxford University Press 1992). See also, Robert B. Fairbanks, "Dallas in the 1940s: The Challenges and Opportunities of Defense Mobilization," in *Urban Texas: Politics and Development*, ed. Char Miller and Heywood T. Sanders (College Station: Texas A & M University Press, 1990), 145–54.

[2] Philip J. Trounstine and Terry Christensen, *Movers and Shakers: The Study of Community Power* (New York: St. Martin's, 1982), 87–90.

In Phoenix a similar recruitment effort was led by the Chamber of Commerce and its booster organization, the Thunderbirds. Prospective investors were invited to visit the city at the Chamber's expense. Takers were escorted about town and presented with dossiers of Phoenix's advantages as a site for industrial location. The general manager of the Chamber "made all of the authorizations regarding what concessions the city would be willing to make in order to attract a given industry." Having targeted the electronic industries, Phoenix soon counted among its new employers Motorola, AirResearch, General Electric, Goodyear Aircraft, Kaiser, and Sperry Phoenix.[3] In Dallas, Banker Robert Thornton led a campaign to expand the city's economy from wholesaling, retailing, banking, and insurance to industry.[4] In San Diego the Chamber of Commerce began to worry about the shape of the postwar economy in 1941, and government leaders and the city's Congressman, Bob Wilson, worked to continue the city's close relationship with the navy. Wilson became an important and articulate advocate not only of San Diego, but also of Cold War defense spending in the 1950s. The navy had already invested heavily in San Diego. Nevertheless, local leaders realized, as Roger Lotchin later explained, that "many if not most, of these military resources [awarded after World War II] could have been put somewhere else." To avoid that outcome, "almost everything the services got in San Diego came from enthusiastic city offers [of land] and much local brokerage of crucial matters." These efforts insured the city's economy and its social character as a navy town.[5]

In Austin the Chamber of Commerce and its secretary, Walter E. Long, had pursued and defended Austin's no-industry growth plan from before the First World War. In the mid 1940s, a small group of businessmen began to argue that the city needed to broaden its economy. As in San Jose, an intense national advertising campaign supplemented efforts to recruit industry. The first indication that the new growth plan might succeed was the continuing federally funded work of the Defense Research Laboratory. Local leaders worked with Lyndon Johnson to enable the University of Texas to acquire the facility, soon renamed the Balcones Research Center.[6]

---

[3] Michael Francis Konig, "Toward Metropolis Status: Charter Government and the Rise of Phoenix, Arizona, 1945–1960" (Ph.D. diss., Arizona State University, Tempe, 1983), chap. 6, esp. 205–16, emphasis added.

[4] Robert Fairbanks, "Dallas in the 1940s: The Challenges and Opportunities of Defense Mobilization," in *Urban Texas: Politics and Development*, ed. Char Miller and Heywood T. Sanders (College Station, Texas: Texas A & M Press 1990), 145.

[5] Richard F. Pourade, *History of San Diego* (San Diego: Union–Tribune, 1977), 7:34. Lotchin, *Fortress California*, 40.

[6] Anthony M. Orum, *Power, Money, and the People: The Making of Modern Austin*

Albuquerque too avoided postwar depression by soliciting continued defense spending. Kirtland Air Force Base continued to expand. Equally important, scientists from Los Alamos laboratories organized a laboratory that soon became the Sandia Corporation. Sandia's future as a site for ordnance engineering and weapons development was assured by the transition from World War II battles to 1950s Cold War.[7]

Accommodating the changes in southwestern cities required sustained activism on the part of local governments. The first generations of reform governments had disappointed their founders in a variety of ways. The continued presence of the very same politicians through a series of charter revisions served in some places as the most visible index of how little political life had changed. By the 1940s local government did not have adequate taxing powers to finance expanding infrastructure or provision of amenities, nor were the propertied voters who controlled the financing of additional debt inclined to approve new bonds. Spending was as problematic as getting. Despite tremendous wartime expansion, some political leaders held fast to pay-as-you-go frugality. This was hardly an adequate philosophy for financing infrastructure and services for new residents, much less continued growth. Cities were falling behind in providing basic services to neighborhoods. Suburbs and older neighborhoods alike complained of neglect; yet neither wanted government to have general taxing powers that would allow spending neighborhood money someplace else. In some cities police and fire departments were demoralized, inefficient, too autonomous from central authorities. At the same time, the desire to annex suburbs, direct growth, and attend to fraying downtowns energized local elites to become more attentive to city government.

In the decade 1945–55, and in some cases well before, the cities of the Southwest were refounded. Efforts to reconstruct local government were a leitmotif of the interwar period, and the pace of reform increased in the aftermath of World War II. The *National Municipal Review* crowed over the increasing numbers of cities adopting the city-manager plan: only twenty-five in 1945, but seventy-nine in 1946, ninety-five in 1948 (this last an all-time high, surpassing the record of 1921), and ninety-three in 1953. "The record rate of adoptions each year since World War II," reported the *Review* in 1953, "indicates the

---

(Austin: Texas Monthly Press, 1987), 229–36. These ideas met resistance from the old guard of business, in firm control of the Chamber of Commerce. One index of the new generation's victory was the forced resignation of Walter E. Long, secretary of the Chamber since before the First World War.

[7] Robert Turner Wood, "The Transformation of Albuquerque, 1945–1972" (Ph.D. diss., University of New Mexico, 1980), 97–101.

council-manager plan will become the prevailing form of local government within the next decade."[8]

Later authors have also drawn attention to the increased efforts of business and political leaders to reorganize and reinvigorate local government at mid-century. Writing in 1961, Lorin Peterson argued that the postwar period saw another *Day of the Mugwump*, as newly energetic elites organized to transform local politics.[9] Peterson discussed the direct descendants of progressive reformers (municipal research bureaus, the League of Women Voters), as well as the press, chambers of commerce, and the increased political activism of business leaders in new or revived organizations (municipal parties, "top brass committees"). Peterson studied twenty large cities. Consistent with precedent, modern mugwumps achieved their greatest triumphs at eliminating corruption and exercising leadership in the South and West. Obviously the numbers are very small, but the pattern is familiar: of the seven cities where Peterson saw greatest governmental change, five were in the South and West (Dallas, San Antonio, New Orleans, Memphis, Seattle).[10]

Three years later Robert Salisbury argued that there was a "new convergence of power" in American cities.[11] Salisbury confined his analysis to cities that had experienced "substantial growth before World War I" and specifically eliminated cities with council-manager government. In Salisbury's cities,[12] looming problems posed by the end of the Second World War (among them, deterioration of the physical plant, particularly downtown, and the dramatic demographic changes of wartime migrations) provoked the greater organization of leaders of large businesses with stakes downtown. In combination with mayors and public sector professionals, they formed the new convergence of power organized to tackle urban problems.

The cities of the Southwest were in the 1940s and 1950s as they had been in the Progressive Era, more successful and ambitious than cities elsewhere at the reorganization of local government. By 1955 almost every large city from Texas west to the Pacific enjoyed nonpartisan city-

---

[8] *National Municipal Review* 43, no. 2 (February 1954): 81.

[9] Lorin Peterson, *The Day of the Mugwump* (New York: Random House, 1961).

[10] The other two were Cincinnati and Kansas City. Peterson, *Mugwump*, sees Dallas as prefiguring events in Pittsburgh and elsewhere (see 92 *ff*).

[11] Robert Salisbury, "Urban Politics: The New Convergence of Power," *Journal of Politics* 26, no. 4 (1964): 775–97.

[12] Presumably the cities of the Northeast and Midwest. It is not too much to say that by choosing this sample, Salisbury eliminated his best cases. Salisbury is dismissive of Peterson, unhappy with the appellation "mugwump." I am happy to grant Peterson the artistic license to call his local leaders "mugwumps," although my own characterization is different. Much of Peterson's argument anticipates the argument of "New Convergence"; see, for example, Peterson, *Mugwump*, 89.

manager government, usually with citywide elections for seats on the city council (among them: San Jose, Phoenix, Dallas, Austin, San Diego, Oklahoma City, and Albuquerque). Exceptions were few. Tucson, Arizona adopted council-manager government but allowed partisan elections. Tulsa retained commission government long after it became a big city. El Paso enjoyed strong-mayor government with aldermen who also served as commissioners.[13] This chapter follows the course of argument in another exception, Houston. Houston adopted city-manager government in 1942 but dismantled it in 1947 in favor of the strong-mayor form.

Phoenix and San Antonio adopted city-manager government in the postwar decade. In other cities elite organization was enough. Albuquerque and San Jose, for example, did not change their city-manager charters significantly after 1917, but in the postwar period elites organized for political action did change the direction of local government. San Jose, San Diego, and Dallas were ahead of the curve. San Diego abandoned commission government in favor of a mayor-council system in 1915. This also proving unsatisfactory, a city-manager charter was offered to the voters in 1929 and defeated, and another offered in 1931, when it passed. Dallas adopted city-manager government a year earlier. Citizens in Austin approved a city-manager charter in 1924, although the resistance of elected officials delayed its implementation several years. Austin did change its charter in 1953, creating a place system. In this system citywide elections were retained, but places on the city council were numbered, and winning required a majority of votes cast (previously the top five vote-getters citywide were declared the winners).[14]

City-manager proponents across the Southwest invoked like arguments; opponents too sounded much alike from place to place, and underlying issues were also largely the same from place to place across city-manager adoptions. For that reason, this chapter considers the Dallas, Austin, and San Diego campaigns along with those in Houston, Phoenix, and San Antonio.

The section that follows, "Persistence against Stone Walls," traces discontents with commission government. "City-Manager Campaigns" describes the campaigns for adopting city-manager charters and the forces that favored and opposed the manager plan. Recurrent efforts to change local government between the world wars were symptomatic of elite dis-

[13] Mark Adams and Gertrude Adams, "Report on Politics in El Paso" (mimeograph, Joint Center for the Study of Urban Politics, MIT and Harvard Universities, 1963), II-1.
[14] David A. Olson, *Nonpartisan Elections: A Case Analysis* (Austin: University of Texas, 1965), 11. Olson reports that fears of single-shot voting, and of election by less than a majority, motivated the change, and that fear of successful African-American candidacies may also have played a role.

content. In Phoenix there were campaigns for charter change in 1923, 1933, 1934, 1936, 1938, and 1948;[15] in Houston there were charter revision campaigns in 1933, 1938, 1942, and 1947. As the need for repeated campaigns indicates, city-manager government was controversial enough that political consensus did not come easily.

The final section of the chapter, "Citizen Action," traces the creation of nonpartisan slating groups. While reformers were energetic in the promotion of new charters, they also recognized that new charters alone would not guarantee the changes in local government they desired. Indeed, the fault of prior strategies was to trust that the work of changing city government was done when new charters were enacted. Institutional change had to be augmented by continued mobilization. The result was the organization of nonpartisan slating groups (NPSGs), which rapidly became the political parties of local politics. There is more than a little irony here. Having denounced political parties for nearly a century, municipal reformers became the devoted organizers of local parties and came to behave much like party leaders themselves.

Persistence against Stone Walls

A decade after the adoption of Progressive Era changes, local leaders may well have felt the "obvious futility" of reform activity. Commission governments failed to control their own departments or metropolitan development; in some places developers effectively looted municipal treasuries; relations with utilities remained strained; voters and banks alike were loathe to finance expanded municipal budgets. Just as local politicians demonstrated their staying power across charter changes, so too old municipal problems persisted. In San Diego, where securing an adequate water supply was always difficult, the council government managed to squander most of the proceeds of a $2 million bond issue by building two dams in the wrong places.[16] Austin, San Diego, and Phoenix continued to have difficulty negotiating acceptable relations with utilities; Albuquerque and Phoenix worried about recruiting new industries. One citizen of Phoenix recalled simply, "Whatever was bad about city government was bad about Phoenix."[17]

---

[15] Michael J. Kotlanger, "Phoenix, Arizona, 1920–1940" (Ph.D. diss., Arizona State University, 1983), 384.

[16] Harold A. Stone, "San Diego," in *City Manager Government in Nine Cities*, ed. Harold A. Stone, Don K. Price, and Kathryn H. Stone (Chicago: Public Administration Service, 1940), 148.

[17] Rhes Cornelius interview, June 22, 1976, Arizona Historical Society.

In the face of these problems, mayors appointed charter commissions to study alternate plans for city government, hold hearings on current difficulties, and propose new city charters (in San Diego a Board of Freeholders was elected for this purpose). As in earlier times, the National Municipal League was contacted, the advice of professors solicited, testimony provided from other cities. San Diego consulted Professors Samuel C. May of the University of California at Berkeley, Edwin Cottrell from Stanford, William B. Munro from Harvard, and George Peterson from San Diego State College. The Board of Freeholders read with interest about developments in Cincinnati, the country's outstanding example of successful reform, and received materials from the National Municipal League.[18] Professor Herman G. James of the University of Texas at Austin, and the secretary of Austin's Chamber of Commerce, Walter E. Long, traveled together to meetings of the International City Manager's Association.[19] In Houston Charter Commission members read Leonard White's *The City Manager*.[20] In Phoenix Alfred Knight, recently emigrated from Cincinnati and a participant in that city's successful reorganization, was a founding member of the Charter Government Committee. The committee, appointed by Mayor Busey to rewrite the charter, also solicited and read materials from the National Municipal League; the league's model city charter "figured prominently in debates and exerted a strong influence" on the committee's work. The Charter Revision Committee also sent the draft of its final recommendations to the League "for criticism and suggestions."[21] Testimony from Cincinnati's success, disillusioned leaders from Galveston, and views of current leaders in local government were presented to charter commissions over months of hearings. Their deliberations complete, the commissions offered new charters—always city-manager charters providing government expanded powers—in municipal referenda and often organized campaigns to insure their passage.

Everywhere local government had financial problems. Austin's city government was largely financed by user or consumer charges rather than property taxes. When revenues were insufficient, Austin borrowed through bond issues, which propertied voters were increasingly reluctant

[18] For the 1928 effort, H. Stone, "San Diego," 153. Minutes of the [San Diego] Board of Freeholders (hereafter MSBDF) June 4, 14, 1929; May 17, 1929.

[19] Frank Staniszewski, "Ideology and Practice in Municipal Government Reform: A Case Study of Austin" (University of Texas at Austin Studies in Politics, Series I, no. 8, 1977), 31.

[20] Minutes of the Houston City Charter Commission (hereafter HCC), May 2, 1938, Houston Municipal Research Center, Houston Public Library.

[21] Dix Price Interview, Arizona Historical Society; Paul Kelso, "Phoenix Charter Arises Anew," *National Municipal Review* 38, no. 4 (April 1949): 178.

to approve. Even without the industrial ambitions of Houston, Austin's government needed greater powers, not only to raise money, but also to regulate utilities and implement zoning.[22] In Houston spending was so far ahead of foreseeable revenues that neither banks nor voters approved further borrowing. Testifying before the Houston Charter Commission in 1938, T. W. Browne, the tax collector, reported that of the $2.00 tax rate (on 50 percent valuation), $1.14 was necessary for retiring debt.[23] George Waters, a city commissioner, reported that the city's deficit of 1931 would not be paid off until 1951.[24]

A related problem was managing the growth of new residential communities. Houston's tax collector attributed the city's onerous debt to its incorporation of suburban areas and with them, their debts.[25] In Houston and also in San Diego, the city council and engineering departments were corrupted by the presence of developers. Houston's commissioner, George B. Waters, explained, "Any developer who comes down to the city hall and persuades the City Council to dump city funds into his land subdivision, is getting that much 'pork,' and any official who does that same thing on his own subdivision is just stealing that much money out of the treasury."[26] In San Diego new communities were financed by special assessment, paying for their own development. This did not completely absolve the city of financial responsibility, however, as the council "let contracts for subdivision development . . . influenced by the pressure brought by companies building streets or selling paving, street lights, or sewer materials. A real estate developer could protect his interests and help his friends by being on the council."[27]

Despite the possibility that their developer might be on the city council, residents of outlying communities felt unrepresented in a system with citywide elections. For this reason the Board of Freeholders appointed in 1929 to rewrite San Diego's city charter spent more time on the issue of district elections than anything else. Neighborhood improvement clubs and commercial clubs testified about the need for districts to protect their interests. Similarly, neighborhood residents sought to protect themselves by requiring that any special assessment be approved by two-thirds of affected voters.[28] The same conversations took

[22] Staniszewski, "Ideology," 35; Harold A. Stone, "City Manager Government in Austin," in *City Manager Government in Nine Cities*, ed. Harold A. Stone, Don K. Price, and Kathryn H. Stone (Chicago: Public Administration Service, 1940), 415, 418, 419.

[23] HCC, box 1, April 7, 1938, 17.

[24] HCC, box 1, March 16, 1938, 9.

[25] HCC, box 1, April 7, 1938, 17.

[26] HCC, box 1, March 16, 1938, 6.

[27] H. Stone, "San Diego," 146.

[28] Minutes of the San Diego Board of Freeholders (hereafter MSDBF), August 23, 1929 (special assessments): October 17–24, testimony for districts.

place in Houston. There Commissioner Frank Holton testified that "eighty or eighty-five per cent of the taxes paid to the City are from south of Buffalo Bayou and I further venture to say that eighty-five or ninety per cent are spent out in the Heights on the north side, and out in the east, and very little is spent out in the south or southwest portion of the city."[29] Commissioner Waters, seeing the inefficiencies of improvements directed by developers, wanted improvement districts and special assessments to pay for municipal work, rather than financing improvements from general funds.[30]

Phoenix suffered from all sorts of corruption. No city manager of any national stature was ever appointed. It was alleged that a paint dealer, Ward H. "Doc" Scheumack, controlled the city council, the awarding of contracts, the city manager, and local public policy from behind the scenes. The police department was corrupt, there was a thriving business in gambling,[31] and the city council itself was corrupt, dividing among members the considerable proceeds from fines levied on houses of prostitution.[32]

Municipal employees of course had large stakes in the organization of local government. Often too they were the best organized group in the electorate, and everywhere municipal employees and labor unions took positions on municipal reform. In Phoenix municipal employees, organized in the City Employees Unity Council, worried that strengthening the city manager's administrative powers would undermine civil service protections; equally threatening was the prospect of change in the union's informal collective bargaining arrangements. The same was true in San Diego, Houston, and Albuquerque.[33] Along with the Central Labor Council of the AFL in Phoenix, the City Employees Unity Council op-

[29] HCC, March 24, 1938, 14–15.

[30] HCC, March 16, 1938, 6.

[31] Paul Roca interview, June 30, 1977 (by N. J. Coulter). Tape at the Arizona Historical Society.

[32] For Scheumack, Konig, "Metropolis Status," 27–28. Harry Rosenzweig recalled that the madams "would be arrested once a month, and all the girls would be arrested, and they just automatically went down and paid the fine, only the fines went in a bag, and every month the council cut it up. . . . Each girl was fined $25 a month into the pot, and the madams—say, forty of them—that's another couple thousand, so there was five, six, seven thousand to divide up among five or six guys every month. And they had a bag man. He'd go down and do the collecting." Transcript, p. 75 (from the collection of G. W. Johnson, Brigham Young University), interviewed July 19, 1976.

[33] MSBDF, September 12, 1930. September 12, 1930, letter from the San Diego County Federated Trades and Labor Council to the Board of Freeholders. "The Fire Department is rather jealous of its present set up, and naturally wants to know that the structure which it has built will be preserved in the charter." James G. Pfanstiel to Nicholas J. Martin, September 12, 1930. In Albuquerque the issue arose later. There too municipal employees enjoyed informal collective bargaining rights, which the Albuquerque Citizens' Committee opposed. See chapter 6 below.

posed the charter proposed in 1948.[34] Similar concerns drove organized labor in San Diego to oppose the charter of 1929. Municipal employees in San Diego not only feared the loss of civil service protections but also objected that the charter proposed in 1929 would supersede protections of state law, including the minimum wage for government employees. The police and fire departments enjoyed the greatest autonomy and self-management, and they were adamant in the defense of departmental prerogatives against proposed powers for city managers.[35] In Houston Herman Wright, an attorney representing the Association of City and County Employees, cautioned that city managers in Amarillo and Dallas had lowered wages to lower municipal debt. Another attorney told a large meeting at the labor temple, "I know of no place where the city manager form of government hasn't worked hardships on two groups—city employees and labor."[36]

Houston had a large, well-organized labor movement outside government's own workforce. Municipal employees and longshoremen had strong organizations for some time; the oil industry was about to be the site of a CIO organizing campaign.[37] In an effort to recruit labor support, Roy Sessions, an organizer for the Oil Workers (a CIO affiliate), was appointed to the Houston Charter Commission of 1938. Citing a pattern of police harassment of legal and peaceful strike activity, Sessions proposed a charter provision to restrict police activities:

> No police officer, deputy, or special officer shall serve in any capacity during a strike within the city unless the majority of the City Council shall determine that there is imminent danger of the loss of life and destruction of property; and order police participation. Under no circumstance shall any police officer or special officer act in the capacity of strike breaker.

Asked to "explain just what the conditions are that he is trying to remedy," Sessions responded that "on innumerable occasions the Police Department has, under orders of course, broken strikes or helped to break strikes." The Police Department restricted the number of picketers without authority, escorted strikebreakers through picket lines, subjected strikers to verbal and physical—sometimes lethal—abuse, and arrested picketers, whom they then were forced to free for lack of charges. Although other commission members assured Sessions of their opposition to police brutality, they countered that the maintenance of order was a regular police function. After prolonged discussion the chairman

---

[34] Konig, "Metropolis Status," 34–35.

[35] Stone, "San Diego"; MSDBF, Pfansteil and Labor Council letters.

[36] Wright, HCC, box 1, May 2, 1938; Myers, *Houston Press*, August 31, 1938.

[37] Clyde Johnson, "The CIO Oil Workers Organizing Campaign in Texas, 1942–3" (typescript, April 1, 1976, University of Texas at Arlington, Labor History Collection).

summed up the views of the rest of the commission: "This thing is conducive to industrial warfare in no man's land. The only possible authority is eliminated." The resolution was dropped.[38]

Finally, leaders of organized labor viewed the city manager as an antidemocratic figure, since the manager was neither elected nor subject to recall. "American democracy," wrote the president and secretary of the San Diego County Federated Trades and Labor Council (of the AFL), "is a challenge to the primary claims made for the city manager system. . . . By charter law a city manager is a created autocrat."[39] Similarly, Herman Wright, attorney for the Association of City and County Employees of Houston and Harris Country, testified, "I have listened with considerable care to the argument of these people who would contend that city manager government automatically will eliminate all politics from city government. I say those people are either idealistic beyond endurance, or else they have closed their eyes to the facts."[40] Lewis Fisher, eight years mayor of Galveston under its commission government, agreed: "never as long as the sun shines and we still maintain a democratic form of government in this country, are we going to eliminate politics."[41]

The several problems of local government did not point to a common solution. For those most concerned with inequities of taxation and distribution—whether older city neighborhoods or newer suburban communities inside the city limits—district representation seemed the solution to problems of inadequate representation, and financing by special assessment seemed their best protection against impoverishment by municipal extravagance.[42] Coupled with the poor reputation of city managers toward city employees and the principled objections to managers, this meant working-class and suburban opposition to managers and to increased taxing powers. For those who felt the several parts of local government too autonomous and its spending too profligate, centralization in the manager and broad-based taxation rather than special im-

[38] HCC, box 2, July 7, 1938, 29–31, July 11, 1938, 61–74. Sessions did not return to the charter commission deliberations. In an interview with the author, Houston labor lawyer Chris Dixie recalled that although police were guilty of most of Sessions's accusations, there was only one occasion on which police actually worked as strikebreakers. Conversation with the author, June 1991.

[39] September 12, 1930, in the files of the MSDBF.

[40] HCC, box 1, May 2, 1938, 55–56.

[41] HCC, box 1, April 18, 1938, 8–9.

[42] Cf. chapter 3 for comparable concerns in Albuquerque when the city's commission charter was being debated. This issue appears repeatedly; see, for example, Becky Nicolaides, "Battle on the Crabgrass Frontier: Society and Political Struggle in a Working Class Suburb of Los Angeles, 1929–1930" (paper delivered at the annual meetings of the Organization of American Historians, 1993) for conflict in a developing suburb about financing the community.

provement districts or special assessment financing seemed the obvious remedy to the ills of local government. These disparate concerns, then, powered the arguments about reorganizing local government when city-manager plans were offered to the voters.

City-Manager Campaigns

From the First World War through the 1940s, efforts to create city-manager governments dominated the reform agenda. Because city-manager proposals were controversial, their advocates could not leave victory to chance. Under the mantle of leadership organizations like the Citizens Charter Committee in Houston or the Citizens' Charter Association in Dallas, supporters of city-manager plans spoke at civic and women's clubs, neighborhood meetings, union halls, churches, over the radio, and to the press; the same people organized precincts and, on the last and most important day, got out the vote. In Austin, the Chamber of Commerce claimed: "Council manager . . . government was adopted after seven years of educational work. This educational work was a non-political [*sic*] activity of the Chamber of Commerce [beginning] in 1917. . . . Following this program the Council-Manager Club organized and directed a campaign until the charter was changed . . . by a margin of 40-odd votes."[43] Proponents of city-manager plans enjoyed enormous press advantages. In San Diego in 1931, the *Union*, *Tribune*, and *Sun* all supported the proposed plan; in Phoenix the *Arizona Republic* and the *Phoenix Gazette* campaigned ardently for the plan as their editor, Eugene Pulliam, became a leading spokesman for the proposal. In Dallas the *Morning News* promoted the plan, to which its editor, George B. Dealy, was wholly committed; a *News* journalist later reported that "all of the daily newspapers supported the plan, and not one cent was spent for advertising with any of them."[44] In each case newspapers offered copious coverage of current political ills and the purported benefits of manager plans, while providing scanty coverage of the opposition. Houston provides a different case. The press was diverse—including several labor and African-American newspapers—and its opinions divided. In addition to local press support, advocates of reform enjoyed the assistance of the National Municipal League's pamphlets, sample editorials, speakers' bureau, and campaign assistance.[45]

[43] Walter E. Long, *Something Made Austin Grow* (Austin: Chamber of Commerce, 1948), 24.

[44] Louis P. Head, "Dallas Joins Ranks of Manager Cities," *National Municipal Review* 19, no. 12 (December 1930): 806–8, 807.

[45] In 1921 the *National Municipal Review* began reporting the numbers of cities re-

Campaigns for city-manager charters, and opposition to them, repeated the familiar themes of argument about local government. Proponents supported their choice with claims of "business-like management," eliminating "politics" and "bossism." Opponents warned of the demise of democracy and rule by "the interests."

Advocates of city-manager government and leaders of newly formed nonpartisan slating groups promised efficiency and lower taxes, clear lines of authority and administration, and government by "better men" rather than "politicians." Efficiency was sometimes promised in the arcane language of efficiency experts (as when an Austin advocate promised that the manager "will eliminate lost motion"[46]), but most often praised for small budgets and low taxes. An attorney for the city of Fort Worth testified to that city's rewarding experience with the city-manager plan under the headlines "Cuts Tax Burden; Miracle of More Work for Same Money Performed There."[47]

Business methods promised not only efficiency and low taxes but also better organization and management. A typical accolade for the clear lines of authority city-manager government would exhibit is found in the San Diego Union, which editorialized that the charter proposed in 1931 provided for "absolutely clear and specific assignment of business management to the manager's office, with ample authority and absolute responsibility. . . . the city's surest safeguard against buck-passing."[48] The Dallas Morning News claimed in 1930 that the city-manager system "demands results in economy and efficiency, and gets these. Each official knows that his hold on the job does not depend on political influence, but on his doing a better job than anybody else. It encourages a man to do his best work."[49] These portraits stood in sharp contrast to current govern-

---

questing assistance and its responses. Vol. 10, no. 5 (1921), for example, reported: "The demand for speakers in city-manager campaigns grows from day to day; the demand goes hand in hand with the demand for the booklet, 'The Story of the City Manager Plan' " (264).

[46] Austin American, August 7, 1924, 3.

[47] Dallas Morning News, October 1, 1930; to these examples many others could be added. The Dallas Morning News declared (October 1, 1930), "Tax Rates Cut When Manager Operates City." A physician visiting Kansas City reported, "I was told everywhere that Kansas City was receiving more efficient and economical government under the city manager system" (Dallas Morning News, October 9, 1930, 1). The Austin American reported (May 27, 1924, 3) that "one year after the city manager plan . . . began" in Beaumont, "the treasury had been built up, improvements were made in every branch of the government, and today there stands 150 miles of paved thoroughfares." The Houston Press (October 1, 1938) chose Cincinnati to draw the moral of the savings of reform: "discredited widely as being one of the nation's worst governed cities" before the adoption of the manager plan, Cincinnati had, a dozen years after, "the lowest tax rate of any American municipality, the lowest light rate, and benefits not provided elsewhere."

[48] San Diego Union, April 4, 1931, 4.

[49] Dallas Morning News, September 5, 1930, part 2, p. 14.

ments' "bickering,"[50] "factionalism," "squabbling," patronage, and "inefficiency" caused by political rather than managerial motives. Leaders of Dallas's women's clubs saw that the council-manager plan "eliminates the discharging of efficient city employes" who in the past "have been replaced by inexperienced, and often incapable, persons in order to pay off political debts."[51] The *Houston Press* editorialized that the "constant battle royal over political plums demonstrates [the] failure of [the] present system."[52]

Not the least of the reasons government could be expected to improve under city-manager government is that it would be manned by better men (and later women). It was often boasted that proposed manager charters had been drawn up by the city's most prestigious civic leaders. In Houston the Charter Commission of 1942 was "composed of 35 outstanding citizens representing all geographical sections of the city, after four months of hearings, debate, and argument"; "They served unselfishly for their city."[53] If adopted, the manager plan would encourage their continued service, not least because the compensation for members of the city council was lowered![54]

In Phoenix Charter Government Committee was characterized this way:

> Each [member] has a high moral reputation. . . . As individuals they are not under the thumb of any boss. Moreover, they are known to have an interest in the people and in promoting civic welfare. They are not in politics for the sake of . . . personal gain. . . . All of them have proved their personal interest in civic work—in boys' clubs, in health activities, in work among minorities, in the welfare of the people of Phoenix.[55]

Their opponents were denounced as politicians, interested in local government for their own financial gain. So the *Houston Press* reported that the street and bridge department had become a patronage machine, at a cost to taxpayers of $200,000 in 1942 alone,[56] and posed the question, "Efficiency or Spoils, Which Shall it Be?"[57] In Phoenix it was argued that the sitting government was corrupt, that too much of the city's budget went to payrolls, and that safeguards against extravagant spending were routinely circumvented. (In Austin, Dallas, and San Diego proponents of

---

[50] *Houston Press*, August 14, 1942, 14.
[51] *Dallas Morning News*, October 5, 1930, part 1, 13.
[52] *Houston Press,* April 16, 1942.
[53] Ibid., August 14, 1942, 1; "served unselfishly," *Houston Press,* October 1, 1938, 4.
[54] *Houston Post*, October 2, 1938.
[55] *Arizona Republic*, October 28, 1949, 6.
[56] *Houston Press*, August 4, 1942.
[57] Ibid., August 14, 1942, 1; July 15, 1942.

the manager form more often argued local officeholders were no better or worse than in most places but suffered from antiquated and inadequate institutions that required change if their cities were to progress.)[58]

Opponents of city-manager charters argued that it was undemocratic, "class government" that would put "big business in the saddle." Contrary to reformers' claims, manager government would be at once expensive and antilabor. Worse, manager charters created institutions that would facilitate centralized machine-building. Finally, city-manager government would increase the influence of hostile outsiders on local government.

Austin's commissioner Harry Haynes made these arguments against the city-manager plan proposed there in 1924. "City managership," he said, "means big business in the saddle." "If the proposed city manager plan [passes] . . . the average citizen of Austin will have about as little to say about the conduct of this city as the negroes have to say about the conduct of the democratic party" and "Austin will be run for the primary benefit of a few big business men."[59]

In Houston in 1942, the Citizen's League for the Preservation of Democratic Government (probably some combination of Democratic party organization and organized labor) published *Facts and Figures*, a tabloid newspaper opposed to the city-manager charter. Its columns exhibit all the arguments commonly made against city-manager government both in other campaigns in Houston and in other cities. *Facts and Figures* saw abundant evidence that the city-manager form was undemocratic. For one thing, advocates of the manager form wanted municipal employees barred from campaigning for or against the charter. Second, both because salaries of elected officials were reduced and because high filing fees were required of candidates, poor men could not run for office. Third, the city manager was appointed not elected. Like the *Houston Press* in 1938, *Facts and Figures* showed Hitler caricatures labeled "city manager" (in 1938 the *Press* had underscored the thought with the caption "you cannot recall me.")

Facts and Figures also argued that city manager charters were hardly a guarantee against corruption or machine building, of which Pendergast's Kansas City was the outstanding case. Nor would the manager system insure growth and prosperity. "In Georgia", *Facts and Figures* pointed out,

> there are no city managers in Atlanta, Augusta, Macon or Savannah, but there are at Cedartown, Cordale, Cornelia, Griffin, and Tifton. . . . Milwaukee with strong-mayor type of government, is known as one of the best governed and

[58] See, for example, *Dallas Morning News*, October 9, 1930.
[59] *Austin American*, August 4, 1924, 1.

operated city [*sic*] in America. . . . The city manager towns in Wisconsin are Delcit, Ft. Atkinson, Janesville, Kenosha, Rhinelander, and Two Rivers.[60]

Finally, opponents claimed the city-manager form was sponsored by outside financial interests and would give outsiders a role in the choice of the city manager. "Do the voters want an imported city manager, named by the International City Managers Association of Chicago, to take away from the elective city officials their voice in the affairs of our city government and make stooges of them?"[61]

Advocates of city manager charters ridiculed these arguments as "bogeymen,"[62] "Bogey Bears, Bad Mans, and Other Hokum to Scare Voters."[63] In Austin Judge White "defied the opposition to show 'one power of the people that is sacrificed under the manager form of government. The only thing that has been changed is that you have one man to operate the city's business instead of five men. . . . with this exception, which relates only to the city's BUSINESS, you have the same charter that you have now.' "[64]

Manager advocates also responded to antimanager arguments by elaborating the democratic arrangements of city manager government. "In all democracies," Austin's A. C. Baldwin explained to a public meeting, "the power of legislation is divorced from the power of administration." The latter of course was the manager's task, the provision of public services to the people. The legislative power, "the making of the laws . . . [protecting] lives, liberty, and property of the people . . . is the supreme power of the people" and fully retained in city-manager government.[65] The *Dallas Morning News* explained that the rise of large cities made old-fashioned town-meeting democracy impossible. In these large communities, voters might elect public officials but then of necessity had to trust them and grant them discretion. Fear of losing subsequent elections and the threat of recall served as checks on politicians' conduct. The discretionary power of the council is "first spent in selecting a highly trained expert in city government. . . . The council acts for the . . . citizens in supervising his work."[66] (Opponents of city managers ridiculed these explanations by calling them "remote control democracy.") In San Diego, which defeated a city-manager charter in 1929, the *San Diego Union* argued on the eve of the second city-charter election in 1931 that since the charter

[60] *Facts and Figures*, July 30, 1942, 4.
[61] Ibid., July 30, 1942, 4.
[62] Judge I. White in *Austin American*, August 7, 1924, 3.
[63] Headline, *Austin American*, August 5, 1924, 1.
[64] *Austin American*, August 7, 1924, 3.
[65] Ibid., August 5, 1924, 1.
[66] *Dallas Morning News*, September 5, 1930, part 2, 14.

had been revised in response its earlier defeat, "to an extent seldom exhibited in politics, this document is the work of the people."[67]

More than in the Progressive Era, municipal reformers worked to undermine the argument that manager government was "class government" by including labor leaders prominently among their supporters and by making direct appeals to labor. The *Austin American* printed long excerpts from a *National Municipal Review* article showing labor's support for the city-manager plan. In the *Review* article, a journalist from Portland, Maine, reported on his survey of organized labor in fifty-three cities. He found them everywhere " 'absolutely sold' on the . . . manager form of government as the most business-like, efficient, and democratic form of government." Union leaders reported they supported the manager plan because "it fixes responsibility, is responsive to popular will, eliminates graft and favoritism, and tends . . . to lessen the shifting of those burdens to all without property."[68] Also in Austin, the conversion of labor leader Victor Pannell from opposition to the city-manager charter in 1921 to support in 1924 was headline news for days, and his arguments quoted at great length.

In Houston there was argument for more than a decade about adopting city-manager government, and the victory of city-manager forces was brief. City-manager charters were defeated in 1933 and 1938. In 1938 the charter had strong support in the wealthy sections of Houston. The city-manager proposal also found support among African-American leaders, who argued, "While it does not give Negroes participation in the primary, it is a step in the right direction."[69] Concessions on pensions for police officers and firemen and provision of a minimum wage for day laborers were insufficient to win the support of organized labor. This was the charter commission that rebuffed Roy Sessions' requests for restraints on police intervention in strikes. There was also anger that another set of amendments (for a mayor-council government) was not offered the public, and the election was denounced by Sessions as a "German plebiscite."[70] Supporters of the proposed charter blamed defeat on the city council for allowing municipal employees to campaign.[71]

Another charter revision commission was appointed and its amend-

[67] *San Diego Union*, April 1, 1931, 4.

[68] *Austin American*, May 22, 1924.

[69] *Houston Chronicle*, September 29, 1938; see also *Houston Post*, September 28, 1938.

[70] *Houston Chronicle*, August 4, 1938. Houston's Commissioner Philip Morin proposed that in addition to the charter commission's manager plan, voters be offered a mayor-council charter with district elections. Morin's proposal had the support of A. J. Bannon, president of the Houston Labor and Trades Council. The charter commission insisted that only one charter—the manager charter—be offered to voters.

[71] *Houston Post*, October 4, 1938, 3.

ments offered to the electorate in 1942. Intense mobilizing efforts brought out more than half again as many voters as the 1938 election, and council-manager government passed. The twenty-nine thousand votes cast in the August election were hailed by the *Houston Press* as a "political miracle." The vote on the amendment creating a city manager was close: 15,809 in favor and 12,839 against.[72] The labor press blamed its own readers for the reform victory, headlining the charter change "Labor Failed to Go to the Polls; City Manager Candidates Win."[73]

Otis Massey, a supporter of the city-manager charter, was elected mayor in 1942 and again in 1944. Anticipating decades of campaign rhetoric across the Southwest after the war, the city's newspapers claimed that city-manager government boasted "a reputation of showing no favors and scrupulous honesty in purpose."[74] The *Labor Messenger*, however, was quick to denounce the regime. "A small self-appointed group of 'better minds' promoted the idea of city manager government in Houston." The same groups nominated candidates for city government and financed their campaigns, "so that in all justice these candidates can be viewed as henchmen of the small group of wealthy citizens who sponsor them." While there were many highly paid officials in this government, the *Messenger* claimed, municipal employees were poorly compensated.[75]

In 1946 the city's municipal employees, having failed to secure a raise, and rebuffed in their assertion of a right to negotiate, went on strike. The job action soon escalated to a "labor holiday" and popular *cause celebre*. Public support was widespread (the city government, for example, was unable to recruit substitutes for striking municipal employees). Deftly avoiding the legal issue of collective bargaining for municipal employees by renaming labor leaders a "citizens' committee," union officials and the mayor together declared victory after a week. On labor's side, striking workers were neither fired nor prosecuted; on the city government's part, no raise was granted, nor was the union recognized.[76]

In the succeeding election, Oscar Holcombe, out of office since 1937, was elected mayor. The *Labor Messenger* hailed his victory: "Houston voters went to the polls Tuesday and cleared the way for the greatest

---

[72] "Miracle," *Houston Press*, August 16, 1942, quoted in Kenneth E. Gray, "A Report on the Politics of Houston" (mimeograph, Joint Center for Urban Studies of the Massachusetts Institute of Technology and Harvard University, 1960), p. II-25; votes cast, *Houston Chronicle*, August 16, 1942.

[73] [Houston] *Labor Messenger*, November 6, 1942, 1.

[74] *Houston Chronicle*, August 31, 1944 (Mayor's scrapbook); see also *Houston Press*, July 7, 1943, 9.

[75] [Houston] *Labor Messenger*, November 3, 1944, 1.

[76] Marilyn Rhinehart, "A Lesson in Unity: The Houston Municipal Workers' Strike of 1946," *Houston Review* 4, no. 3 (Fall 1982): 137–54.

improvement program in the city's history. At the same time, they unmistakably declared their dissatisfaction with the city-manager form of government."[77] Holcombe himself declared his victory "a mandate from the . . . people . . . to no longer be governed by the city manager system" and promised to ignore the charter to the extent he legally could.

The next spring Holcombe launched a campaign to change Houston's government to the strong-mayor form. The four years under the city-manager government were denounced for lack of progress and democracy. World War II images of dictatorship in Germany and Italy were compared to the city-manager form; the heroic struggle of American armed forces for democracy overseas recalled to energize the struggle in Houston. In July 1947 Houston voters endorsed the government Holcombe wanted, and the city's flirtation with city-manager government was over.[78] The success of opponents of municipal reform may be attributed to the city's well-organized labor movement and the political skill of Holcombe. Although city-manager government was opposed by organized labor, and especially city-government employees, almost everywhere, in Houston these forces were simply more numerous and more politically experienced than in other cities. Once Massey's administration seemed to aim at withdrawing long-standing prerogatives of municipal employees, the fate of city-manager government was sealed.

Elsewhere, for all their financial advantage and superior press support, city-manager advocates did not coast to victory, but they did win. Victory in Phoenix was unequivocal, with about 9,544 voters (14 percent of adults) approving charter changes nearly 2 to 1. The same was true in Dallas, although support for the charter there was uneven. The charter carried by more than 2 to 1 (8,899 to 4,239).[79] Levels of support in the city varied dramatically. *Dallas Morning News* journalist Louis P. Head reported in the *National Municipal Review*: "In some precincts, especially in the better residential areas, the vote for the charter ran as high as 18 or 20 to l. In only [sic] 18 of 60 precincts were there majorities against, these being in the industrial districts."[80] In Austin the margin of victory was

[77] [Houston] *Labor Messenger*, November 8, 1946, 1.

[78] Gray, "Houston," provides a good account of these changes, pp. II-21–II-31. For campaign rhetoric, see Holcombe's 1947 radio charter campaign speeches (Holcombe papers, box 4, folder 3, Houston Municipal Research Center) and press coverage, especially the *Houston Chronicle*, for July 20–27, 1947. Also in 1947, the Texas legislature passed the state's right-to-work law, including a provision that public employees could neither bargain collectively nor strike. Rhinehart, "Lesson," 151.

[79] Harold A. Stone, "Dallas," in *City Manager Government in Nine Cities*, ed. Harold A. Stone, Don K. Price, and Kathryn H. Stone (Chicago: Public Administration Service, 1940), 287.

[80] Head, "Dallas Joins."

very small, with charter amendments carrying by 2,463 to 2,443. Of seven wards, five defeated the charter, but the two "silk stocking" wards, approving charter amendments by 3 to 1 margins, carried the day.[81]

In San Diego the initial referendum for the council-manager plan was defeated. Opposition from municipal employees and outlying neighborhoods took their toll in the 1929 vote. A second Board of Freeholders was elected, which was attentive to concerns both of municipal employees (making concessions on departmental prerogatives and pensions) and neighborhoods (designing a system of ward designations for city council members, albeit with citywide elections). When this board's work was submitted to the public in 1931, city-manager government was approved.

In San Antonio the first attempt to win voter approval for city-manager government failed (1945), and city-manager advocates needed to wage several campaigns before a new charter passed in 1951. Here, as in other cities, proponents of the manager charter left nothing to chance. The Citizens Committee conducted "a highly targeted and personalized strategy aimed at motivating and turning out a known electorate,"[82] as "mugwumps concentrated their campaigns in the north and south, largely ignoring the Negro and Latin American districts."[83] This concentrated effort brought results. The 1951 election "marks something of a watershed in participation terms. While the total vote cast in Hispanic precincts increased, Anglo voting boxes showed an enormous increase, on the order of three times the 1949 level."[84]

In San Antonio, and also in Phoenix, Dallas, and Austin, promoters of city-manager charters paused only briefly to celebrate their hard-won victories. "We cannot permit the work we have done," argued one Citizens Charter Association leader in Dallas, "to be wasted by turning the government over to the politicians."[85] To preclude that possibility, leaders of city-manager campaigns turned to the organization of nonpartisan slating groups to take control of local government.

Citizen Action

In San Antonio, Dallas, and Phoenix, events after the passage of charter amendments quickly revealed that victory was more apparent than real.

[81] Staniszewski, "Ideology," 32.

[82] Heywood Sanders, "The Creation of Post-War San Antonio: Politics, Voting, and Fiscal Regimes, 1945 to 1960" (paper prepared for the annual meeting of the Southwestern Social Science Association, San Antonio, Texas, March 1991), 17.

[83] Peterson, *Mugwump*, 196.

[84] Sanders, "Creation," 16.

[85] Carolyn Jenkins Barta, "The *Dallas News* and Council-Manager Government" (M.A. thesis, University of Texas at Austin, 1970), 40.

In San Antonio, elections soon after the adoption of a new city charter in 1951 disappointed charter supporters, provoking the formation of the Good Government League.[86] In Dallas supporters of the city-manager charter adopted in 1931 did poorly at the polls in the 1930s. This was enough warning for the promoters of city-manager government who, led by banker Robert L. Thornton, organized the Citizens Charter Association to field candidates for office.

In Phoenix, city manager James T. Deppe (allegedly working in alliance with the reputed behind-the-scenes boss of Phoenix, Ward H. Scheumack) remained firmly in control of the city council. Even revelations of serious misdoing on Deppe's part—padding the budget, avoiding competitive bidding for city projects, financial mismanagement—did not persuade the council to dismiss Deppe.[87] Writing in the *National Municipal Review*, Arizona State University Professor Paul Kelso observed, "There are many persons in Phoenix who believe that . . . it would be prudent to form a citizen's organization . . . to take advantage of the opportunity for better government offered" by changes in the charter, an idea quickly endorsed by the *Phoenix Gazette*.

Two generations of Phoenix elites joined forces to form the Charter Government Committee (CGC), having already worked together to rewrite the charter. Dix Price, president of the Young Democrats, and Ron Webster, president of the Young Republicans, agreed to put partisanship aside and organize a group to govern Phoenix. At the same time, their elders in the Chamber of Commerce, led by Alfred Knight, had come to the same decision. "We used to say," Dix Price recalled, "they had the money and the time and the Young Democrats and Young Republicans had the enthusiasm and the ideas."[88] All accounts (including Price's) agree that it was Alfred Knight who had the ideas. Knight's leadership was important because earlier he had participated in successful reform efforts in Cincinnati; Knight not only played an important role initially, but also continued active as an important fund raiser for the CGC. Later, Price recalled their plan of action:

> We agreed we'd raise money, elect candidates, and then we would disband. And that, I think, was the real secret of Charter Government . . . disband as a committee. It did not stay in existence as a committee to tell anybody what to do. Our theory was, base it on sound principle . . . pick good capable honor-

---

[86] L. L. Sanders, "How to Win Elections in San Antonio The Good Government Way, 1955–1971" (M.A. thesis, St. Mary's University, 1975), 7, and John A. Booth and David R. Johnson, "Power and Progress in San Antonio Politics, 1836–1970," in *The Politics of San Antonio, Community, Progress, and Power*, ed. David R. Johnson, John A. Booth, and Richard J. Harris (Lincoln: University of Nebraska Press 1983), 21–23.

[87] Konig, "Metropolis," 35–39.

[88] Dix Price interview, October 18, 1978, Arizona Historical Society.

able candidates; third, get them elected, and then four, get out of their way and avoid every possibility of string pulling and people saying that it was the government of the big business of the town behind the scenes.[89]

Citizens surely recognized the city's most important business leaders in the executive committee and the slate of candidates of the CGC. The first slate fielded set the course for later years by including wealthy business and civic leaders, among them Barry Goldwater, Leslie Kober, Hohen Foster, and Harry Rosenzweig.

Alfred Knight's presence in Phoenix may have been fortuitous, but the influence of the Cincinnati experience was typical. In 1924 citizens in Cincinnati organized to replace its corrupt Republican regime with nonpartisan city-manager government. Afterward the City Charter Committee nominated candidates for office on the "Charterite" ticket, and a decade later it was clear that the machine was trounced and the reform administration would often succeed itself. In 1934 the National Municipal League published a pamphlet, *The Cincinnati Plan of Citizen Organization for Political Activity*, distilling the lessons of Cincinnati's successful municipal revolution. "The most tragic error made by political reformers," the pamphlet declared, "is the confusion of political machines with political parties." Political machines rewarded their workers with employment and favors, an organizing strategy bound to bring out those with self-serving motives, founding the parties in venality. A party organized by reformers would be manned by those who desired good government; in a fair fight, the amateurs would be able to defeat the professionals.[90] Like the founders in the 1790s, reformers' aversion to parties gave way to recognition of their utility: "Political parties are necessary," *The Cincinnati Plan* explained, "political parties are requisite for the proper functioning of democracy."[91]

From reformers' point of view, the creation of a local political party was simply "adopting for political purposes the same sort of association that has proved successful in other community work" (the community chest or chamber of commerce, for example). A citizen board of directors contributed their time and hired full-time paid executives to run the organization. This small paid executive staff was supplemented by a large corps of volunteers. Volunteers' work was critical, canvasing neighborhoods, distributing literature, making sure that "on election day the worker knows whose votes may be counted upon and whose attendance

[89] Ibid.
[90] Commitee on Citizens' Charter Organization of the National Municipal League, *Cincinnati Plan of Citizen Organization for Political Activity* (New York: National Municipal League, 1934), 17.
[91] *Cincinnati Plan*, 5.

at the polls is desired."[92] Those who could be counted on were not the voters of the machine's old delivery wards. The pamphlet reported approvingly that one achievement of Cincinnati reformers was an increase in turnout in outlying residential wards and decreasing turnout in the central city wards that long had provided heavy support for the machine.[93]

Although NPSGs served as the parties of local politics, they were in crucial ways different from true political parties. For one thing, unlike political machines, citizens who worked at ward, precinct, and block organizing were always unpaid.[94] This was particularly important for poll watchers. "In the organization of any municipal party," experienced NPSG organizers from Cincinnati reported, "the temptation comes to pay workers at the polls in certain places where it seems to be very difficult to secure volunteers." Giving in to this temptation will discourage volunteers "of the type desired," since they will worry about being perceived as mercenary. "It was found to be much better to secure men and women as volunteers from other parts of the city who would go into the tough wards and serve as witnesses and challengers than to pay persons in these localities."[95]

Richard S. Childs saw another difference from political parties as critical to NPSG success. This was the ability of NPSGs to control their membership:

Unlike the Republican and Democratic organizations . . . they can and do resist self-serving boarders attracted by their success and opportunities. The Dallas Citizens Charter Association is a private association and its governing board can control its . . . membership. So can the officers of the Cincinnati City Charter Committee . . . or the Phoenix Charter Government *Committee*. In San

<hr/>

[92] *Cincinnati Plan*, 10. The pamphlet describes party organization in detail. The Cincinnati Committee had complete parallel organizations of men and women, which functioned somewhat differently. "Men and women are energized into action in political matters by slightly different impulses. The women will work to conserve good government, and the ward chairman, precinct captains, and block workers will respond to the appeal to maintain the good government that has been obtained by their efforts." Because women were "more idealistic," they were "more ready to do their share of preparation in advance of the actual fighting." By contrast, "men appreciate the necessity of organization, but are more apt to postpone action until the conflict is actually joined because they require the stimulus of combat," 10. Without attributing the difference in effort to men and women's natural attributes, the 1949 version of the pamphlet also noted: "It has been found practical for the women's organization to get into action first. The men's organization becomes active in the last few weeks before an election when intense campaigning is necessary." *Citizen Organization for Political Activity* (National Municipal League, 1949), 11.

[93] *Cincinnati Plan*, 16.

[94] *Cincinnati Plan*, 7.

[95] *Cincinnati Plan*, 16.

Antonio it is the Good Government League but it, too is really a committee; you can't force your way into it as a matter of legal right! In Dade the Independent Citizens for Better Metro can renew its ranks with like-minded adherents as it pleases. . . . The more careful they are to become a hardly perennial, keeping their ranks from erosion or pollution, the better![96]

Other reformers may not have expressed this sentiment, but the practice of NPSGs made it clear that the thought was a common one.

NPSGs held their meetings in private, and their membership was controlled. The method of assembling slates of candidates was also peculiar to NPSGs, which avoided candidates who put themselves forward. Just as their campaigns claimed, NPSGs sought out "civic leaders" rather than leaders who desired political careers. NPSG leaders were sometimes defensive and sometimes boastful about the secret and closed proceedings of their organizations. In Phoenix Margaret Kober explained, "We don't like the fact that we're criticized . . . that a little group of people get in a closed room . . . and select a handful of people and put them up. But I don't know any better way."[97] In Dallas a Citizens' Charter Association leader simply declared the policy that was common: "Anyone who asks for a place on the council is never considered."[98] Writing about San Antonio, L. L. Sanders argued that secrecy and privacy allowed the Good Government League to perform the interest-aggregating and coalition-building functions of political parties while insisting in its public statements that "politics" was irrelevant in cities, in which government could simply pursue the interest of the whole.[99]

The stories of Phoenix and Cincinnati were replicated across the Southwest.[100] Dallas, "following the pattern of the Cincinnati citizens' organization," organized "an effective political machine" first for the campaign to adopt the charter and then to field candidates for office.[101] In Albuquerque, leaders who better envisioned postwar growth mobilized to defeat Clyde Tingley in 1946. Although Tingley was still a member of the commission, he was in the minority and cast the only vote opposing major annexations of the city's suburbs (on the grounds that it

[96] Richard S. Childs, *The First 50 Years of the Council-Manager Plan of Municipal Government* (New York: National Municipal League, 1965), 103–4, italics in the original.

[97] Mrs. Leslie Kober (Margaret) Interview, June 18, 1976, transcript, p. 16, in G. W. Johnson's collection.

[98] Peterson, *Mugwump*, 116.

[99] L. L. Sanders, "How to Win Elections," 11.

[100] For the role of nonpartisan slating groups in electoral politics, see Louis Fraga, "Domination through Democratic Means," *Urban Affairs Quarterly* 23, no. 4 (June 1988): 528–55. Fraga provides a history of NPSGs, their rationale and promotion by the National Municipal League, and their dominance of city politics in San Antonio, Dallas, and Abilene.

[101] Stone, "Dallas," 287, 5.

was too expensive). Later the Albuquerque Citizens' Committee (ACC) was organized, a descendant of citizens' action groups organized on particular issues (for example, the Citizens' Committee for a Fair Bus Franchise). The ACC fielded its first slate of candidates in 1954. By 1960 the committee decided that backing qualified men was not adequate to the city's political needs, and its chairman announced that the ACC would operate "more as a non-partisan municipal political party," opening its membership and taking public-policy stands.[102]

In San Antonio the president of the Chamber of Commerce invited sixty citizens to his home to found the Good Government League (GGL) in December of 1954. Like their counterparts in Dallas, GGL leaders were anxious to keep local government out of the hands of politicians. Not only did the GGL present slates of candidates at election time, but it also consulted with leaders of the African-American and Mexican-American communities on public policy. As these consultations were held in secret, the GGL's accommodation of diverse interests never appeared publicly to contradict the notion of pursuing the good of the whole city.[103] In Austin, a smaller and shorter-lived NPSG was organized in the late 1920s, but quickly ceded holding office to the city's popular politicians (as described *supra*, chapter 4). In 1953 business leaders organized to change to charter to create a place system on the city council. Afterwards an informal caucus of representatives of the Chamber of Commerce, downtown (as opposed to outlying) retailers, banks, real estate, and construction interests organized and endorsed slates and supported bond referenda. There too support from the city's African-American and Mexican-American community was solicited quietly. David Olsen reported, "Little information of group and party endorsement . . . became public knowledge. Group endorsements were negotiated privately."[104]

In other cities somewhat less formal and even less public elite organizations were organized in the 1940s and 1950s. In Austin an informal caucus including representatives of "the larger banks, stores, and law firms," as well as former officeholders, nominated candidates for office in

---

[102] Wood, "Transformation," 104–16, 144–45, 248.

[103] John A. Booth and David R. Johnson, "Power and Progress in San Antonio Politics, 1836–1970," in David R. Johnson, John A. Booth, and Richard J. Harris, *The Politics of San Antonio: Community, Progress, and Power* (Lincoln: University of Nebraska Press, 1983), 23. On accommodating communities of color, L. L. Sanders, "How to Win Elections the Good Government Way," 6, 11. GGL philosophy was expressed by one interviewee thus: "Rational decisions cannot be made in open public debate. . . . debate on public issues must be removed from public view in order to reach a workable consensus" (11).

[104] The place system was a change from a system in which the top five vote-getters won seats on the council, even if they did not gain a majority of all votes cast. This seemed necessary after an African-American candidate came close to winning a seat under the old system. Olson, *Nonpartisan Elections*, 10, 17, 31.

the 1950s and 1960s.[105] In San Jose the Progress Committee, a group of merchants, attorneys, industrialists, and property owners, was organized in 1944. It aimed first to oust Charles Bigley and his city manager, Clarence Goodwin, from office. This accomplished, the Progress Committee turned its attention to its second goal, industrial recruitment. In Oklahoma City a reenergized Chamber of Commerce selected and funded candidates for municipal office; in Houston the 8-F Crowd, in Fort Worth the Seventh Street Gang, and in San Jose the Book of the Month Club (successor group to the Progress Committee), while not selecting candidates for office, set the agenda for local politics.[106]

One hundred years after the first municipal reform campaigns in the old cities of the Northeast, leaders in the large cities of the Southwest were poised to bring big-city reform to life. They had written the rules of local politics to their own best advantage, and they were organized to win the game.

---

[105] Olson, *Nonpartisan Elections*, 31.

[106] Richard M. Bernard, "Oklahoma City, Booming Sooner" in *Sunbelt Cities: Politics and Growth since World War II*, ed. Richard M. Bernard and Bradley R. Rice (Austin: University of Texas, 1983), 213–34; Barry Kaplan, "Houston: The Golden Buckle of the Sunbelt," in ibid., 196–212; "Fort Worth: Great Expectations—Cowtown Hars and Tortoises," in *Urban Politics in the Southwest* ed. Leonard F. Goodall (Tempe: Arizona State Univeristy Institute of Public Admnistration, 1967), 46–67; Trounstine and Christensen, *Movers and Shakers*, chap. 4.

Six

The Statesman Joins It

WRITING IN 1962, Edward Banfield and James Q. Wilson presented affluent suburbs as the home of reform government. In Winnetka, Scarsdale, and Berkeley, they explained, there was a citizen consensus about the style and functions of local government. At the same moment Banfield and Wilson were writing about Winnetka, Scarsdale, and Berkeley, the cities of Austin, Dallas, San Antonio, San Jose, San Diego, Albuquerque, Phoenix, Forth Worth, and Oklahoma City were also governed by city-manager regimes, and most of these cities had nonpartisan, citywide elections. The years around 1960 may be considered the apogee of big-city reform government. The coalitions and nonpartisan slating groups (NPSGs) supporting municipal reform were no longer new to government, and their governments were not yet shaken by the challenges of citizen assertiveness and unsettling federal programs the 1960s brought.

The key accomplishment of southwestern reform regimes at midcentury was the creation of political communities that looked much like Winnetka, despite governmental agendas substantially more ambitious and social settings that were considerably more diverse. In the large cities of the Southwest, without parties or districts, civic associations and nonpartisan slating groups offered those "best qualified to serve," and their candidates rarely faced significant opposition. Political life revolved around an apparent consensus on local government's priorities. City councils were neither geographically nor demographically representative. Political leaders were rarely career politicians, more often civic and business leaders, Anglos, and affluent. Each of these cities was many times larger than Winnetka, and none boasted its social homogeneity. Winnetka was a very affluent bedroom suburb.[1] Much smaller than the big cities of the Southwest, Winnetka was without many places of employment, not competing for growth opportunities in the national market, not seeking to annex suburbs of its own.

---

[1] Winnetka's population in 1960 was 13,368; median family income was $20,166. Not only was Winnetka's median family income three or four times that of any large southwestern city, but also, in seven large southwestern cities in 1960 (Albuquerque, Austin, Dallas, Phoenix, San Antonio, San Diego, and San Jose) only four *census tracts* (of 609)—two in Dallas, one in Phoenix, and one in San Diego—are comparable to Winnetka in median family income.

All of these differences were likely to affect local politics; two are of primary importance. First, greater demographic diversity fostered another and more complex list of issues for local government. In addition to the low taxes, schools, parks, and libraries demanded by middle- and working-class neighborhoods alike were the political agendas of less affluent neighborhoods and communities of color. These communities not only wanted the low taxes, good schools, parks, and libraries of their more affluent neighbors but also low-income housing, lower utility rates, and eased assessments for municipal improvements. Communities of color campaigned against police brutality and for open housing, voting rights, desegregation, and access to public employment. A second difference between southwestern cities and the suburbs cited by Banfield and Wilson is that the cities pursued growth strategies requiring aggressive elite organization and a long list of government initiatives.

The primary vehicle for the creation of political community in southwestern cities was a set of rules tending to decrease participation in local politics. Reformers wrote the rules to win the game of local politics. In the first section below, "Writing the Rules," I trace institutional arrangements and participation in local politics, showing that participation was dramatically lower in big southwestern cities than in the big northeastern cities that were descendants of political machines. The subsequent section, "Campaigning and Persuading," sketches political contests in the 1950s. In this setting the discourse of local politics was narrow, and "Outs" sounded much like "Ins."

"Winning the Game" presents three elections near 1960. Those who voted were not a representative sample of the citizenry. Rather, turnout in Anglo affluent and middle-class areas exceeded turnout in other neighborhoods, providing a plurality of the electorate. Thus reformers succeeded at creating Anglo middle-class political communities in diverse metropolitan settings. "The Political Community of Big City Reform" summarizes the distinguishing characteristics of the political system in southwestern cities at mid-century.

Writing the Rules

Political leaders have resources both to hamper participation in politics and to encourage participation. In 1967 Stanley Kelley argued that "those in power" might construct an electorate "to a size and composition deemed desirable"[2] by writing the rules of registration to keep

---

[2] Stanley Kelley, Jr., Richard E. Ayres, and William G. Bowen, "Registration and Voting: Putting First Things First," *American Political Science Review* 61, no. 2 (June 1967): 375.

unwanted voters from the polls. Writing about participation and mobiliz-ation in national politics, Steven Rosenstone and John Hansen empha-sized the importance of politicians' efforts to mobilize voters. Demon-strating the effects of politicians' mobilizing work, Rosenstone and Hansen concluded that the "strategic choices of political leaders . . . de-termine the shape of political participation."[3]

The big reform cities of the Southwest provide excellent cases for these arguments. Here are both all the devices known to depress turnout, and well organized efforts to mobilize selected constituencies. The rules were written to include substantial *obstacles to voting*, of which difficulty reg-istering to vote, the poll tax, and the literacy test were most important. There were also less formidable but effective deterrents, for example, the siting of polling places. *Barriers to representation*, especially citywide elections, discouraged voting. In addition, other arrangements *discour-aged voting* by making municipal politics less visible or less comprehen-sible, or by lowering the value of the vote. Nonpartisanship, nonconcur-rent elections, noncompetitveness of elections, lack of descriptive or geo-graphical representation, and scanty press coverage of local elections functioned in these ways. The result was just what was intended: political life in the regimes of textbook reform was politics of low participation. The costs of voting were very high; the payoffs low.

Urban statesmen were also attentive to the mobilization of their likely supporters. Just as the Cincinnati Plan recommended, nonpartisan slat-ing groups fielded poll watchers and precinct organizers to their likely supporters. The significance of recruiting voters, perfectly obvious to ma-chine politicians and NPSG organizers alike, has been confirmed for po-litical scientists by Rosenstone and Hansen's work.

Fortuitously, several studies of voting and turnout examine big cities in 1960, the heyday of big-city reform. Subsequent studies have confirmed their major findings. The discussion below briefly reviews these findings and then turns to ask the same questions for big reform cities.

Obstacles to Voting

Beginning, as the voter must, with registration, Stanley Kelley and coauthors studied the effects of registration requirements on turnout in 104 large cities in the presidential election of 1960. Registration was not only first but also important: 78 percent of the variation in turnout could be accounted for by the variation in rates of registration.[4]

---

[3] Steven J. Rosenstone and John Mark Hansen, *Mobilization, Participation, and De-mocracy in America* (New York: Macmillan, 1993), 36.

[4] Kelley, "Registration," 362.

Proximity to the election of the closing date for registration was the most important determinant of rates of registration. The further in advance registration was required, the lower the registration.[5] Convenience of registration was found to affect not only how many people registered but which people registered. Difficulties in registration did not affect all voters equally: where costs were high, socioeconomic differences became relatively more important. Later analyses confirmed the findings that registration is the most important determinant of voting, that the further in advance of an election registration is required the lower registration rates will be, and that early closing dates most depress voting among the poor and people of color.[6] Kelley also found that literacy tests were also strongly related to rates of registration, although the effects outside the South were modest.[7] "Thus," Kelley concluded, "local officials, by varying the convenience of registration procedures, may be able to affect appreciably not only the size but also the composition of local electorates."[8]

Discouraging Voting

Municipal elections received systemic attention at the same time. In 1962 the staff of the *Municipal Year Book* surveyed 729 cities of more than twenty-five thousand population; 574 sent usable returns reporting votes cast in their most recent municipal election. The returns were examined by Eugene C. Lee, Robert R. Alford and Lee, and Ruth B. Dixon.[9] Each

---

[5] Ibid., 366–67. Kelley's findings suggested that advancing the closing date from one month before an election to one week before the election would increase registration by "about 3.6%."

[6] Rosenstone and Hansen, *Mobilization*, 207–9.

[7] Analysis of the 1952 presidential election by Rosenstone and Hansen showed that literacy tests reduced the probably that African-Americans would vote by 16.0 percent, poll taxes by 10.2 percent, and periodic registration by 11.6 percent. Rosenstone and Hansen, *Mobilization*, 199.

[8] Kelley, "Registration," 367. Cf. 369: "When costs of registering are high," wrote Kelley, "difference . . . in the . . . variables affecting . . . motivation . . . education, for example . . . will account for a considerable part of the variation in rates of registration." Where barriers were low, convenience of arrangements for registration became relatively more important. In contrast to system characteristics, which depressed the effects of individual characteristics on voting, for registration some socioeconomic factors were important across systems: a higher proportion of young people and nonwhites in a city's population was associated with lower rates of registration, while a higher median educational attainment was associated with higher rates of registration (364).

[9] Eugene C. Lee, "City Elections: A Statistical Profile," *Municipal Year Book, 1963* (Chicago: International City Managers' Association, 1963), 74–84; Robert R. Alford and Eugene C. Lee, "Voting Turnout in American Cities," *American Political Science Review* 62, no. 3 (September 1968): 796–813; Ruth B. Dixon, "Predicting Voter Turnout in City Elections" (M.A. thesis, University of California, Berkeley, 1966). All three essays are writ-

of these authors found that the institutional arrangements of local politics had significant impacts on turnout. The rules of reform government were without exception associated with lower turnout: nonpartisan elections exhibited lower turnout than partisan elections; manager and commission cities had lower turnout than mayor-council cities, nonconcurrent elections brought fewer voters to the polls than concurrent elections.

Political parties, or their absence, were associated with sizeable differences in turnout. Lee showed that nonpartisan cities had significantly lower turnout than partisan cities. Rosenstone and Hansen's findings about mobilization also provide validation for case-study hypotheses about why nonpartisan systems were more discouraging to working-class than middle-class voters. Willis D. Hawley and Eugene C. Lee argued that the organizations that take the place of parties in nonpartisan systems—civic groups, the chamber of commerce, the League of Women Voters, and so on—are groups with middle-class memberships. The result was a greater gap between middle-class and working-class turnout than in national elections, and more Republicans elected to city councils than would have been if candidates had been identified by party.[10]

Looking at concurrent elections, Dixon showed that nonpartisan elections were associated with five points lower turnout than partisan elections in mayor-council cities and fifteen points lower turnout in reform

---

ten from the same data set, although for a variety of reasons each essay uses a slightly different number of cities from the survey. The authors made various decisions that are in my view unfortunate. For example, Lee and Alford group commission-government cities with mayor-council cities as "nonmanager" cities, rather than grouping the two reform types together. Lee and Alford also only look at nonconcurrent elections, thereby eliminating the highest turnout cities. Nor do Lee and Alford look at the cumulative effects of various reform provisions (e.g., nonconcurrence, nonpartisanship, city-manager government). Dixon does chart cumulative effects but offers no consideration of region and its possible effects. I have tried to recover this large data set, but it is no longer with the ICMA nor with the home institutions (current or former) of the authors cited here.

[10] Willis D. Hawley, *Nonpartisan Elections and the Case for Party Politics* (New York: Wiley, 1973); Eugene C. Lee, *The Politics of Nonpartisanship: A Study of California City Elections* (Berkeley: University of California Press, 1960). David Greenstone and Paul Peterson offered parallel observations for nonpartisan Detroit, where the union movement performed the party functions listed by Lee. There working-class voters were not severely disadvantaged by nonpartisan electoral systems, and more Democrats were elected than would have been if candidates had party labels. J. David Greenstone and Paul E. Peterson, *Race and Authority in Urban Politics: Community Participation and the War on Poverty* (New York: Russell Sage, 1973). There are some similar examples in the Southwest (Olson speaks of labor precinct organizations in Austin), but their scope was very limited. The same arguments suggest why, later, community organizations are critical to insurgent political movements in nonpartisan cities. See Katherine Underwood, "Process and Politics: Multiracial Electoral Coalition Building and Representation in Los Angeles' Ninth District, 1949–1962" Ph.D. diss., University of California, San Diego, 1992), who makes this argument about the Community Service Organization in Los Angeles.

cities.[11] Looking at elections in 461 cities, nonpartisan cities exhibited median of 30 percent of adults voting, while in partisan cities the median was 50 percent of adults voting.

Form of government was also associated with turnout difference. Lee showed that median proportion of adults voting dropped with municipal reform: 50 percent of adults voted in mayor-council cities, 38 percent voted in commission cities, and 27 percent voted in city-manager cities. Independent election dates (nonconcurrence) were also associated with lower turnout. Lee showed that in cities with independent elections, median turnout of adults was 29 percent in municipal contests, while in cities where municipal contests were concurrent with state and national elections median turnout was 50 percent of adults.[12]

Finally, Dixon estimated the cumulative effects of reform arrangements on turnout. Cities with mayor-council government and partisan, concurrent elections had a median turnout of 51 percent in local elections; commission or manager cities with nonpartisan independent elections had a median turnout of 24 percent.[13]

Findings about the relationship of rules to turnout in cities meant that aggregate data contradicted well known relationships among individual characteristics and turnout. Alford and Lee observed that "the . . . correlation of registrants voting with education is the opposite of the well known individual correlation" and "cities with highly ethnic populations and less educated populations have higher voting turnout."[14] Dixon found "no relation at all between the proportion of people of high social status a city contains and the proportion voting in local elections."[15] Similarly, although Kelley found that education retained its importance in the aggregate, income had only a modest relationship to rates of registration. Finally, both Kelley and Alford and Lee found that once the impact of institutional arrangements was taken into account, the independent effect of region was greatly diminished.[16]

Rules and Turnout in Big City Reform

The data examined by Kelley, Alford, Lee, and Dixon were nationwide samples, and the large number of cities in their survey suggests that there are many Winnetkas, many less affluent suburbs, and many small cities in

[11] Dixon, "Predicting," 13 (these are concurrent elections).
[12] Lee, "City Elections," 83.
[13] Dixon, "Predicting," 12.
[14] Alford and Lee, "Voting Turnout," 882 (this is for 282 cities with nonconcurrent elections).
[15] Dixon, "Predicting," 53.
[16] Kelley, "Registration," 370, Alford and Lee, "Voting Turnout," 804.

their data. To study big-city reform, I looked at a smaller set of large reform cities: Phoenix, Albuquerque, Austin, Dallas, San Jose, San Antonio, and San Diego. All of these cities had nonpartisan city-manager government and nonconcurrent elections. Four cities—Phoenix, Albuquerque, San Antonio, and Dallas—also had strong nonpartisan slating groups and so may be said to represent fully institutionalized reform. Data were also collected for three cities that may be termed machine descendants. New York, Chicago, and New Haven all had strong party organizations, substantial patronage resources, and concurrent elections. Another difference between the reform cities and the machine descendants is that the reform cities all had citywide elections for the city council, while the machine descendants had district representation on the city council.

The founders of big-city reform government were attentive to the rules of local politics. Beginning again with registration, the big reform cities studied here required registration substantially before election day. New Mexico required registration before the thirtieth day before an election, except that no registration was required for property holders to vote on municipal bonds. California allowed registration up to fifty-three days before an election. Arizona required registration four months in advance of primary elections and six weeks before general elections; in addition, Phoenix required annual registration for municipal elections, and the only site of registration was the city clerk's office downtown.[17]

In Texas the poll tax served as registration. The tax was payable between October 1 and January 1 annually for the subsequent election season; in Houston, municipal elections were in November. As David Olson explained for Austin, where municipal elections were in April:

> Even though the termination date is only two weeks prior to the filing date for city council candidacies in the odd-numbered years, it is three months in advance of the party primaries in the even-numbered years. The result is high registration in the years of party primaries and general elections to state and national offices, and low registration for the odd-numbered years of local elections. In effect city council campaigns do not become publicly visible until after the registration period has ended.[18]

---

[17] I divided states into three groups: those that allowed registration as late as two weeks before an election (17), those that allowed registration only up to thirty days before an election (18), and those that required registration more than thirty days before the election (11; four states were unclassifiable with the information I had). All the big reform cities studied here were in the last group, states requiring the longest advance registration. On where to register in Phoenix, see Brent Whiting Brown, "An Analysis of the Phoenix Charter Government Committee as a Political Entity" (M.A. thesis, Arizona State University, 1968), 47. For Albuquerque's exception to registration requirements for voting on municipal bonds, documents in the city clerk's office, election files.

[18] David Olson, *Nonpartisan Elections: A Case Analysis* (Austin: University of Texas, 1965), 3.

Both the requirement that the tax be paid well in advance of elections and its high price ($1.75 in 1960; about $21 in 1995 dollars) deterred voting.[19]

Literacy tests were important in Texas and Arizona. Arizona's NAACP claimed poll watchers in Phoenix "harassed and intimidated" voters "in precincts heavily populated by the poor." In particular, voters in African-American and Hispanic precincts were met "with forceful demands that they read portions of the Arizona constitution as proof of literacy."[20] As this testimony suggests, the literacy test, like the poll tax, was particularly aimed at African-Americans and Mexican-Americans.

The big reform cities also have all the elements associated, in the data sets examined by Lee, Alford, and Dixon, with depressed turnout: elections were citywide, nonpartisan, nonconcurrent, and in city-manager cities.

Turnout—that is, percent of all *adults* voting—from 1946 to 1963 is shown in table 6-1. The differences between the reform cities and the machine descendants are dramatic. In Phoenix, Albuquerque, and Dallas average turnout was below 20 percent over the whole period (and only 10.8 percent in Dallas), while New York, Chicago, and New Haven have averaged, respectively, 43.6 percent, 54.3 percent, and 57.3 percent of adults voting in municipal elections. Consistent with other authors' findings that aggregate demographic characteristics contradicted the relationship of individuals' characteristics to turnout, machine descendant turnout is higher despite the presumed disabilities of populations more heavily foreign-born and less well educated (see table 6-2).

Reformed cities may also be compared with the machine descendants on competitiveness. (Kelley also found that competitiveness was related to registration, citizens being more likely to register in cities with more competitive political systems).[21] Table 6-3 shows competitiveness in municipal elections in selected cities for the years 1946–63. The most important information in the table is that city politics was not very competitive in any of the six cities for which it is measured. With that observation in

[19] Constance E. Smith, *Voting and Election Laws* (New York: Oceana, 1961), Arizona, p. 68; California, p. 69; New Mexico, p. 80; Texas, p. 85. The same states also had steep residence requirements. Kelley found these did not seem, in the aggregate, to be effective deterrents to turnout, but the finding is counterintuitive. In Texas, for example, the poll tax was levied on those resident in the state prior January 1. Mobility, however, is related to turnout, and a possible turnout depressor for the high growth cities of the Southwest in the 1950s. The states that were homes to machine descendants did not make things much easier: New York had a literacy test; Illinois and Connecticut required registration no later than 28 days before an election. Arizona and California also had literacy tests.

[20] These allegations were later directed at William Rehnquist. Peter Irons, *Brennan vs. Rehnquist: The Battle for the Constitution* (New York: Knopf, 1994), 58–59.

[21] Kelley, "Registration," 365.

TABLE 6-1
Turnout in Municipal Elections, 1947–1963 (percentage of adults voting)

	Big-City Reform							Machine Descendants		
	San Antonio	San Jose	San Diego	Austin	Phoenix	Dallas	Albuquerque	Chicago	New York	New Haven
1945	7.9	—	—	—	—	*	—	62.9	—	—
1947	21.4	29.4	23.4	12.4	10.5	7.9	18.1	—	—	51.2
1948	—	—	—	—	13.9	—	18.9	—	—	—
1949	23.2	36.8	—	14.5	31.9	8.1	—	—	45.8	63.5
1950	—	—	—	—	—	—	28.4	49.7	46.3	—
1951	17.7	30.2	33.1	16.5	24.5	4.6	24.8	—	—	—
1953	19.2	—	—	—	14.5	9.4	—	—	40.3	67.6
1954	—	—	—	21.1	—	—	31.4	—	—	—
1955	11.9	18.5	30.2	22.1	12.4	0.6	10.9	54.8	—	62.1
1957	11.1	18.2	—	—	10.6	16.2	—	—	41.0	61.1
1958	—	—	—	6.3	—	—	16.7	—	—	—
1959	14.8	14.1	21.1	—	17.5	17.6	14.7	47.5	—	58.1
1960	—	—	—	10.1	—	—	—	—	—	—
1961	16.1	52.6	—	—	17.5	19.3	—	—	44.8	57.7
1962	—	—	—	18.7	—	—	21.3	—	—	—
1963	NA	—	—	—	30.0	13.9	14.1	56.6	—	57.3
Average	15.9	28.5	42.2	15.2	18.3	10.8	19.9	54.3	43.6	59.8
Median	14.8	14.5	28.7	15.5	14.5	9.4	18.5	54.8	44.8	59.4

Sources: Election Returns for Albuquerque and Phoenix (1959–1963) and for San Diego, San Jose, and Chicago are from their respective Offices of the City Clerk. For Austin, "Elections, 1924–1979" (City of Austin, Public Information Office, 1979). For Dallas, Carolyn Jenkins Barta, "The Dallas News and Council-Manager Government" (M.A. thesis, University of Texas Austin, 1970), 155–66. For Phoenix, 1945–1957, Brent Whiting Brown, "An Analysis of the Phoenix Charter Government Committee as a Political Entity" (M.A. thesis, Arizona State University, 1968), appendix G. For San Antonio, *San Antonio Express,* 1945–1961; L. L. Sanders, "How to Win Elections in San Antonio: The Good Government Way, 1955–1971" (M.A. thesis, St. Mary's University, 1975), 69–71. For New Haven, Robert Dahl, 1945–1955, *New Haven Register,* 1957–1963. For New York, *New York Times,* 1949, 1953, 1957; *World Almanac,* 1951 (New York: World Telegram, 1951), 1950; *World Almanac,* 1962 (New York: World Telegram, 1962), 1961, 42.
*Unopposed.

TABLE 6-2
Social Characteristics of Selected Cities, 1960

	Median Years Education	Median Family Income	% Foreign Born
Albuquerque	12.4	$6,626	2.2
Austin	11.9	$5,116	2.3
Dallas	11.8	$5,976	1.9
Phoenix	11.8	$6,117	4.4
San Antonio	9.6	$4,766	6.8
San Diego	12.2	$6,614	7.0
San Jose	12.1	$6,949	8.5
Chicago	8.9	$6,738	12.3
New Haven	8.8	$5,864	13.2
New York	10.1	$6,091	20.0

Source: U.S. Bureau of Census, *County City Data Book, 1967* (Washington, D.C.: Government Printing Office, 1968), table 4.

mind, it is also clear that the big-city reform elections are even more lopsided than elections in the machine descendants.

Because 1960 is the apogee of big-city reform in the Southwest, this discussion of the general characteristics of municipal elections in big reform cities and machine descendants appropriately concludes by comparing the elections immediately preceding and following 1960. While an average of 18.7 percent of adults voted in thirteen[22] elections in reformed cities, an average of 49.8 percent of adults voted in six elections in the machine-descendant cities. Over the whole period, in Chicago proportionately three times as many adults (more than half of the city's adults) voted as in Phoenix (less than 20 percent): four times as many adults voted in New York as in Dallas (44.8 percent vs. 10.8 percent); three times as many adults voted in New Haven as in Albuquerque (59.4 percent vs. 18.5 percent). In these big reformed cities, politics was simply not as prominent in the lives of most people as it was in the Northeast. The young David Greenstone, having written a "Report on Politics in Detroit" for Edward Banfield's City Politics project, was next sent to San Diego. There he was taken aback by "an extraordinary lack of interest in local politics among the citizenry."[23]

[22] Elections immediately before and after 1960 were averaged. Austin held an election in 1960, hence there are thirteen rather than fourteen elections in the seven-city computation. If the election before, the election after, and 1960 are included for Austin, the seven-city average only changes by .1 percent.

[23] J. David Greenstone, "Report on Politics in San Diego" (mimeograph, Joint Center

TABLE 6-3
Competitiveness of Elections in Selected Cities, 1945–1963

	Chicago	New York	New Haven	Phoenix	Dallas	Albuquerque
1945			55.2		100[a]	
1946		56.7				57.8
1947	58.7		54.5		73.0	53.7
1949		56.9	50.5	59.9	64.5	
1950						—[b]
1951	56.2		50.0	79.9	70.6	52.0
1953		60.7	51.0	67.1	69.5	
1954						76.7
1955	54.6		65.4	64.3	100*	78.3
1957		71.2	69.4	81.7	58.9	
1958						66.6
1959	71.4		61.8	70.9	52.1	51.6
1961		50.9	53.5	71.8	51.7	
1962						63.8
1963	55.6		64.9	52.7		—[b]

Source: Computed from election returns; see note to table 6-1 for sources.

Note: Competitiveness is measured in Chicago, New York, Phoenix, and Dallas by the proportion of all votes cast for mayor received by the winning candidate. In New Haven, number given is percentage received by the winner of the votes for the two major-party candidates. In Albuquerque, where election was to the city commission, competitiveness is measured by the percentage of votes cast for the winning candidate with fewest votes, of that candidates' votes and the votes cast for the loser with the largest number of votes. Thus the Albuquerque winners' majorities, shown here, are smaller than the majorities of other winners of commission seats in the same elections.

[a] Incumbents unopposed.

[b] Data unavailable.

Campaigning and Persuading

Campaigns and elections in big reform cities in the 1950s had their own character and rhetoric. Candidates did not campaign as individuals, boasting their achievements; in many places candidates themselves did not campaign at all. Rather, campaigns were usually launched for tickets or slates. Where there were nonpartisan slating groups, these became the focus of campaigning. Belying reformers' antipathy to parties and party loyalty, the banner of the NPSG claimed the allegiance of candidates and voters.

for Urban Studies of the Massachusetts Institute of Technology and Harvard University, 1962), II-6.

Candidates for office proclaimed their commitment to the principles of reform government (usually expressed as commitment to the city charter). In Dallas, the "candidates of the Citizens Charter Association are the only ones publicly committed to retaining the council-manager form of government, which has proved highly successful here";[24] while in Albuquerque the Citizens Committee began its platform with a commitment to "operate the City within the framework of the city manager form of government."[25] Like the nineteenth-century reformers who promised to be "untrammeled by party pledges," twentieth-century reformers pronounced their central goal as the good of the whole city. In Phoenix it was claimed that since the Charter Government Committee was really a "citizen's political action committee" rather than a political party, "once elected," a city council member "had no obligations to anyone except the citizens."[26] In Dallas, the Citizens Charter Association "seeks only the good of Dallas."[27]

The good of the whole city meant its continued growth. Interviewing the leaders of the Good Government League of San Antonio, L. L. Sanders wrote, "The definitive parameters of . . . representing the community as a whole were formulated by businessmen. . . . they wanted growth and expansion."[28] A contemporary observed in San Diego, "in most elections, candidates have lined up to a man in favor of more industry, more jobs and development of Mission Bay."[29]

Slating-group nominees were presented not as politicians but as the city's successful businessmen and most selfless civic leaders, reluctantly entering the electoral arena to promote the interests of the city as a whole (while their opponents were characterized as self-interested politicians). In Dallas "nonpolitical and unselfish service as the city's board of directors [that is, service on the city council] implies a high degree of turnover. . . . These men do not make politics a career."[30] In Albuquerque, the Citizen's Committee argued on behalf of one of its nominees, "Judging from [his] record of civic service and business accomplishments, we have no doubt he will prove to be an outstanding commissioner."[31]

---

[24] *Dallas Morning News*, April 1, 1947, V-4, quoted in Carolyn Jenkins Barta, "The *Dallas News* and Council-Manager Government" (M.A. thesis, University of Texas at Austin, 1970), 70–71.

[25] *Albuquerque Journal*, April 8, 1958, 7.

[26] *Phoenix Gazette*, November 3, 1969, 15.

[27] *Dallas Morning News*, April 1, 1947, II-2, quoted in Barta, "*Dallas News*," 71.

[28] L. L. Sanders, "How to Win Elections in San Antonio the Good Government Way" (M.A. thesis, St. Mary's University, 1975), 17.

[29] Robert F. Wilcox, "San Diego: City in Motion," in *Urban Politics in the Southwest* ed. Leondard Goodall (Tempe: Arizona State University Press, 1967), p. 155.

[30] *Dallas Morning News*, February 18, 1951, III-3, quoted in Barta, "*Dallas News*," 83.

[31] *Albuquerque Journal*, April 6, 1958; for a similar claim, ibid., March 3, 1966, 2.

Frugality, efficiency, and professionalism in public administration were the announced operating principles of these governments. Frugality and efficiency were best demonstrated by low taxes. "Charter government has brought to the city of Phoenix not only a stable government," argued former Phoenix mayor Hohen Foster, "but also a stable tax rate."[32] Commitment to professional public administration was contrasted with patronage employment. In Dallas the Citizens Charter Association made sure "our city departments are free to discharge their daily chores without pressures."[33] In Phoenix

> One of the blessings the Charter Government movement has brought to management of municipal affairs . . . is the nonpolitical nature of city jobs. From city manager to trash collector, including along the line policemen, firemen, engineers, stenographers, and all others, employees get and keep their jobs without having to lick the boots of some petty politician.[34]

Slating groups called upon voters to remember the days of inefficiency, expense, and perhaps corruption that preceded their ascent to power, and to contrast their own record of businesslike management, honesty, low taxes, and rapid, orderly growth with the record of their predecessors. The *Dallas Morning News* editorialized in 1951, "The CCA has brought Dallas the cleanest municipal government it has ever known. It sponsored the city manager form. . . . it eliminated collusion between local racketeers and persons in authority."[35] In 1966, The *Albuquerque Journal* reported "The Albuquerque Citizens Committee platform . . . praises the recent past and holds out high hopes for the future," claiming that "ACC candidates have since 1954 been successful in meeting increased needs and desires of the city's residents."[36] Nor were voters permitted to forget that Albuquerque was declared an All American City in 1957,[37] as was Phoenix in 1950 and again in 1958.[38] In Phoenix every municipal campaign was accompanied by a retelling of the "boss-ridden old days before an angry citizenry formed the CGC movement to throw the rascals out."[39]

[32] *Phoenix Gazette*, November 3, 1959, 15. For a similar claim in Dallas, see Barta, "*Dallas News*," 34.; for Albuquerque, see *Albuquerque Journal*, April 7, 1958.

[33] *Dallas Morning News*, April 1, 1963, 1, quoted in Barta, "*Dallas News*," 109.

[34] *Phoenix Gazette*, November 4, 1963, 4 (editorial).

[35] *Dallas Morning News*, January 6, 1951, III-2, quoted in Barta, "*Dallas News*," 82. In 1967 the *News* editorialized: "Dallas has gained national note for its clean, businesslike city government. CCA-backed candidates have played leading roles in compiling a record of excellence"; March 26, 1967, c-2, quoted in Barta, "*Dallas News*," 121.

[36] *Albuquerque Journal*, March 4, 1966, F-6.

[37] *Albuquerque Journal*, April 8, 1958, 7.

[38] Paul Kelso, *A Decade of Council-Manager Government in Phoenix, Arizona* (Tucson: University of Arizona, 1960), 6.

[39] *Phoenix Gazette*, November 4, 1963, 4 (editorial), and see also November 6, 1963,

Opposition candidates for office for the most part echoed the claims of the Ins. "Outs" also formed nonpartisan slating groups, with names much like those of the Ins (for example, the Dallas Voters' League and the Good Government League in Albuquerque in 1959). The most loyal of oppositions, Outs insisted that their love for the city charter was even greater, their commitment to professional public administration deeper, and that if elected they would be even more frugal and efficient than the Ins, and they would be even more effective at promoting growth. In Albuquerque the opposition slate in 1962 advertised, "Realizing that the City Commissioners are . . . charged by the people with the efficient operation of city government, we pledge ourselves to stand squarely behind the city manager form of government in its purest form."[40] In Phoenix in 1963, one opposition candidate for mayor "stressed that he supports the Charter Government principle," while another pledged not to change the council-manager form of government.[41] Endorsing an opposition candidate for mayor in 1961, the *Dallas Morning News* insisted he had been "steadfast in support of the council-manager system that lifted Dallas to an enviable position."[42]

Insurgents promised not only to maintain manager government, but also to administer it more efficiently. The Economy Ticket in Phoenix in 1953 denounced the "squandering of taxpayers' money"; two years later the Taxpayers Ticket promised tax reduction; in 1963 insurgents promised "a more efficient, economical city administration."[43] In Dallas in 1949 the opposition charged the Citizens Charter Association with inefficiency and mismanagement[44]; in Albuquerque local government was criticized for poor administration[45] and failing to promote growth.[46]

There was a leitmotif of more trenchant opposition. Phoenix and Dallas witnessed recurrent campaigns for district representation on the

---

35, "for story telling how Phoenix city charter was revised to provide a foundation for new and better municipal government," and November 2, 1959, "First Charter Candidates Cleaned Up Political Mess," 15. Similarly, in Houston "inertia, uncertainty, wrangling [and] subordination of all things to politics . . . [was] blighting municipal progress" before the adoption of council-manager government (*Houston Press*, July 7, 1943, 9).

[40] *Albuquerque Journal*, April 2, 1962, B3.

[41] Kenneth Stites, Jr., "A Study of Nonpartisanship—The 1963 Phoenix Municipal Primary Election," (M.A. thesis, Arizona State University, 1964), 101.

[42] *Dallas Morning News*, March 19, 1961, quoted in Barta "*Dallas News*," 103–4.

[43] For 1953, 1955, see Stites "Study of Nonpartisanship," 54–55; *Phoenix Gazette*, November 4, 1963, 33.

[44] Barta, "*Dallas News*," 72–73.

[45] *Albuquerque Journal*, March 11, 1966, 1; in 1958 Property Owners' candidate Poorbaugh promised "we'd quit spending so much money" (*Albuquerque Journal*, April 2, 1958, 15).

[46] *Albuquerque Journal*, March 25, 1966, 8.

city council, political parties, or elected mayors. In 1947 the All Dallas, GI, and Veterans' Party (which had CIO support) won a seat on the Dallas Council. In 1949 the Democratic party called for district elections in the city, and the Change the Charter Association called for mayor-council government.[47] The opposition slate in Phoenix (all of whom were registered Democrats) in 1951 called for ward representation and partisan elections, in 1957 the opposition Democratic Charter Government Ticket also called for partisan elections, and in 1961 there was another call (this time from the right) for a strong mayor and ward representation.[48] In San Antonio the Better Government League campaigned for a strong-mayor system and descriptive representation.[49]

In response to these criticisms, NPSGs sometimes included insurgents on subsequent tickets or invited representatives of African-American or Mexican-American communities or organized labor to be on executive committees or appear on slates. The Citizens Charter Association in Dallas, for example, responded to criticisms in the 1947 campaign by offering more representative slates, offering a place on the ticket to a prominent AFL leader in 1953, and promising more services and city jobs to African-American voters.[50] Nevertheless, the CCA was charged with being a machine guilty of cronyism and favoritism.[51]

In Phoenix the African-American *Arizona Sun* was published from 1942 to 1963. In 1946 the *Sun* reported a "political study council" was proposed to promote "intelligent participation in politics," and two years later the paper announced the organization of the Arizona Voters' League in Phoenix. The League's platform included Fair Employment Practices legislation for both Phoenix and Arizona, prohibition of discrimination and segregation in education, health, and employment, better and more secure employment opportunities in state government, an end to discrimination in the National Guard, housing codes, and the promotion of voter registration in Maricopa County (Phoenix) and Arizona.[52] The African-American *Houston Defender* published its platform in 1954, calling for equal work and pay opportunities for Negro

[47] Barta, "*Dallas News*," 72.

[48] Brent Whiting Brown, "Phoenix Charter Government Committee," 48–49 for 1951, 53 for 1957, 56–57 for 1961.

[49] L. L. Sanders, "How to Win," 28.

[50] Robert B. Fairbanks, "The Good Government Machine: The Citizens Charter Association and Dallas Politics, 1940–1960," in *Essays on Sunbelt Cities and Recent Urban America*, ed. Robert B. Fairbanks and Kathleen Underwood (College Station: Texas A & M University Press, 1990), 136–38.

[51] Barta, "*Dallas News*," 89, 94. Among other things, it was noted that the street in front of the *Times Herald* was improved within days of the paper's endorsement of the CCA slate in 1959 (Fairbanks, "Good Government Machine," 143).

[52] *Arizona Sun*, May 31, 1946, 1, August 27, 1948, 1.

workers, suppression of lynching, more African Americans in the police and fire departments, paving and drainage in "colored residential areas," and a housing code. Each paper served its entire state; both papers reported both on local politics and progress and setbacks across the country for African-Americans.[53] The *Sun* reported with approval Mayor Busey's condemnation of school segregation in Arizona; the next year, the *Sun* reported that while Phoenix public schools remained segregated, both Phoenix parochial schools and Prescott public schools were integrated.[54] Asking an end to racial segregation in the state, the *Sun* declared, "While more cattle rustlers than Negroes have been lynched within the boundaries of the state . . . Arizona generally stands with the South in it attitude toward Negroes."[55] Outside the Black community, of course, probably hardly anyone read this press. Phoenix, Dallas, and Houston also had labor papers, providing a sometimes critical reading of local government. Houston's *Labor Messenger*, for example, reported that the city maintained a "polo field for the rich but won't maintain the zoo for the Poor."[56] Thus, there were alternative voices in local politics, but most likely they were not heard beyond a restricted audience.

At midcentury municipal reformers governed the big cities of the Southwest and enjoyed a rhetorical monopoly in public discourse about local government. By *public* discourse I mean discourse "heard" by all citizens. This monopoly followed in the first instance on vanquishing completely the opposition, so that it—in particular, party politicians—had no role in local political life. There were a few critics of local government, like Austin's Emma Long, but citywide elections and the activities of nonpartisan slating groups meant Long was the exception. In most places there were no elected voices of opposition.

Reformers and their opponents alike proclaimed their allegiance to businesslike local government administered frugally, efficiently, and professionally. They agreed that the city's business and civic leaders were its appropriate political leaders, promoting growth and governing the city with only the best interests of the whole citizenry in mind. Reformers were shielded from criticism by enthusiastic and boosterish local mass media. Often the major newspapers were owned by men who strongly supported reform and nonpartisan slating groups. The *Dallas Morning News* and the *Arizona* (later *Phoenix*) *Gazette* serve as prominent exam-

---

[53] *Houston Defender*, April 10, 1954, 7. The *Sun*, for example, covered not only local politics, but the progress and setbacks of African-American politics elsewhere, including the police brutality in Los Angeles, the fate of the Scottsboro boys, court rulings on miscegenation and other civil rights issues.

[54] *Arizona Sun*, September 24, 1948, 1; February 18, 1949, 1.

[55] Ibid., February 18, 1949.

[56] (Houston) *Labor Messenger*, September 12, 1941, 1.

ples.[57] There were other views of city politics, found in labor and minority presses, but the major papers (as well as, later, television broadcasts) excluded or misrepresented opposition voices.

Campaigning and persuasion were undergirded by organization. The Good Government League in San Antonio "planned inclusion of minority groups" and took care "to insure that all major geographical areas [were] represented on the ticket" (at least early in its career).[58] In Phoenix the Charter Government Committee likewise worried about a balanced ticket, which in the 1950s meant a woman (occasionally), perhaps a Catholic, a Jew, and a Mormon in addition to Anglo men of other Protestant denominations.[59] NSPGs also organized for elections. The Albuquerque Citizens' Committee created "an effective precinct organization" with hundreds of volunteers in the 1950s.[60] In 1960 the chairman of the Albuquerque Citizens Committee declared that while their "basic principle remains unchanged," the committee would henceforth act as "a nonpartisan municipal political party, following basic political activities that apply to any party."[61]

Winning the Game

A closer look at municipal contests circa 1960 reveals the coalitions supporting reform regimes. Three elections, two prototypical good-government triumphs and one with a very strong insurgent candidacy,

[57] For Dallas, Barta, "*Dallas News*" for San Diego, J. David Greenstone, "Report." Greenstone observed, "The power of the press in San Diego seems real enough, to the satisfaction of most of my conservative informants and the outrage of the liberals" (V-24). Greenstone cites devastating criticism of the *Union* by prominent Democrat Lionel Van Deerlin in *San Diego Magazine*. One example from presidential politics was the *Union*'s characterization of Thomas E. Dewey as "two-term governor of New York" while Adlai Stevenson (although he was governor of Illinois) was described in the *Union* only as "the twice-defeated candidate for President." Van Deerlin concluded that the *Union*'s bias was not confined to election coverage: "It continues round the calendar, attentive as Moscow's *Pravda* to the party line" ("Report," V-26, V-7).

[58] L. L. Sanders, "How to Win," 6, and Bill Crane, "San Antonio: Pluralistic City and Monolithic Government," in *Urban Politics in the Southwest*, ed. Leonard Goodall (Tempe: Arizona State University Institute of Public Administration, 1967), 134.

[59] Brent Whiting Brown, "Phoenix Charter Government Committee," 68; see also G. Wesley Johnson, "Generations of Elites and Social Change in Phoenix," in *Community Development in the American West: Past and Present Nineteenth and Twentieth Century Frontiers*, ed. Jessie L. Embry and Howard A. Christy (Provo: Brigham Young University, 1985), 97.

[60] Dorothy I. Cline and T. Philip Wolf, "Albuquerque: The End of a Reform Era" in *Urban Politics in the Southwest*, ed. Leonard Goodall (Tempe: Arizona State University Institute of Public Administration, 1967), 15.

[61] Robert Turner Wood, "The Transformation of Albuquerque, 1945–1972" (Ph.D. diss., University of New Mexico, 1980), 248.

show the popular base of reform support.[62] The typical reform victories are Sam Mardian's election as mayor of Phoenix in 1959 and the success of the Albuquerque Citizens' Committee (ACC) ticket in 1962. The more closely contested election is from Austin in 1961.

Mardian's victory was overwhelming, as Mardian received 29,027 votes while his opponent, Russell Kapp, garnered 11,742. Readers of the *Phoenix Gazette* probably found the campaign wholly predictable. The *Gazette* ran a series of articles explaining how the Charter Government Committee (CGC) came to office as a reforming group, curing the many ills of local government in the 1940s. (The headline of the fourth article was "First Charter Candidates Cleaned Up Political Mess.") The *Gazette* also gathered quotes from the city's former mayors, endorsing the CGC ("Charter Policy Best Way, Claim Phoenix Mayors"). Opposition criticism of the CGC, offered gently as the Kapp campaign insisted on its own support for the city's charter, was ridiculed as echoing the song, "Anything You Can Do, I Can Do Better." In the wake of victory, with 68.5 percent of the vote in his favor, mayor-elect Mardian thanked the voters by declaring the election "a tremendous vote of confidence for ten years of progress and prosperity for Phoenix under the Charter Government administrations."[63]

In Albuquerque the Citizen's Committee fielded almost a thousand volunteers to get out the vote for its sixth electoral contest. The ACC slate of Westfall, Heilman, and Brown was endorsed by the *Albuquerque Journal*. The occupations of the three men—an engineer, real-estate agent, and businessman—represented, in the *Journal's* view, the ideal skills for a city commission. The ACC was opposed by challengers with varied constituencies. Clarence Davis was an incumbent member of the commission (but not an ACC supporter), with a constituency in the affluent Heights. Larry Felicetti and Fred Chavez were Valley politicians, the second supported by the GI Forum. Another Valley politician, Orlando Ulivarri, campaigned against proposed municipal bonds. Opponents denounced the ACC as a vehicle of vested interests, and reported on its large campaign fund, "much of it collected from local contractors." The opposition platform pledged to recruit new industry, raise wages of municipal

---

[62] The elections were chosen as follows: 1960, as I argued above, is the apogee of reform regimes. Chapters 5, 6, and 7 examine seven big cities with citywide, nonpartisan elections and city-manager government in the 1950s. Of these, two have not kept voting returns for polling places (San Jose and San Diego), so elections could not be studied. Three are in Texas (Dallas, Austin, San Antonio); of these, Austin is both the smallest and has the best secondary literature on its elections, making it the best case for this chapter. Phoenix and Albuquerque also kept election returns by polling place.

[63] *Phoenix Gazette*, October 30, 31, November 1–3, 1959; for Mardian's statement, November 11, 1959, 10.

employees, and of course support city-manager government. The Albuquerque Citizens' Committee won all three seats by comfortable margin. The least popular ACC candidate received 10,990 votes, while the most popular of the challengers received 6,232 votes. After the election ACC officials declared a "great victory . . . that shows the confidence of the people in the future of Albuquerque."[64]

In contrast to the Phoenix and Albuquerque contests, the Austin runoff in 1961 was a fiercely contested and very close race, decided by 68 of 20,664 votes cast. Emma Long and Bob Armstrong were competing for a seat on the city council. Long was well known to Austin voters. First elected to the city council in 1948, Long initially campaigned on the virtues of a wife and mother, claiming, "The city needs a good housekeeper." Once in office Long made herself the champion of ordinary voters, an opponent of subsidies to developers and utilities, and a supporter of civil rights. Long opposed telephone rate hikes; supported municipal employees' demands for wage improvement; secured legislation to subsidize the assessments of less affluent homeowners for street improvements and then stretch out payments of the homeowners share; supported integration of public places and, later, a fair-housing ordinance. Long retired from politics in 1959 but tried to return in 1961 (the election examined here). Although Long lost in 1961, she won in 1963, and remained on the council until 1969.[65]

Returns for these three elections were examined to discover the demography of the electorate, support for incumbent regimes, and the sites of opposition to them. I divided each city into relatively homogeneous sections of affluent, middle-class, and lower-middle-income/working-class, and poor voters (see table 6-4).[66]

[64] *Albuquerque Journal*, April 1, 1962, 1, 2; April 2, 1962, 1, 5. This election campaign included portents of the disarray of the 1960s. Valley residents complained about flooding; the *Journal* reported that the fast expansion of the 1950s included much shoddy work, and many utility extensions already required repairs (April 1, 1). After the election the *Journal* reported, "Voter Approval of City, County Bond Issue to Lead to Tax Boost for Property Owners" (April 4, 1962, 1).

[65] Anthony M. Orum, *Power, Money, and the People* (Austin: Texas Monthly Press, 1987), chap. 8.

[66] The constraints of available data shaped these choices. Phoenix retained voting information by precinct as well as a map of the city's precincts. These are not coterminous with census tracts, which are larger. Austin and Albuquerque kept voting information by polling places; although the addresses of polling places are listed, the precinct boundaries are unknown. Albuquerque and Austin were about the same size, but Albuquerque had 95 polling places, while Austin had only 37; this meant that inferences about where people voted in Albuquerque were much more difficult (more polling places meant more neighborhoods were close to more than one polling place). These limits on information put a premium on contiguity of sections, making them less homogeneous than if politicians and the Bureau of the Census had conspired on boundary lines (as they did in New York).

TABLE 6-4

Demographic Characteristics of Neighborhoods in Austin, Phoenix, and Albuquerque, ca. 1960

	Population	Voting-age Population	% Hispanic	% Black	Median Income
Austin					
Affluent	27,857	16,986	2.0	6.3	$8,111
Middle Income	84,475	49,812	6.3	6.1	$5,615
Low Income	32,166	20,906	5.1	18.4	$4,486
Poor	42,047	21,988	38.8	39.8	$2,920
Total	186,545	109,692	12.8	15.1	$5,116
Phoenix					
Affluent	57,133	33,891	1.7	0.1	$8,544
Middle Income	212,914	125,757	2.7	0.1	$6,804
Low Income	91,794	55,917	11.8	5.1	$5,038
Poor	46,253	22,550	39.7	20.3	$3,881
Total	408,094	238,115	9.2	4.8	$6,117
Albuquerque					
Affluent	37,454	22,881	5.8	0.5	$8,614
Upper Middle Income	59,485	29,121	8.8	0.0	$7,770
Middle Income	47,235	27,723	17.3	1.9	$6,229
North Valley (low income)	34,134	18,587	41.9	0.8	$5,119
South Valley (poor)	22,744	12,867	60.7	9.6	$3,798
Total	201,052	111,178	21.7	1.8	$6,637

Source: U.S. Bureau of the Census, Census of Population and Housing, 1960: Census Tracts, Final Report (Washington, D.C.: Government Printing Office, 1961), PHC (1)=4 (Albuquerque), PHC (1)=11 (Austin), PHC (1)=117 (Phoenix).

Note: Polling places grouped using census tracts.

Austin developed much like the well known Burgess concentric circle model, with poorer residents near the center and more affluent residents toward the suburbs. Austin's African-American neighborhood stretched eastward on the south side of the city. Albuquerque divided between the Heights, to the east of downtown, and the Valley, on the city's west side. The Heights were in some places affluent, elsewhere middle class, and almost entirely Anglo. Lower-middle-income Anglos lived to the southeast. The Valley, largely Hispanic, was more financially comfortable in the north (which was 40.9 percent Hispanic), and poorer in the south (60.7 percent Hispanic), which was near downtown. Albuquerque's Valley trailed southwesterly to outside the city limits. This southernmost part of the Valley, where residents of course could not vote in Albuquerque elections, was more Hispanic than the north Valley (58 percent), housed more residents than the south Valley inside the city limits, was poorer than the Valley inside the city limits, and was closer to downtown than most of the Heights.

Phoenix grew in a fairly uniform north-south gradient, with the wealthy in the north and the poor in the south (at the 1959 election, much of poor south Phoenix remained outside the city limits). In each city the lowest income communities are also the place most African-American and Spanish surnamed families resided. Even in Albuquerque, the city least segregated by ethnicity, the wealthiest areas are almost exclusively Anglo, and the poorer areas predominantly Hispanic.

I divided Austin and Phoenix into four, and Albuquerque into five, residential districts. Albuquerque's division reflects residents' own understanding of the city's social geography (confirmed by the census): three areas of the city east of downtown represent affluent, middle, and upper-middle-income, predominantly Anglo, communities, while two areas west of downtown demarcate the north and south Valley. In each city the affluent districts had median family incomes well above $8,000 and were almost exclusively Anglo. Middle income communities had median family incomes of $6,804 in Phoenix and $5,615 in Austin. Albuquerque's upper-middle-income community had median family income of $7,770, and its middle-income community had median family income of $6,229. These communities too had few residents of color. Albuquerque's middle income communities appear more comfortable than the middle-income communities in the other cities both because Albuquerque as a whole had a higher median family income (itself an artifact of city boundaries excluding the poorest neighborhoods), and because affluent voters in the northeast corner of the city could not be segregated from their middle-class neighbors and so are included with them.

In all three cities, the low income areas had median family incomes between $4,500 and $5,100. The low income communities were mostly Anglo working class families, although about a fifth of residents in low-income areas were African-American or Hispanic. In Phoenix the low income section was almost 17 percent African-American and Hispanic, in Austin 23.5 percent; in Albuquerque 19.2 percent. Albuquerque's north Valley, with comparable income, was 41.9 percent Hispanic (and less than 1 percent African-American). The poor in each city had median family incomes under $4,000, and African-American and Hispanic residents constituted the great majority of the poor. Phoenix's poor residents were 20.3 percent African-American and 39.7 percent Hispanic; in Austin the city's poorest fifth were about 40 percent African-American and 40 percent Hispanic; Albuquerque's south Valley was 60.7 percent Hispanic and 9.6 percent African-American.

TABLE 6-5
Turnout and Voting Returns in Austin, Phoenix, and Albuquerque, ca. 1960

	Turnout (%)	% of Vote for Winner[a]	% of Vote for Alternate Slate[b]	Distribution of Votes for Winner (%)	Distribution of Total Population (%)
Austin					
Affluent	26.8	70		35	15
Middle Income	18.3	47		47	45
Low Income	9.8	52		12	17
Poor	12.3	23		7	23
Total	16.8	50		100	100
Phoenix					
Affluent	20.7	83		20	14
Middle Income	18.5	71		58	52
Low Income	10.1	58		18	23
Poor	10.0	50		4	11
Total	17.5	70		100	100
Albuquerque					
Affluent	25.9	60	21	30	19
Upper Middle Income	30.1	53	21	38	30
Middle Income	15.4	43	33	15	24
North Valley (low income)	19.4	33	47	9	17
South Valley (poor)	19.3	41	47	8	11
Total	22.5	49	29	100	100

Source: Computed from election returns collected from respective Offices of the City Clerk in Albuquerque, Phoenix, and Austin.

[a] Percentage of the total vote for the Albuquerque Citizens' Committee in Albuquerque; the percent of the total vote for Armstrong in Austin; the percent of the total vote for Mardian in Phoenix.

[b] Percentage of the total vote for the 'alternate' slate in Albuquerque. The remaining vote was won by scattered candidates in Albuquerque.

As shown in earlier tables, turnout was (relative to machine-descendant cities) low in each of these cities. Only Albuquerque squeaked above 20 percent turnout; Phoenix and Austin were well below (see table 6-5). Although the available information is imperfect, it does allow estimates of turnout in each city's communities. These estimates suggest that turnout was highest in affluent neighborhoods within each city. In Phoenix and Austin, turnout in affluent neighborhoods was more than double the turnout of working-class and poor neighborhoods. In all three cities, middle-class neighborhoods looked much like affluent neighborhoods in turnout (in

Albuquerque the middle-class area exceeded the affluent in turnout). Similarly, the lower-income and poor sections were close in turnout. The result was that more affluent neighborhoods were a substantially larger portion of the electorate than of the city as a whole.

Differences in turnout were reinforced by differences in support for candidates. In each city strong majorities of the affluent supported the regimes in power. In Phoenix 83 percent of the affluent, in Austin 70 percent of the affluent, and in Albuquerque 60 percent of the affluent voted for incumbents. Middle-class communities were not far behind. Everywhere, support for incumbents varied with income: the poorer the voting community, the less support it offered the incumbent.

Across these similarities and NPSG victories, there were different underlying realities. In Phoenix Charter Government could fairly claim widespread voter endorsement: of more than eighty precincts, only three went to Mardian's opponent. In Albuquerque, although the Citizens' Committee won, it did so only by gaining large margins in affluent and middle-class neighborhoods. Elsewhere the ACC won pluralities, but less than half of votes cast. In the north Valley the ACC claimed only 33.4 percent, and in the south Valley 41 percent of the votes cast. Although the other votes were scattered, their totals suggested that an attractive alternative might have carried the Valley and perhaps placed a commissioner on the city council.

In Austin's close election, incumbents left nothing to chance. Not only were the rules written to hinder voting in communities likely to be unhappy with incumbents, but also, polling places were more convenient for communities likely to support Austin's incumbents. More votes were cast for Long than for Armstrong in the general election, although lacking more than 50 percent of the votes cast, Long was forced into a runoff. (Before creation of the place system in 1953, Long would simply have won the election.) Turnout differences were key to Armstrong's victory: if the turnout of poor voters had matched the turnout of affluent voters, Long would have won by the comfortable margin of 489 votes. Of course, in Austin in 1961 that insight had all the wisdom and futility of the observation that if wishes were horses, beggars would ride.

In the aftermath of their victory, Long's opponents acted to weaken the voting strength of those likely to support her. Before the 1963 elections, six polling places were moved. Among these two were in lower-income neighborhoods near the center of the city, and another was taken from an African-American elementary school.[67] Despite these efforts, Long won

---

[67] Comparison of polling place lists for 1961 and 1963, City Clerk's Office, Austin, Texas.

a seat on the city council in 1963, and was reelected to two more terms before retiring.[68]

The Political Community of Big-City Reform

The election victories traced here reveal much of the general pattern of big-city reform, the broad arrangements in place across the Southwest for voting and elections, and the political communities these arrangements created. Municipal leaders wrote the rules of local politics to present obstacles to voting: difficult registration well in advance of elections, the poll tax, and literacy tests. The organization of elections also discouraged voting, as nonpartisan, nonconcurrent elections lowered the visibility of elections, and citywide balloting diminished the value of the vote by preventing descriptive representation. These arrangements had their intended effect of low turnout, particularly among poorer voters and people of color. At the same time, political leaders made concerted efforts to mobilize likely supporters, and these efforts too were rewarded.

The three elections described here are examples of regimes of sustained political ascendancy. Everywhere the institutions of local politics depressed participation and turnout. Only one in five or one in six adults voted in local elections. Voting differences among communities suggest that only one in ten poor or working-class adults voted in local elections, one in four of their more affluent neighbors. Nonpartisan slating groups, although they had widespread support in some places, were most strongly supported by affluent Anglo voters.[69]

[68] City of Austin, "Elections, 1924–1979" (Austin: City of Austin, Public Information Office, 1979), 20–22 for Long's tenure. Not all council races in Austin were as polarizing as the 1961 runoff between Emma Long and Bob Armstrong. For the next municipal election, in 1963, David Olson found different configurations of support for different council candidates. Three were elected by Bourbon coalitions of affluent west-side voters and African-American voters from the city's southeastern precincts. One veteran council member, Ben White (first elected 1951), won every precinct except for one of the precincts with a large Mexican-American population. White was one of only two candidates who won strong support from lower-income Anglos to the city's south, no doubt because he was a resident of the city's south side himself. The other candidate who won that support, as well was the election, was Emma Long. White and Long differed from the other victors by winning the strong support of lower-income rather than affluent Anglo voters. Olson also looked at turnout and found it no different than it had been in 1933! There was a single exception: "Latin" turnout, Olson found, had tripled. Olson, *Nonpartisan Elections*, 71–80 for electoral coalitions, 88 for turnout.

[69] Heywood Sanders has shown that the shape of the San Antonio electorate changed dramatically over the period of the city's refounding from 1945 to 1960, providing a good example of political leaders reshaping the electorate by discouraging some and mobilizing others. Sanders argued that Hispanic voters were the most reliable supporters of bond

Emma Long's sustained career of opposition in office was unmatched in the urban Southwest. By contrast, in machine-dominated Chicago the antimachine Fifth Ward, and sometimes an affluent North Side ward, were able to elect a series of opposition city councilmen who kept vigorous criticism alive (while being, it must be admitted, wholly unsuccessful at influencing public policy). In the Southwest, the costs of mounting citywide campaigns and the requirement of gaining more than half the votes cast proved insurmountable barriers to most challengers.

Nonpartisan slating groups—the Charter Government Committee in Phoenix, the Citizens' Charter Association of Dallas, the Albuquerque Citizens' Committee, and comparable groups elsewhere—governed without effective challenge. In Dallas, for example, the Citizens' Charter Association elected all but twenty-five of the 182 city council members between 1931 and 1969, claimed the allegiance of a majority of council members in every year except 1935–38, and lost only one seat on the council between 1939 and 1959.[70] *Every* member of the city council in Phoenix from 1949 to 1975 was a nominee of the Charter Government Committee.[71] In Albuquerque the Citizens' Committee controlled city government from 1954 to 1966.[72] In San Antonio, Good Government League nominees won seventy-seven of eighty-one council races between 1955 and 1971.[73]

Continued ascendancy without significant challenge meant political leaders in fully institutionalized reform cities had no incentive to recruit diverse voters to support them, nor any reason to increase participation. Like the party bosses of late-nineteenth-century industrial cities, the civic statesmen of city government in the Southwest could, at midcentury, confidently expect to win again and again with the constituents already

---

issues before the inauguration of city-manager government in 1951. The vote for the new charter in 1951 "marks something of a watershed in participation terms. while the total vote cast in the Hispanic precincts increased, Anglo voting boxes showed an enormous increase, on the order of three times the 1949 level." In the wake of the new charter's adoption, Anglo participation remained high while Hispanic participation waned. After 1955 "Anglo voters . . . [provided the] support necessary to pass bond proposals." Heywood T. Sanders, "The Creation of Postwar San Antonio: Politics, Voting, and Fiscal Regimes, 1945 to 1960" (paper prepared for the annual meeting of the Southwestern Social Science Association, San Antonio, March 1991).

[70] Barta, "*Dallas News*," 131.

[71] Bradford Luckingham, "Phoenix: The Desert Metropolis" in *Sunbelt Cities*, ed. Richard M. Bernard and Bradley Robert Rice (Austin: University of Texas Press, 1983), 319.

[72] D. I. Cline, "Albuquerque, The End of the Reform Era," in *Urban Politics in the Southwest*, ed. Leonard Goodall (Tempe: Arizona State University Press, 1967.

[73] David R. Johnson, "San Antonio: The Vicissitude of Boosterism" in *Sunbelt Cities*, ed. Richard M. Bernard and Bradley Robert Rice (Austin: University of Texas Press, 1983), 240.

recruited to politics. It is not too much to say that the political regimes of big-city reform rested squarely on the shoulders of the white Anglo-Saxon Protestant middle class; the great achievement of big-city reform regimes was that they created political communities much like Winnetka in social settings that were considerably more diverse. This was accomplished by writing the rules to win, by organizing to mobilize prospective supporters and bring them to the polls, and by failing to annex communities less likely to support incumbent regimes.

Reform candidates were so successful in the postwar period as to be unbeatable. The invulnerability of reform regimes rested on their popularity with the small electorates of big reform cities. The very popularity of reform regimes among voters encouraged political opponents to compete with reformers on their own terms, even though this was almost always a losing strategy. That said, it remains to be see why these governments were so popular with voters, what kind of government big-city reform provided, and what goods it delivered to its constituents.

Seven

And Takes the Credit

ACROSS the United States, the 1950s and 1960s were decades of growth and transformation for cities. Insufficient capital investment during the Depression and Second World War, followed by the return of veterans and, in the Southwest, immigration from other areas of the country, raised enormous demands for investment in infrastructure, utilities, and housing. Postwar prosperity and the baby boom meant there were not enough houses, roads, playgrounds, schools, parks, or libraries anywhere. *Business Week's* description of Albuquerque after the war might have been written about many cities:

> People have brought a painful housing squeeze to Albuquerque. . . . All sorts of other shortages cropped up. The electric company ran out of meters to install in houses. The telephone company got 5,000 phones behind, and still hasn't wiped out the backlog. Schools bulged, and sewers overflowed. The city and the utilities, as they jumped from one job to another, began to feel as though they were trying to dam a flood with a sieve.[1]

In Dallas one reporter lamented, "Dallas' municipal problems seem endless. . . . The city needs more of everything."[2] In the Southwest the rapid annexation of suburbs to keep pace with (or even better, outpace) settlement was a high priority. Federal assistance was forthcoming for highways and airports. In some cities leaders were planning renewal of downtowns even during the war; once federal funds were available, urban renewal was considered in every city hall.

Big-city reform governments served their core constituents well, assisting the development of new middle-class communities and providing parks and schools. There were also in these cities communities that were considerably less well served, and less visible in local politics. Their situation and discontents are also part of the portrait of big-city reform presented here. Together, the rules of local politics, the discourse of elections and governance, the services government provided and those it withheld, brought big-city reform to life.

---

[1] "Albuquerque: Bombs Build Boom Town," *Business Week*, May 13, 1950, 60.

[2] Allen Quin, "Tomorrow's Dallas," *Dallas Morning News* reprint, July 1957, 12, quoted in Carolyn Jenkins Barta, "The *Dallas News* and Council-Manager Government" (M.A. thesis, University of Texas at Austin, 1970), 81.

Growth's Agenda

Like Teaford's nineteenth-century city governments, the city governments of the postwar era managed triumphs of building, management, and expansion. City governments improved airports, expanded and upgraded sewers and water systems, built highways, and extended roads, water, electricity, and sewerage to new suburban communities. The tremendous energy and money required for these undertakings were justified both by the manifest need for public improvements and by progrowth rhetoric. As one San Jose mayor recalled, "We were all boomers then."[3]

Growth was not merely ideology. Southwestern cities grew dramatically in both population and area. Population growth was fueled by the settlement of returning veterans and the migration of employees and prospective employees of new industries. Between 1950 and 1960, the populations of Austin and Dallas grew by 50 percent; Albuquerque and San Jose doubled; Houston and San Diego nearly so; Phoenix quadrupled in numbers. The population growth shown in table 7-1 reflects as well the aggressive annexation of surrounding areas by southwestern city governments, shown in table 7-2. Dallas got an early start, in 1945 doubling its area in a single week. In 1960 San Antonio and Dallas were almost twenty times their area in 1950; San Diego, near the bottom of the list, merely doubled. One Phoenix official explained the city's goal: "We wanted to avoid the St. Louis model, where suburbs strangle the city. . . . We didn't want white flight, or brain drain, or whatever you call it, so we annexed."[4] The same image haunted the city manager of San Jose, who also explained the relationship between annexation and fiscal health: "If you wanted to grow and be able to pay the bill, you had to annex surrounding areas to the city. . . . you couldn't sit on your hands. Pretty soon you would become like Bakersfield and St. Louis, an enclave. . . . bottled up, your tax rate would put you out of the running for new industries."[5] In some places annexation was controversial, as surrounding towns resisted joining cities or quickly incorporated to protect themselves from annexation without consent. Annexation of surrounding areas was facilitated by state governments, testimony to the influence of the Southwest's large cities in their state capitals. Texas had "the most liberal annexation law in the nation," allowing home-rule cities to annex

[3] George Starbird, "The New Metropolis, San Jose between 1942 and 1972" (San Jose: Rosecrucian Press, 1972).

[4] Bradford Luckingham, *Phoenix: The History of a Southwestern Metropolis* (Tucson: University of Arizona Press, 1989), 162.

[5] Anthony P. Hamann, quoted in Philip J. Trounstine and Terry Christensen, *Movers and Shakers: The Study of Community Power* (New York: St. Martin's Press, 1982), 93.

TABLE 7-1
Population of Selected Southwestern Cities, 1950 and 1960

	1950	1960	% Change
Albuquerque	96,815	201,189	109
Austin	132,459	186,545	41
Dallas	434,462	679,684	56
Phoenix	106,818	439,170	311
San Antonio	408,442	588,042	44
San Diego	334,387	573,224	71
San Jose	95,280	204,196	114

Source: U.S. Bureau of the Census, *County and City Data Book, 1962* (Washington, D.C.: Government Printing Office, 1962), table 6.

unincorporated areas without the consent of residents.[6] New Mexico allowed for the creation of arbitration boards to mediate between cities and resisting suburbs. Since, however, the sole criterion the boards could use was the ability of the city to provide services to proposed annexations, mediators were bound to favor Albuquerque.[7] At the urging of San Jose and suburban schools, California passed a law relieving annexed communities from joining metropolitan unified school districts. San Jose annexed "long narrow strips . . . capturing the cross roads which the administration told us were to be the shopping centers of the future— where the sales tax would be. Then they were orchards and two-lane roads. We knew if we got the biggest corners, the subdivisions would follow into the city."[8] San Antonio too used that technique. Annexation might also be coerced through the provision of utilities and water.[9] Phoenix negotiated reduced commercial property tax rates with outlying industrialists to persuade them not to resist annexation; the city govern-

[6] Barta, "*Dallas News,*" 81, quoting *Dallas News* reporter Allan Quin.
[7] Later legislation was even more generous to the city. In 1964 New Mexico passed legislation allowing incorporated municipalities to take in any unincorporated area encircled by the city for five years, without securing consent of the residents. Robert Turner Wood, "The Transformation of Albuquerque, 1945–1972" (Ph.D. diss., University of New Mexico, 1980), 104–5, 465.
[8] Starbird, "New Metropolis," 4.
[9] Albuquerque doubled the water rates for those outside the city limits when they rejected annexation (Wood, "Transformation," 104–5). Pp. 464–69 describe conflict and coercion over annexations in metropolitan Albuquerque. In San Jose, the city's sewerage monopoly was its "greatest weapon in the annexation wars. . . . What water was to Los Angeles, sewage was to San Jose" (Trounstine and Christensen, *Movers and Shakers,* 97).

TABLE 7-2
Land Area of Selected Southwestern Cities,
1950 and 1960 (square miles)

	1950	1960
Albuquerque	48	58
Austin	13	45
Dallas	13	254
Phoenix	17	187
San Antonio	7	148
San Diego	99	195
San Jose	17	56

Source: U.S. Bureau of the Census, County and
City Data Book, 1962 (Washington, D.C.: Government Printing Office, 1962), table 6.

ment also wrote pamphlets, held meetings, and generally propagandized
suburbanites about the advantages of joining the city.[10] However controversial annexation may have been in some instances, by 1960 southwestern cities were the envy of northeastern and midwestern mayors for
their success at gobbling up their own sprawling suburbs. This meant
that in Phoenix, for example, by 1960 nearly three quarters of the population resided in communities that had been outside the city limits in
1950.[11]

Annexation and construction of infrastructure sometimes leapfrogged
older, poorer communities while streets and utilities were provided for
newer communities further from the center. In Phoenix and Albuquerque, poor African-American and Hispanic communities closer to downtown remained outside city limits until the end of the 1950s, while affluent new developments further from the center were targeted for annexation. Similarly, San Diego failed to annex San Ysidro, a poor Mexican-
American community, until 1957.[12]

[10] Michael Francis Konig, "Toward Metropolis Status: Charter Government and the
Rise of Phoenix, Arizona, 1945–1960" (Ph.D. diss. Arizona State University, Tempe,
1983), 96–115.
[11] Luckingham, Phoenix, 162.
[12] Election maps for Phoenix show that the southernmost part of the city—its black
community—was annexed just in time for the 1960 census. Similarly, much of the Valley
remained outside Albuquerque until 1960 or later; the poor Hispanic community just
southwest of Albuquerque remains independent at the time of this writing. For San Ysidro,
Donald V. Kurtz, "Politics, Ethnicity, Integration: Mexican-Americans in the War on Poverty" (Ph.D. diss., Anthropology, University of California, Davis, 1970), 6. The San Ysidro
case is not exactly comparable because the community is fifteen miles from downtown San
Diego.

One consequence of remaining outside city limits was exclusion from municipal water and sewerage. In 1948 the front page of the *Arizona Sun* displayed a photograph of Milton McDuffie, clad in overalls, walking five blocks with his bucket to get water for his family. McDuffie lived in South Phoenix, a poor and largely African-American community not yet annexed to the city of Phoenix, which was served by the independent East Broadway Water Company. Only between midnight and 5 A.M. was there sufficient water pressure in South Phoenix; at other times the taps were dry or nearly so. While residents of Phoenix paid $2 monthly for 13,500 gallons of water, residents of South Phoenix paid $5 to $7.50 per month for the little water they got. Beginning in 1948, the community petitioned Phoenix for annexation and for the city to condemn the East Broadway Water Company. The South Phoenix Civic Organization was granted a hearing before the city council in January 1962, and a month later the council directed community representatives to the Corporation Commission. In March 1962 the community, now inside the city limits, was still campaigning to be rid of the East Broadway Water Company.[13]

Inclusion within the city boundaries did not guarantee provision of utilities, and Phoenix was not alone in failing to provide the most basic services to communities of color. In Albuquerque, former Mayor Louis Saavedra recalls, in the mid-1960s "we could see outhouses, you know, a stone's throw from outside City Hall. And even with all this great scientific [expertise] that many of these persons brought to politics they couldn't see their way to bring the least improvements to the center city . . . whereas they were quite eager to . . . extend utilities and other services to the perimeter."[14] Sewerage was finally provided in the Valley in 1972. In Albuquerque and in San Antonio, poorer Mexican-American communities lacked drainage, and heavy rainfalls flooded many homes (a problem not fixed in either city before the 1980s). In Austin as late as 1969 the first priorities of communities designated for Model Cities funds were paving and drainage.[15]

---

[13] *Arizona Sun*, May 21, 1948, 1; January 25, 1962, 1; February 1, 1962, 1; March 1, 1962, 1.

[14] Louis Saavedra interview, May 18, 1994.

[15] Cecelia Babcock Smith, "The Austin Model Cities Program" (M.A. thesis, University of Texas, Austin, 1970), 51. Paving was also an issue in Albuquerque and Phoenix. Professionals in the Albuquerque city government determined required right-of-way if streets were to be paved; in the Valley, where many dirt roads were too narrow to meet this requirement, they were simply not paved (Saavedra interview). In Phoenix, the south side's representative to the state house of representatives voted no on a three-cent gas tax increase for street paving because he had no confidence his district would benefit. "The holes [in my district] get deeper, while many on the North side [are repaired]." *Arizona Sun* February 22, 1962, 1.

Municipal governments assisted developers who were creating communities in the empty spaces far from the center. In Austin city government provided streets and utilities, water and wastewater service in new subdivisions. When development outpaced the city's ability to provide these amenities, forcing developers to build streets and utility connections, city government repaid developers "five times the revenue from new customers for ten years, or until the developer's costs were totally recouped." (Later this was reduced to twice the revenues until costs were recouped.) The city also paid interest on the unpaid balance of developers' costs.[16] In San Antonio builders and developers frequently requested annexation, not least, one imagines, because "once the area became part of San Antonio, the city reimbursed developers for capital improvements."[17] In Albuquerque, as the costs of suburban development mounted, city government became more demanding of developers. The city's planning commission was not inclined to impose costs on developers. Themselves prominent among Albuquerque builders, developers, and engineers, planning commission members agreed that a proposal requiring builders to pay for utilities and paving in new subdivisions was "an infringement on a man's right to develop his own property." Closer both to the budget and to taxpayers, and "painfully aware of the shortfall of money in the city coffers," the City Commission hesitated only briefly before overruling the planners and enacting the proposal. Community builders were also required to donate land for parks in new subdivisions.[18]

The developing neighborhoods encouraged by city governments were for affluent, working-class, and middle-class families ready to purchase homes. Yet in the crush of postwar growth, decent, affordable housing

[16] Austin was more generous in this regard than any other city in Texas. By contrast, Dallas paid nothing to developers. Austin subsidies were taken away in 1974–75. Frank Staniszewski, "Ideology and Practice in Municipal Government Reform: A Case Study of Austin" (Austin: University of Texas, Studies in Urban Political Economy, no. 8, 1977), 36–38, 48.

[17] Eighty-seven percent of the land annexed was done so forcibly, however. Arnold Fleischmann, "The Politics of Annexation: A Preliminary Assessment of Competing Paradigms," *Social Science Quarterly* 61, no. 1 (March 1986): 133, 137. Fleischmann has also shown that the dynamics described here were not peculiar to the Southwest, "The Territorial Expansion of Milwaukee: Historical Lessons for Contemporary Urban Policy and Research," *Journal of Urban History* 14, no. 2 (February 1988): 147–76. David G. Bromley and Joel Smith have shown that southern and western cities account for most annexed land, although cities in other regions also annexed as they were able, even after the Second World War. The authors attribute greater area annexation by the South and West to greater distances between cities, lower density development, failure of suburban communities to incorporate, and friendlier state governments. "The Historical Significance of Annexation as a Social Process," *Economics* (August 1973): 194–309.

[18] Wood, "Transformation," 176–77.

was hard to find. Immediately after World War II, there was great de-mand for low-income housing, especially for veterans; later, real-estate inflation made buying a first home difficult. The Federal Housing Act of 1949 provided assistance to cities for building low-income housing, but creating local political support was tricky. In Phoenix in 1946 the *Arizona Republic* reported "3000 vainly seek housing here," while the Public Housing Authority was holding 843 unfilled applications for low-income housing from veterans. That year Mayor Ray Busey appointed a committee to study the housing problem, and the city chose three[19] sites for low-income housing projects. The city also planned to rehabilitate the Harry Cordova project for Hispanic veterans. The rehabilitation was halted by community objections, which were sustained by local courts; when higher courts reversed lower court rulings, the project was stymied by exhaustion of federal funds.

Phoenix Housing Authority (PHA) proposals for new projects were opposed by the Chamber of Commerce. PHA professionals mounted a detailed and persuasive defense of their work. Existing low-income housing had won commendations from federal officials; the projects were financed with bonds payable only by the PHA (taking no funds from general revenues); the documented need was great; building the projects would provide employment opportunities. For several years construction proceeded on the proposed housing, despite Chamber opposition. In 1956, however, the federal government provided an opening for opponents of public housing by asking for changes in the Phoenix housing code. The city's newspapers campaigned vigorously against concessions to the federal government, and in 1961 the city council revoked the housing code entirely, making the city ineligible for federal funds.[20] San Diego did not seek funds under the Housing Act, most leaders believing that—absent slums of the sort common in the East—existing housing was adequate; Albuquerque did not build low-income housing either in the 1930s or in the 1950s.[21] Austin and Dallas were more generous in the provision of low-income housing, taking advantage of both the 1949 act and funding under the earlier Wagner-Stegall Act.[22]

---

[19] One Hispanic, one African-American, and one Anglo; all federally funded housing was segregated.

[20] Konig, "Metropolis Status," 164–81; a bitter account of the city's abandonment of efforts to provide low-income housing is provided in Richard L. Gilbert, Jr., "Phoenix Unreborn" *Reporter* 9 (November 21, 1963).

[21] David Greenstone, "A Report on Politics in San Diego" (mimeograph, Joint Center for Urban Studies of the Massachusetts Institute of Technology and Harvard University, 1962), VI-35–VI-36. This view was not shared by African-American leaders. For Albuquerque, Harry Kinney interview, July 25, 1994.

[22] Anthony M. Orum, *Power, Money, and the People: The Making of Modern Austin*

The immediate and best rewarded beneficiaries of successful growth strategies were the leaders of southwestern growth coalitions. Most prominent were bankers and real estate developers, joined by retailers from both outlying and downtown areas. When the *Saturday Evening Post* reported on "The New Millionaires of Phoenix," most of them were housing developers.[23] Bankers had interests not only in downtown, but also in the mushrooming mortgage market in outlying areas.[24] The ascendancy of these interests explains the priorities of municipal government's growth agenda (geographic expansion and construction of middle-class housing, industrial recruitment, airport improvement, highway construction) as well as its limitations (halting efforts to provide low-income housing, and grudging commitments to downtown).

In Phoenix Del Webb, a developer of both residential communities and shopping malls, and Sam Mardian, also a developer of residential communities, were prominent in the Charter Government Committee, as were the executives of the city's largest banks. The 1950s were "a time when Frank Snell could still, as members of the elite had done for several decades, sit down for lunch at the Arizona Club with a few friends and develop either public or private policies for Phoenix, as the occasion demanded."[25] Similar characterizations of the leaders of the growth coalition, and their decision-making style, could be offered for Austin, Albuquerque, San Jose, Dallas, and San Diego. In Dallas, Robert Thornton and the Dallas Citizens' Committee gathered commercial, industrial, and property interests around a table to chart a course for the city's growth and continued good order. In Albuquerque all the members of the plan-

---

(Austin: Texas Monthly Press, 1987), 132–35, 169–72. Robert B. Fairbanks, "The Good Government Machine: The Citizens Charter Association and Dallas Politics, 1930–1960," in *Essays on Sunbelt Cities and Recent Urban America*, ed. Robert B. Fairbanks and Kathleen Underwood (College Station: Texas A & M University Press, 1990).

[23] Harold H. Martin, "The New Millionaires of Phoenix," *Saturday Evening Post*, September 30, 1961, 25–30.

[24] Larry Schweikart, "Financing the Urban Frontier: Entrepreneurial Creativity and Western Cities, 1945–1975," *Urban Studies* 26, no. 1 (February 1989): 177–86; Lynne Pierson Doti and Larry Schweikart, "Financing the Postwar Housing Boom in Phoenix and Los Angeles, 1945–1960," *Pacific Historical Review* 58, no. 2 (May 1989): 173–94, explain that downtown (and also older) bankers were late to recognize the possibilities of the mortgage market; their assets were also inadequate to the demand. Younger bankers and financiers were more innovative, forming ties to eastern banks and reaping the benefit of the rising demand for mortgages.

[25] Konig, "Metropolis Status," 137, 179–80; G. Wesley Johnson, "Generations of Elites and Social Change in Phoenix," in *Community Development in the American West: Past and Present Nineteenth and Twentieth Century Frontiers*, ed. Jessie L. Embry and Howard A. Christy (Provo: Bringham Young University, 1985), 94–98, Peter Wiley and Robert Gottlieb, *Empires in the Sun: The Rise of the New American West* (New York: G. P. Putnam's Sons, 1982), 166–73. The quote is from Johnson, "Generations of Elites," 98.

ning commission were developers, engineers, or real estate investors, and the Albuquerque Citizens' Committee was supported by Dale Bellamah and other major builders. In San Jose, the Book of the Month Club "provided a forum for coordinating public investments policies with the development interests of the private sector."[26]

This did not mean that there was no conflict about growth policies among businessmen and political leaders. In San Diego, Albuquerque, and Phoenix, there was conflict between outlying commercial interests and downtown business interests. The economic prominence of outlying commercial interests, and their presence within the cities' political boundaries, stalled or stymied plans for urban renewal to rebuild downtowns in each of these cities.[27] From a city hall perspective, this was the down side of having annexed the suburbs: downtown real estate and financial interests were challenged in their dominance of local government by outlying interests, and downtown suffered as a result. By contrast, there was greater agreement on investment in airport improvements, utility extension to new communities, roads and highways, and of course, annexation.

Paying the Piper

The critical link between the growth ambitions of southwestern leaders on one hand and the electorate on the other was the financing of expansion through municipal general obligation bonds.[28] The propertied electorate might brake expansion by refusing to approve proposed bond issues. In 1959, for example, Valley (poorer) residents in Albuquerque failed to approve a proposed bond issue to fund municipal parks, appar-

---

[26] Heywood T. Sanders, "Beyond Machine and Reform: The Politics of Postwar Development in Sunbelt Cities" (paper prepared for delivery at the annual meeting of the American Political Science Association, Washington D.C., 1984), 16.

[27] For Albuquerque, see Wood, "Transformation," 229; the *Arizona Sun* cautiously endorsed urban renewal November 7 1957, 3, hoping uprooted African-Americans would be relocated within the city limits; a second article a week later announced that the project had been approved by city government, but withheld endorsement (November 14, 1957, 1). In San Diego there was continuing controversy about downtown versus suburban priorities, Greenstone, "Report," V-5–V-27.

[28] It remained true that it was important that the bonds be marketable, and at a reasonable rate. George Starbird explained San Jose's strategy: "[The city manager] conceived the idea that we should make periodic trips to the bond underwriting houses in the East, telling our story. We would create a favorable market which would reflect when we put out bonds. On a strict basis of classification, San Jose voters were carrying a heavy load indeed, and the bonds shouldn't go as well as they did, but the glamour we painted into the picture for the underwriters salesmen, would go with them all throughout the Middle West where, I guess, everyone wanted to invest in California if they couldn't live there." ("New Metropolis," 5).

ently from the conviction that the parks would not be in their part of town.[29] In San Diego resistance to rebuilding downtown doomed bond offerings in 1962.[30] To preclude defeat at the polls, growth supporters organized campaigns to advertise the benefits of growth and the importance of supporting increased public debt. In San Jose (where a two-thirds of the property owners were required to approve public offerings), the Book of the Month Club financed campaigns in support of bond issues.[31]

Voters had good reasons to approve of municipal government. A standard campaign claim was efficiency, and there is some evidence to support it. Table 7-3 shows employees and per capita spending for common functions (highways, police and fire protection, sanitation, general administration, libraries, parks, and recreation). Big-city reform governments did spend somewhat less than machine descendants and hire fewer municipal workers to perform common functions. In every case, big reform cities employed fewer municipal workers per 10,000 population than the average for cities in their respective size class. The machine descendants, except Chicago, hired more freely.[32]

Reformers frequently claimed credit for keeping property taxes low. Table 7-4 shows tax burdens per capita for common functions of local government in twelve cities.[33] Except for San Antonio and Phoenix, taxes for common functions in big reform cities were not appreciably lower than the tax burden in New Haven and Jersey City, and in Albuquerque and Dallas they were higher. Moreover, since property taxes were a less important source of municipal revenue in big reform cities than in machine descendant cities, reformers' claims to keep taxes low was a carefully crafted appeal: once sales taxes and user charges were added to the citizens' contribution, the tax burden in big reform cities looks heavier.

The last column in table 7-4 shows the per capita debt burden in each city. This represents the entire debt, not only the debt accrued in performance of common functions. Austin's very high debt surely reflects the

[29] Wood, "Transformation," 15, and see below.

[30] Richard F. Pourade, *History of San Diego* (La Jolla: Copley Books, 1977), 7:199.

[31] H. Sanders, "Beyond Machine," 14–16.

[32] There are only five cities in New York and Chicago's size class (over 1 million). Municipal employees per 10,000 population for the other three are Philadelphia, 121.1; Los Angeles, 98.5; Detroit, 107.9.

[33] Of course the whole tax burden of the machine descendants is much greater, since these cities also had substantial school, welfare, and education expenses. This suggests that one reason for higher participation in machine-descendant cities is that so much was at stake: whether the citizen's interest was parks, libraries, public health, or streets, the buck stopped in the same place. By contrast, big reform cities had a much smaller list of functions.

TABLE 7-3
Local Government Employment and Spending, 1960

	Population (in thousands)	Employees	Employees per 10,000 Residents for "Common Functions"	Average Employees/10k Residents in Cities of Similar Size[a]	Spending per Capita on "Common Functions"
Reform Cities					
Albuquerque	201	1,723	85.6	97.2	47.3
Austin	187	1,890	101.3	91.2	46.2
Dallas	680	6,993	102.9	111.8	48.3
Phoenix	439	3,083	7.2	91.2	36.2
San Antonio	588	3,773	64.2	111.8	32.1
San Diego	573	4,534	79.1	111.8	38.7
San Jose	204	1,228	60.1	97.1	52.4
Machine Descendants					
Chicago	3,550	34,803	98.0	117.0	64.2
New Haven	152	1,501	98.7	91.2	44.6
New York	7,781	102,656	131.9	117.0	64.2

Sources: Spending per capita for 'common functions' are from the U.S. Bureau of the Census, *County and City Data Book, 1962* (Washington, D.C., Government Printing Office, 1962), table 6. 'Common functions' are highways, police and fire, sanitation, water, parks, recreation, libraries, and general administration. Number of employees are from the U.S. Bureau of the Census, *Government Employment, 1960* (Washington, D.C.: Government Printing Office, 1960).

[a] The average number of employees per 10,000 residents for cities in the same size group. The size groups (determined by the Census Bureau) were more than 1 million, 500,000–999,999, 100,000–499,999, 200,000–399,999, 100,000–199,999.

city's generous policies toward developers. Albuquerque and Dallas accumulated debts comparable to those of Jersey City and Chicago. The other four reform cities came closer to living within their means.

Taken together, these tables suggest that big-city reform government was somewhat more frugal than machine descendants, but not dramatically so. It could hardly have been otherwise. Even without providing paving, grading, and sewerage to poorer communities, the aggressive growth policies of municipal governments were expensive. Two days after the Albuquerque Citizens' Committee victory at the polls in 1962, the *Albuquerque Journal* delivered the bad news: "Voter Approval of City, County Bond Issues to Lead to Tax Boost for Property Owners."[34]

[34] *Albuquerque Journal*, April 5, 1962, 1.

TABLE 7-4
Financing Local Government, 1960

	Taxes per Capita for 'Common Functions'	Taxes plus Charges per Capita	Debt (in 000's)	Debt per Capita
Reform Cities				
Albuquerque	$50.11	$72.04	$47,133	$234
Austin	$16.13	$40.80	$74,396	$399
Dallas	$55.73	$72.49	$166,225	$245
Phoenix	$29.66	$45.41	$87,206	$199
San Antonio	$26.20	$35.02	$111,973	$191
San Diego	$42.89	$71.55	$44,705	$78
San Jose	$46.74	$70.50	$26,109	$128
Machine Descendants				
Chicago	$62.75	$37.81	$828,239	$233
New Haven	$41.36	$58.77	$50,984	$335
New York	$71.15	$112.98	$6,042,467	$777

Sources: U.S. Bureau of the Census, *County and City Data Book, 1962* (Washington, D.C.: Government Printing Office, 1962), table 6. U.S. Bureau of the Census, *Government Employment 1960* (Washington, D.C.: Government Printing Office, 1960).

Delivering the Goods

What collective benefits was local government able to deliver? The wish list Banfield and Wilson report for Winnetka—parks, libraries, and excellent schools—was secondary to the growth agenda. "There is no remaining bond money for a city hall building, parks, and recreation facilities, or library," the *Albuquerque Journal* explained, even though previous bond issues were meant for them. All the money had been spent on utilities and paving.[35] Municipal governments did provide parks and libraries. Table 7-5 shows public libraries in six reform cities and four machine descendants.

The distribution of branch libraries shows the challenge of providing amenities to keep pace with growth. Austin, Jersey City, and New Haven, the smallest cities, have more libraries relative to the population than any of the other cities. Dallas, Phoenix, and San Diego had barely begun branch library systems in 1960. San Antonio, despite its poverty, provided as many community libraries, relative to its population, as Chicago.

[35] Ibid., April 1, 1962, A14.

TABLE 7-5
Public Libraries in Selected Cities, 1960

	Public Libraries	Population per Branch
Albuquerque	4	50,298
Austin	7	26,737
Dallas	6	91,410
Phoenix	3	146,390
San Antonio	9	65,302
San Diego	3	191,072
Chicago	56	63,400
New Haven	7	21,714
New York	158	49,261

Sources: Albuquerque Bernalillo Telephone Directory (Mountain States Telephone, October 1960) p. 12; *Austin Telephone Directory* (Southwestern Bell Telephone, December 1962), 57; *The Red Book* (Chicago Yellow Pages) (Chicago: Reuben H. Donnelly, 1960), p. 1128; *Greater Dallas Alphabetical Telephone Directory* (Southwestern Bell Telephone, May 1960) 134; *Public Libraries Survey* (New Haven: City Clerk's Office, November 10, 1961); *Manhattan Telephone Directory* (New York: New York Telephone, 1960); *Queens Telephone Directory* (New York: New York Telephone, 1960); *The Bronx Telephone Directory* (New York: New York Telephone, 1960); *Brooklyn Telephone Directory* (New York: New York Telephone, 1960); *Staten Island Telephone Directory* (New York: New York Telephone, 1960); *Phoenix Metropolitan Yellow Pages* (Mountain Bell, January 1973), 526, construction dates checked with library staff; *San Diego Yellow Pages Directory* (Pacific Telephone, October 1971), construction dates checked with library staff; *San Antonio Alphabetical Telephone Directory* (Southwestern Bell Telephone, 1961), 88.

The sites of the reform-city branch libraries show local government's solicitous posture toward its core constituents, as well as some concern for equity. All the cities have central libraries downtown. Once these were desegregated, they were available as well as convenient to less affluent patrons living near the city's center. In addition, Austin, Phoenix, and Albuquerque each had one branch library in a community of color, Harmon (Phoenix) and Carver (Austin) for African-Americans and Griegos in the north Valley in Albuquerque.[36] For African-American residents in several cities, inadequate and segregated library facilities were a source of complaint. In Austin Bill Kirk waged a patient war of attrition on segregation of the public libraries by requesting ever greater numbers of books be sent to the Carver Branch. To maintain that facilities were equal, if separate, the main branch always sent the requested books. With main branch librarians exasperated by a request for the *Great Books*, the city council conceded that Blacks might use any library branch in December of 1951.[37]

The remaining branch libraries were strategically located to serve local government's strongest supporters. Five branch libraries in Austin were in affluent (one) or middle-class (four) communities that provided large margins for Armstrong in 1961: Tarrytown, Rosedale, Travis Heights, Colonial Hills, and Allandale. In Albuquerque the remaining neighborhood branches were in very affluent neighborhoods in the Heights, one just east of the University of New Mexico's south campus, and the other in a newer community further east; each of these is in a census tract with median family income over $8,000. In Phoenix the single branch library was in a lower-middle-class Anglo neighborhood, the only neighborhood library in the three cities so placed.[38] That branch aside, it is fair to say that without segregation there would have been no libraries in neighborhoods below the median income in Austin, Phoenix, or Albuquerque.

San Antonio's public libraries provide evidence of shifting priorities as local government changed under the aegis of big-city reform. The city's relatively large number of branches (compared to other big-reform cities) was a legacy of politics is the 1920s and 1930s. The city's oldest branch library, the Carver, was established for the city's African-American population in 1925, testimony to the political skill of the city's most prominent black politician, Charles Bellinger. In the 1930s the city placed small branch libraries in San Antonio's low-income housing projects; in 1960 four of these remained. Under the new city-manager regime inaugurated in 1951, several library studies were written, but no new funding or building occurred through 1962. In that year the Library Board voted to close the four public-housing branches as well as three other older branches. The next year the first new branch of the city library built since

---

[36] Houston more directly named its branch for African-Americans: "Colored Branch."

[37] Orum, *Power, Money*, 200–201.

[38] Both this branch and Harmon may have been built as community libraries before the neighborhood was part of the city. Like Harmon's neighborhood, the area around did not strongly support the CGC in 1959, giving the NPSG only 50.3 percent of its vote. Paul Kelso reports that Charter Government rebuilt the central library and "in 1960 conducted a study to learn the most advantageous sites for branch libraries" (*A Decade of City Manager Government in Phoenix*. 30).

1930 was opened in a newer, Anglo, affluent community on the city's northwest side. The 1960 census count is a deceptive snapshot of a library system between two quite different political regimes, one attentive to lower-income constituents, and the other, big-city reform, in which these residents were politically unimportant.[39]

Municipal parks and recreation departments provided parks, pools, and golf courses. Austin and Phoenix invested heavily in land for parks and recreation; Austin also benefited from contributions of large portions of land for natural reserves and parks.[40] In Phoenix, charter government was particularly proud of the twelve-hundred-acre Papago Park, bought from the state government in 1959, and an archaeological site where a Native American village was reconstructed. Phoenix had also built forty-eight smaller parks and ninety-seven school playgrounds by 1960.[41] Albuquerque required developers to set aside 4 percent of the land in new developments for parks.[42] This requirement bore fruit in the Heights, the rapidly expanding affluent and middle-class section of the city. By 1960 the Heights was scattered with fifty small parks and green areas. In the Valley the only parks were adjacent to schools, and these sometimes private.

In the sweltering Southwest, public swimming pools provided recreation and relief. Phoenix had ten public pools in 1960, six in poor neighborhoods and four in middle-class neighborhoods. Austin's government had built twenty-one pools by 1960, seven in the city's poor and lower-middle-class neighborhoods, six in its affluent neighborhoods, and eight in middle-class areas. In Albuquerque the small number of publicly developed swimming facilities were for less advantaged communities. Albuquerque boasted a "beach" on the Colorado River, created by Clyde Tingley in the 1940s, and two public pools by 1960.

Family recreation was not the only object of municipal parks departments. Municipal golf courses were built everywhere, particularly for the pleasure of more affluent constituents, as well as to provide green space to their neighborhoods. In Austin in 1951, community leader Everett

[39] Heywood T. Sanders, "Rethinking Lineberry and Urban Service Delivery: Politics, Dollars and Libraries in San Antonio" (paper prepared for the annual meeting of the Urban Affairs Association, Indianapolis, April 1993). On the basis of his historical study of San Antonio, Sanders concludes that Robert Lineberry (*Equality and Urban Policy: The Distribution of Municipal Public Service* [Beverly Hills: Sage, 1977]) was "just plain wrong." Looking at six cities, I am persuaded that Sanders was just exactly right.

[40] The existence of large parks available to the whole community (once they were desegregated) makes counting neighborhood parks less relevant. I do count pools, however, below.

[41] Papago Park was the only acreage added to the city's public parks in the decade 1950–60. Kelso, *Decade*, 29.

[42] Wood, "Transformation," 177.

Givens was promised a golf course for the African-American community in response to support for an upcoming bond issue. After the election Givens went to the city council, where the extravagance of constructing another golf course was immediately protested. The result—integrating the existing municipal golf course—was perhaps what Givens intended.[43] In 1960, Austin had two public golf courses, one on the west side just south of affluent Tarrytown, and one near middle-class Hyde Park. Phoenix had two golf courses just north of downtown in Encanto Park and was planning two more.[44]

The provision of public amenities was not very high on the agenda of big-city reform governments. This seems to have been particularly true in Albuquerque and Phoenix, with their tiny library systems and smaller park systems. There parks were better provided for middle-class and affluent communities, pools for less affluent communities. Austin built more of everything and distributed it less equitably, the middle-class and affluent communities receiving almost all the amenities save those originally designed as the segregated library, park, and community recreation center for African-Americans. (With this in mind, it is hardly surprising that Austin elections sometimes looked like class warfare.)

City governments in big reform cities did not manage the school systems, which were in the hands of county governments or independent school districts. Yet since schools are so very salient to residents' sense of well being, they deserve some attention here. A gross measure of community satisfaction with public schools may be found in the proportion of children attending public schools (the remainder attending private schools). Table 7-6 shows the proportion of elementary-school children and high-school students in the public schools in big reform cities, machine descendants, and the affluent suburbs of Scarsdale and Winnetka. By comparison either to the affluent suburbs or to the machine-descendant cities, big reform city schools received overwhelming endorsement from parents. Parents in the big reform cities were much more willing than parents in machine descendant cities, and as willing as parents in Scarsdale, to send their children to public school. For the machine-descendant cities, higher attendance in private schools is no doubt attributable in part to the many Catholic children attending parochial schools. (In the southwestern cities too most private schools are parochial schools.) This hardly takes away from the accomplishment of

[43] Orum, *Power, Money*, 213. Orum does not claim that integrating the existing course was Givens's goal.

[44] The two additional golf courses were for Palo Verde, in a newer and more affluent neighborhood, and Papago Park. Kelso, *Decade*, 29. For Austin, Enco (Humble Oil and Refining Company) Austin-San Antonio Map and Visitors' Guide (Convent Station: General Drafting, 1962).

TABLE 7-6
Percentage of Students in Public Schools, 1960

	Grades 1–8	Grades 9–12
Big City Reform		
Albuquerque	83.5	87.3
Austin	93.1	95.4
Dallas	92.6	94.1
Phoenix	90.0	91.6
San Antonio	83.2	85.9
San Diego	94.2	89.3
San Jose	93.1	92.1
Suburbs		
Scarsdale	87.3	87.0
Winnetka	71.3	76.9
Machine Descendants		
Chicago	65.0	68.3
New Haven	73.9	78.8
New York	69.2	77.7

Source: U.S. Bureau of the Census, *Census of Population, 1960* (Washington, D.C.: Government Printing Office, 1962), table 73, vol. 1, parts 4, 6, 8, 15, 33, 34, 45.

big-reform-city schools: parochial school attendance provides strong evidence that where there is a preference for private schools, families find resources to support them, even without the resources of Winnetka's affluent families.[45]

In Albuquerque the same neighborhoods that strongly supported the Albuquerque Citizens' Committee organized to influence the public high schools. Scientists and engineers arriving at Sandia Labs and Los Alamos in the 1940s were dismayed by Albuquerque high schools. The curricula were not providing adequate preparation for college; math and science classes were neither rigorous nor advanced. For a decade beginning in the mid 1940s, these parents were defeated in their efforts to change the schools by the complacency of the school bureaucracy and the city's "traditional spokesmen," particularly the editor of the *Albuquerque Journal*.

As in many other places, the launching of Sputnik squelched complacency and made converts to the demand for more math and science (also, among other things, Russian). The Sandia Corporation itself promoted

[45] Data are not provided here for the presence of Catholics, since the census does not ask questions about religion. Of course, some children in Catholic schools were not from Catholic families.

and supported revisions in the curriculum. A corporation memo, "Plans for Improving Science and Mathematics Teaching in New Mexico," detailed ten initiatives—from providing summer funds for public school teachers to providing employees to teach in the schools—which were implemented in succeeding years. The critical change was upgrading course offerings. The first high school to upgrade its curriculum, Highland High, added Chemistry II, Biology II, Analytical Geometry, and Russian in 1958. By 1960 the three Heights high schools offered a rich array of advanced courses, while the Valley high schools waited longer for those they did get, and did without others. Valley High, for example, added Chemistry II and Biology II four years later than Highland, and was not offering Russian or Analytical Geometry as late as 1970.[46] The result of more than a decade of organization and campaigning by middle-class parents and their largest employer, then, was dramatically improved college preparatory high-school curriculum for their children.

Valley residents were less aggressive on behalf of their children, but Heights residents and Sandia also had plans for Valley students. In 1964 the city's Technical Vocational Institute (TVI) was established. TVI was "specifically designed to provide marketable vocational skills to those students, largely from the disadvantaged groups, who were not going on to college and who desperately needed such skills to compete economically."[47] Thus the mobilization that led to better preparation for college in the Heights delivered vocational training to the Valley. Similarly, in Dallas recruitment of electronics industries was accompanied by expanded provision of vocational training in the public school system. Surely students who were not going to college benefited from technical and vocational education. Those who know TVI best insist, "Those students get jobs." Without disparaging that accomplishment, we can observe that the students who went to TVI did not have equal opportunities to pursue college-preparatory high-school education.

Everywhere there was complaint about inequities in public education. When the Civil Rights Commission held hearings in Phoenix in 1962, poor schooling for the black community was a prominent issue. In response to *Brown vs. Board of Education*, Phoenix had closed the African-American Carver High School. The reason was not a desire to integrate schools; rather, *Brown vs. Board* provided an opening for Phoenix to reap the savings of not maintaining Carver. Carver's students sim-

---

[46] William M. Hales, Jr., "Technological In-migration and Curricular Change: Educational Politics in Albuquerque, 1945–1965" (Ph.D. diss., University of New Mexico, 1970). See also, "HS Graduation Requirements Hiked," *Albuquerque Journal*, April 9, 1958, 1.

[47] Hales, "Technological In-migration," 173.

ply traveled greater distances to other high schools in the city.[48] Parents in Tempe brought a suit against segregation of Hispanics in the town's school system. In San Diego, where most city leaders were very happy with the school system and citizens voted themselves a large tax burden to support schools generously, African-American and Hispanic leaders voiced criticisms.[49]

Writing about San Antonio, David Johnson and John Booth cautioned, that "the pursuit of progress is one thing; its distribution is another."[50] In the big reform cities of the Southwest, governments targeted the distribution of progress to their strongest political supporters. The same constituency fashioned government's agenda. In these cities the relatively short wish list of the affluent and middle class edged aside the longer lists of other communities. Less comfortable citizens also wanted low-income housing, social services, and public hospitals. Machine-descendant cities provided these services; southwestern city governments left them to county government, private charity, or the market.

Among community leaders there was a range of responses to inequities and lapses in public provision. As leaders in San Diego admired the city's school system and were happy to see it generously supported, so they more generally were satisfied with the performance of city government and oblivious to its deficits, insensitive to its failings for some communities.[51] In Albuquerque the city manager was "sort of oblivious to minorities."[52] In Phoenix, Charter Government leaders made overtures to the African-American community and insisted that their government made progress on issues of discrimination. Barry Goldwater and Harry Rosenzweig supported the organization of the NAACP and the Urban League in Phoenix, Rosenzweig reported advances in the public employment of African-Americans. Austin have-nots found a champion in Emma Long. Even her commitment, however, was limited: in 1956, when Blacks proposed a campaign of civil disobedience to integrate the city's buses, Long declined to support it.[53] In San Diego African-American leaders listed police brutality and lack of employment opportunity in city government as community grievances. The city's administration, in re-

[48] Calvin Goode, "The Glory that Was Carver High School" (remarks delivered at the opening of the African-American Cultural Center in Phoenix, May 1994) (typescript given to the author by Mr. Goode).

[49] Greenstone, "Report," VI-22–VI-29.

[50] Preface in *The Politics of San Antonio: Community, Progress, and Power*, ed. David R. Johnson, John A. Booth, and Richard J. Harris (Lincoln: University of Nebraska Press, 1983), ix.

[51] Greenstone, "Report," V-62, VI-23.

[52] Author's interviews, May 1994.

[53] Orum, *Power, Money*, 254–55.

sponse to a demand for a Commission on Human Relations, argued the presence of the Urban League was enough. While African-American leaders saw discrimination in housing as a problem, Anglos thought segregation was "self-imposed."[54] In San Antonio, "a paternal sense of fairness" informed the Good Government League's aggregation of diverse interests; in Dallas an interventionist elite assertively managed relations among disparate communities.[55]

Low public awareness of disparities and differences seems to have been universal. In San Diego, African-American grievances were "not communicated" to their fellow citizens, as Anglo neighborhoods were "relatively sealed off from the Negro community" and the Mexican-American community as well. In Phoenix the chairman of the Housing Authority despaired, "the northern half of Phoenix doesn't know how the southern half lives. The average Phoenician is interested [only] in his home, job, and recreation."[56]

Textbook Reform

In the 1940s and 1950s, reformers proposed, and saw adopted, new arrangements for local politics. The same reformers organized nonpartisan slating groups to govern their cities. Good government organizations promised, and frequently delivered, efficient administration of the delivery of common services, sustained economic growth, low property taxes, honest government, and adequate public services. Small wonder these governments and the good government organizations that provided their officials were very popular with their limited electorates. The successes of municipal reformers encouraged their opponents to compete on the same terms, but this was almost always a losing strategy. Reformers were unbeatable on their own terms because they delivered satisfactory goods and services to the great majority of voters.

The political community of southwestern cities was a limited one and increasingly so over the course of the postwar period. In Phoenix thirty-four of forty-two city council members elected between 1949 and 1963

---

[54] Greenstone, "Report," V-62–V-66.

[55] For San Antonio, L. L. Sanders, "How to Win Elections in San Antonio the Good Government Way, 1955–1971" (M.A. thesis, St. Mary's University, 1975); for Dallas, Robert B. Fairbanks, "The Good Government Machine: The Citizens Charter Association and Dallas Politics, 1930–1960," in *Essays on Sunbelt Cities and Recent Urban America*, ed. Robert B. Fairbanks and Kathleen Underwood (College Station: Texas A & M University Press, 1990), 125–50.

[56] Konig, "Toward Metropolis," 172.

lived in the northern half of the city at the time of their election.[57] Banfield and Wilson observed the same lack of geographical representation in Berkeley, where "six sevenths of the city officials live on the fashionable 'hill' although more than half the population of the city lives in the low income south and west districts."[58] And in Albuquerque "by 1965 all five commissioners lived in the [well educated, affluent, Anglo] Heights"; from 1954 to 1966 not one resident of the poorer, more Mexican-American and Black Valley served on the city commission.[59]

The residents of Albuquerque's Heights were ardent reform supporters. "Heights residents are zealous," wrote Dorothy I. Cline,

> about "taking politics out of City Hall" and preventing encroachments by the commission on the powers of the [manager]. They believe the well-governed city must be administered by professionally trained, politically neutral executives, utilizing scientific, technical knowledge and modern business methods. Although the corporate, scientific, and research communities are not opposed to the social service functions of government, their advocacy of rational and efficient government coincides with the interests of the middle-class business community—espousing economy, conservative budgetary and taxation policies, an the ideals of individualism.[60]

Whether libraries, schools, or efficient services were the measure, local government rewarded their votes and like-mindedness handsomely.

The limited political community of textbook reform lived within the larger and more diverse communities of big southwestern cities. The best example of the division between the political community and the social community is the exclusion of lower-income neighborhoods, especially communities of color, from annexation by city governments intent on growth and annexation. From the perspective of the diverse metropolitan community, many citizens were less well served than public officials claimed, because some neighborhoods were entirely excluded, because local government was not as frugal as it claimed to be, because the collective benefits government distributed were targeted to the government's core constituents, and because the agenda of local government was limited. A different perspective was expressed well in Phoenix, when federal civil-rights officials held hearings in February 1962. Spokesmen for the

[57] Brent Whiting Brown, "An Analysis of the Phoenix Charter Government Committee as a Political Entity" (M.A. thesis, Arizona State University, 1968), 68.

[58] Edward C. Banfield and James Q. Wilson, *City Politics* (New York: Vintage, 1966), 161.

[59] Dorothy I. Cline and T. Phillip Wolf, "Albuquerque: The End of a Reform Era," in *Urban Politics in the Southwest*, ed. Leonard E. Goodall (Tempe: Arizona State University, 1967), 16.

[60] Cline and Wolfe, "Albuquerque," 13.

city's administration argued that progress was being made, and civil-rights laws could only cause backlash. On the other side, advocates of legislation claimed "all our real and certain progress has been made in response to laws." More succinctly, the president of the Maricopa County NAACP commented, "those people in government and the Pulliam press believe that they know how to solve the problems facing the Negro in Phoenix, which they do not."[61]

In addition to their popularity with Anglo middle-class voters, good-government organizations enjoyed political dominance because the rules of local political life made it nearly impossible to successfully compete against them at the polls. Like their predecessors, reformers at midcentury governed political systems of very low participation. By comparison to machine-descendant cities, electoral coalitions supporting local government in reform cities were narrow, resting squarely on the shoulders of the WASP middle class.[62]

The institutional arrangements of municipal reform more dramatically affected the many than the few. Heywood Sanders has argued persuasively that in San Jose and Albuquerque, relations among developers, property owners, and political leaders were much like those between New York's Boss Tweed and his propertied supporters. "Tweed's political accomplishment," Sanders argues, "did not lie in public plunder." Rather, Tweed "created for a brief period a system which radically reduced the cost of urban expansion and land development in New York City, provided the possibility of greater financial rewards from growth, and simultaneously provided both public and private benefits from increased street construction and extension." Tweed's program of street construction and proposed elevated railways was financed by eased special assessment terms, allowing the property tax to remain low. In this way Tweed managed "a new level of public capital investment necessary

---

[61] *Arizona Sun*, February 8, 1962, 1.

[62] In "The Poverty of Urban Services in the Land of Plenty," Peter A. Lupsha and William J. Simbieda construct an elaborate theory for the lower level of service provision in sunbelt cities. Lupsha and Simbieda identify eight conditions for service provision: favorable values among local elites, wealth, population growth, proximity to service-providing communities, equal and advanced politicization of the citizenry, supportive local political culture, shared views of equity, and complexity (in *The Rise of the Sunbelt Cities*, ed. David C. Perry and Alfred J. Watkins [Beverly Hills: Sage, 1977], 169–90). My own view is that causes and effects are here considerably confused; much of this lists suggests simply that if everyone agrees on services, there will be services. Alas, disagreement is endemic, except in Winnetkas. Cottrell's argument that political representation is the critical determinant, which Lupsha and Simbieda critique, seems both more economical and more persuasive. C. L. Cottrell, "Municipal Services Equalization in San Antonio, Texas: Exploration in China Town" (St. Mary's University Department of Urban Studies, 1976). The political representation argument also explains disparity among neighborhoods within these cities.

to the wave of private development and building that was to engulf New York City." In the process Tweed gained the support of many builders and their workers, real estate investors, and residents with newly paved streets.[63] Relations among political leaders, property owners, and public finance was, Sanders argued, much the same in San Jose and Albuquerque as these cities embarked on large scale expansion in the postwar period. "Albuquerque's politicians," for example, "and its engineering firms were historically joined in a marriage of joint benefit, economic return and growth promotion."[64] Both in the Southwest and in Tweed's New York (although Sanders does not mention this), the legacy of these arrangements was burgeoning debt. Indeed, it was Tweed's mismanagement of sales of municipal bonds that was his downfall. In the Southwest, annexation—which spread costs to an ever increasing population— postponed the political cost of accumulating indebtedness. In sharp contrast to the values of economy, conservative budgetary practice, and individualism cited by Dorothy Cline, the new millionaires of Phoenix, Dallas, San Jose, and other southwestern cities built their fortunes on activist local governments. The close ties among banking, political, construction, and real estate elites and the uneven benefits big-city reform distributed provoked historian Arnold Hirsch to comment that the self-proclaimed Good Government factions of southwestern cities might more credibly have been called Rapacious Land Developers on one hand and Businessmen United for Minority Repression on the other.[65]

The civic statesmen of big-city reform would have given a different account of themselves. Looking over the postwar period, these leaders could claim to have planned and managed unprecedented growth. Civic statesmen recruited industry, saving their cities from postwar recession; they also coordinated the gargantuan effort of building and capital investment to provide homes, roads, water, and electricity for their rapidly growing populations. More, under their aegis, public schooling was upgraded and modernized; parks, pools, and golf courses were built, libraries provided, airports expanded, tax rates controlled. Not only did big-city reform governments provide quality services and amenities, they also did so without scandal at the top of the municipal hierarchy or patronage at the bottom.

Of these achievements voters were frequently reminded. At each itera-

[63] Sanders, "Beyond Machine," 19.

[64] Ibid., 21; see also Heywood Sanders, "Building a New Urban Infrastructure: The Creation of Postwar San Antonio," in *Urban Texas, Politics and Development*, ed. Char Miller and Heywood T. Sanders (College Station: Texas A & M Press, 1990), 154–73.

[65] National Endowment for the Humanities and the National Science Foundation, Conference Panel Commentary, "The Sunbelt: A Region and Regionalism in the Making?" Miami, November 1985.

tion of the argument between reformers and politicians, and after each political victory, the word of "good government" was made flesh in electoral arrangements, political institutions, policy processes, and governmental outcomes of all sorts. Generations of municipal reformers named, described, and practiced "good government," good politics, good administration, and good public policy. For the small political communities in these cities, as for the Heights residents Cline described, "Culture and structural circumstance [reinforced] each other; the environment made plausible the ethos that affirmed it.[66] Because the municipal reform movement was empowered, by its victories, to set its own standards and then live up to them, "good government" and all that went with it were, within the political community they created, self-evident. Affluent and middle class voters knew what good government was, they knew they had it, and they knew it was good. Exhibiting low voter turnout and an absence of significant competition, oblivious or indifferent to South Phoenix, Albuquerque's Valley, East Austin, San Ysidro, and like communities across the Southwest, local politics was a community of shared values, expectations, and satisfactions.

[66] Here I am paraphrasing Swidler: "In settled lives . . . culture and structural circumstance seem to reinforce each other. This is the situation about which . . . Clifford Geertz . . . writes so persuasively: culture is a model of and a model for experience; and cultural symbols reinforce an ethos, making plausible a world-view which in turn justifies the ethos." Ann Swidler, "Culture in Action: Symbols and Strategies" *American Sociological Review*, 51, no. 2 (April 1986): 278.

Eight

The Politician and the Crowd

IN 1960 the formidable supports of reform regimes seemed impervious to the scattered discontents of local politics. Supporting reform governments were a set of rules making successful opposition extremely difficult, a public discourse that justified government priorities and institutions, relatively efficient delivery of quality services to a majority of the electorate, and a well-organized elite that, over a long period, maintained a consensus both among themselves and with a plurality of the electorate about the goals and arrangements of local politics. Potentially unsettling these arrangements were the rising costs of local government, lacunae in the provision of services and amenities, divisions among economic elites, and increasing activism for civil rights, both locally and nationally.

The deficiencies of local government were voiced by increasingly assertive opponents in elections. Insurgent candidates declared "father knows best" government inadequate, decried city government's indifference to the less fortunate, and chafed at politicians' ignorance of neighborhood concerns. For the first time in the postwar period, insurgent candidates did well in elections. These elections are described in the first section below, "Challenges at the Polls." The subsequent section, "Then Comes the Politician," describes the political impact of electoral challenges. One result was that in the 1960s and 1970s local politicians worked to respond to discontents with city government, more openly accommodating competing claims than in the 1950s. Intermittently, more liberal administrations took the place of dominant NPSG administrations. Big-city reform governments accepted federal funds for urban renewal, model cities, and the war on poverty. With federal funds came the complicated consequences that participation in these programs created.

In the same years, civil rights advocates challenged the institutional arrangements of local politics in the courts; "Contests in Court" traces legal argument about the rules of local politics. By the middle of the 1970s, communities of color were not alone in their dissatisfaction with big-city reform. "Rewriting the Rules" explains the appearance of coalitions supporting rewriting the rules of big-city reform to change city council elections from citywide contests to election by districts. "And All the Crowd" assesses the import of this most recent refounding of the big cities of the Southwest.

Challenges at the Polls

In the 1960s the underpinnings of big-city reform began to give way. The political unanimity of the central constituency of local politics—Anglo middle-class voters—unraveled as neighborhoods resisted the increased costs of government, resented the thin offering of amenities, became sympathetic to the War on Poverty and civil rights agendas, or (somewhat later) supported limited, managed, or no-growth policies for their cities. In the same years, War on Poverty initiatives amplified the voices and increased the political leverage of communities campaigning for civil rights and more equal treatment by city government.

One symptom of these developments was that the character of political opposition changed, losing some of its "me too" quality and calling for changes in the direction of local government. In Phoenix, Albuquerque, San Antonio, and Dallas, opposition slates in the mid-1960s denounced local government as unrepresentative and undemocratic, and supported public housing, increased efforts on behalf of teenagers, or other liberal measures, and particularly solicited the support of minority communities. These challenges did not entirely displace "me too" opposition or challenges from homeowners who felt oppressed by their tax burden and insufficiently supplied with amenities. Rather, the number and range of opposing candidates increased.

In Albuquerque in 1966, the People's Committee for Better Government named a slate of lawyer Pete Domenici, engineer Harry Kinney, and Santa Fe foreman John Gurule. Gurule, a Hispanic, was a resident of the Valley and active in veterans' affairs. Enjoying the support of a contingent of former Albuquerque Citizens' Committee (ACC) members but also showcasing Gurule, the People's Committee could claim better to represent the city's diversity. Promising more "openness" in city government, to raise the wages of municipal employees, and to curtail the autonomy of the city manager, the People's Committee enjoyed the active support of the city's unions, which broke with tradition and endorsed council candidates for the first time since the Second World War.[1]

In Dallas in 1965, Elizabeth Blessing led the ticket of the Dallas Charter League against incumbent mayor Erik Jonsson, who led the Citizens' Charter Association (CCA) ticket. "I have no dedication," announced Blessing, "to the status quo, to closed meetings, closed doors, and closed minds. The 'father knows best' approach is not good enough for the city." The League's program included expanding the police force, restor-

---

[1] Robert Turner Wood, "The Transformation of Albuquerque, 1945–1972" (Ph.D. diss., University of New Mexico, 1980), 256–57.

ing public health efforts, and building public housing in West Dallas. The same election saw the first African-American candidates for the city council (one on the League's ticket, one as an independent). Calling the League "outsiders," the CCA campaigned against "politicians," "especially . . . those whose business accomplishments record no notable successes." Mayor Jonsson dismissed his opponent with the remark that Blessing belonged back in her kitchen.[2] By this time criticism had spread to the national media, as *Fortune* and the *Wall Street Journal* explained how business had failed Dallas.

In Phoenix in 1963, the challenging Action Citizens' Ticket (ACT) nominated a former Democratic member of Congress, Richard Harless, for mayor, placed an African-American and a Mexican-American on its slate for the city council, and enjoyed the active support of the city's Central Labor Council.[3] The ACT platform called for greater efforts against crime, poverty, and illiteracy, especially on behalf of the city's teenagers.[4] "The administration has grown lax in services and concern for the young people," Harless charged.[5] The *Arizona Gazette* denounced the ACT as a vehicle of "two selfish interest factions, the small political cadre of organized labor and the radical liberal wing of the Democratic party."[6] In the same election, the Honesty, Economy, and Representation (HEAR) ticket fielded candidates promising that a HEAR administration "will not annex more territory until the city can afford proper city services for all of its present areas," opposing a housing code, and insisting "present ordinances . . . are adequate to deal with problems of health and welfare."[7]

In San Jose in 1962, the insurgents were middle-class homeowners who felt overtaxed and underserved.[8] In Austin a more diffuse unhappiness meant "challengers could agree that they opposed pro-business incumbents, but could not agree among themselves on any form of electoral cooperation or on how they might combine, if elected, to form a new majority on the council."[9] In San Antonio, beginning in 1961, a

[2] Carolyn Jenkins Barta, "The *Dallas News* and Council-Manager Government" (M.A. thesis, University of Texas, Austin, 1970), 112–15.

[3] Leonard E. Goodall, "Phoenix: Reformers at Work," in *Urban Politics in the Southwest*, ed. Leonard E. Goodall (Tempe: Arizona State University Press, 1967), 120.

[4] Kenneth Stites, Jr., "A Study of Nonpartisanship: The 1963 Phoenix Municipal Primary Election" (M.A. thesis, Arizona State University, 1964), 69.

[5] *Arizona Gazette*, November 4, 1963, 12.

[6] Ibid., November 11, 1963, 1.

[7] Stites, "Nonpartisanship," 69.

[8] Philip J. Trounstine and Terry Christenson, *Movers and Shakers: The Study of Community Power* (New York: St. Martin's Press, 1982), 99.

[9] David M. Olson, "Austin: The Capital City," in *Urban Politics in the Southwest*, ed. Leonard E. Goodall (Tempe: Arizona State University Press, 1967), 34.

series of opposition tickets appealed to working men, the poor, African-Americans, and Mexican Americans; denounced the Good Government League (GGL) as a "machine"; and advocated better wages for public employees, recruitment of industry, and provision of recreation facilities in less advantaged communities. GGL defense began with complacency in 1961, escalated to active campaigning in the Mexican-American community in 1963, gained vehemence during the candidacy of independent Pete Torres in 1967, and closed the decade in 1969 by denouncing incumbent Torres as allied with "a small violence oriented group" that threatened "bloodshed" were Torres reelected. (He was.)[10]

Elections were more closely contested than in the 1950s, as opposition slates did better at the polls than the insurgents of the 1950s. Their popularity increased competitiveness and, in some cities, brought more voters to the polls (see table 8-1). Heretofore invulnerable NPSGs took their first losses. In Phoenix in 1963, turnout jumped to 53 percent of registered voters, up from 29 percent in 1961. The Charter Government Committee (CGC) lost on the south side of the city (home to Phoenix's communities of color), and its candidate for mayor was forced into a runoff, the first since the CGC was formed in 1949. Not only did the CGC lose outright on the city's south side (which it had carried comfortably in 1961), but also saw support for the ticket plummet on the north side, always the home of the CGC's most faithful and enthusiastic supporters.[11] In Dallas independent candidates won greater representation on the city council by 1963 than at any time since 1937, and although the challenger, Elizabeth Blessing, lost the race for mayor in 1965, another independent won a seat on the city council. In Albuquerque the People's Committee won all three commission seats in 1966, benefiting from strong support in the newly annexed areas in the south Valley. Pete Torres's victory in 1967 marked the first loss ever for San Antonio's Good Government League.

This was just the beginning of election-year challenges to dominant NPSGs. In Phoenix in 1965, the Charter Government Committee lost a city council seat to a challenger; although the CGC regrouped, it lost the mayoralty in 1973, and in 1975 lost the mayoralty and four of six city

[10] L. L. Sanders, "How to Win Elections the Good Government Way, 1955–1971" (M.A. thesis, St. Mary's University, 1975), 18–49.

[11] The precinct loss in the northwest was to the ultraconservative HEAR ticket. Brent Whiting Brown, "An Analysis of the Phoenix Charter Government Committee as a Political Entity" (M.A. thesis, Arizona State University, 1968), 61–62., Goodall, "Phoenix," 120–21. The highest vote getter for city council on the ACT ticket received 35,000 votes, while the lowest vote getter on the CGC ticket received 37,851 votes (Ibid., 120). Support in the northwest quadrant fell from 75 percent in 1961 to 53 percent in 1963, in the northeast quadrant from 76 percent in 1961 to 61 percent in 1963 (Brown, "Analysis," appendix C).

THE POLITICIAN AND THE CROWD

council seats. That was the last CGC slate.[12] In San Antonio the Good Government League suffered fatal divisions in the same year. In Albuquerque the vanquished Citizens' Committee joined forces with the People's Committee after 1967, but the new People's Committee never achieved the dominance of the old Albuquerque Citizens' Committee.

Then Comes the Politician

In response to challenges at the polls and escalating civil rights activity, incumbent NPSGs nominated more diverse slates for election, offered democratizing reforms in city government or NPSG organization, and embraced limited liberal policy initiatives. Some administrations made these concessions while insisting that they were staying the course. Dallas's mayor Erik Jonsson, the *Wall Street Journal* explained, "is no flaming liberal. But he is a pragmatist." Jonsson accepted federal assistance for slum clearance in Dallas because he recognized "Private enterprise . . . won't get the job done."[13] Others declared their commitment to making local policy outcomes more equitable. There were also concessions to civil rights demands. These efforts did not, in any city, take the center of the political stage; there were neither John Lindsays nor Frank Rizzos in the big reform cities of the Southwest. Rather, liberalizing and War on Poverty efforts represented marginal, and in some places only fleeting, changes in government's agenda. Nevertheless, these initiatives meant the political accommodation of diverse demands was brought out of secret negotiations, there was greater public recognition of diversity and inequality, and made it considerably more difficult for politicians to blithely claim that public policy served "the good of the whole."

Slates for municipal office, appointments to city commissions, and municipal workforces were made more diverse. In San Antonio in 1963, the Good Government League actively campaigned in Mexican-American neighborhoods for the first time and added four Spanish-surnamed candidates to its slate for the city council. Two years later the GGL nominated an African-American minister for the city council. In the 1965 election in Phoenix, the Charter Government Committee placed an African-American educator and a Mexican-American union official on its slate,

---

[12] The *Phoenix Gazette*'s obituary for the slating group concluded, "Charter's noble principle of slating candidates who represent virtue and civic achievement seems esoteric at a time when more down-to-earth problems trouble big city residents." Bradford Luckingham, *Phoenix: The History of a Southwestern Metropolis* (Tucson: University of Arizona Press, 1989), 181.

[13] *Wall Street Journal*, November 17, 1967, 1.

TABLE 8-1
Turnout in Municipal Elections, 1965–1989 (percentage of adults voting)

	Big-City Reform							Machine Descendants		
	Albuquerque	Austin	Dallas	Phoenix	San Antonio	San Diego	San Jose	Chicago	New Haven	New York
1965	—	16.8	13.3	18.8	10.7	—	50.5	—	53.9	47.2
1966	25.1	—	—	—	—	—	—	—	—	—
1967	16.0	24.1	16.6	19.1	8.9	36.7	62.0	51.1	45.7	—
1968	—	—	NA	—	—	—	—	—	—	44.4
1969	—	25.8	—	26.8	17.5	—	55.2	—	48.2	44.4
1970	—	—	—	—	—	—	—	50.5	49.7	—
1971	21.4	33.3	8.0	13.5	NA	42.7	60.2	50.5	49.7	—
1972	—	—	—	—	—	—	—	—	36.5	31.8
1973	—	35.5	8.6	13.1	13.7	—	40.2	—	36.5	31.8
1974	14.5	—	—	—	—	—	—	32.4	42.0	—
1975	—	35.2	13.2	13.1	13.7	25.9	51.6	32.4	42.0	—
1976	—	—	—	—	—	—	—	—	37.1	26.8
1977	27.3	25.8	6.2	19.2	23.6	—	40.0	—	37.1	26.8
1978	—	—	—	—	—	—	—	40.2	34.1	—
1979	—	NA	7.4	21.5	18.2	23.7	46.6	40.2	34.1	—
1980	—	—	—	—	—	—	—	—	26.2	22.9
1981	31.1	25.7	9.9	12.3	28.7	—	—	—	26.2	22.9

Year										
1982	—	—	—	—	—	—	38.2	—	—	—
1983	—	25.9	1.9	22.1	NA	29.2	—	62.8	35.8	—
1984	—	—	—	—	—	—	47.6	—	—	—
1985	30.7	21.8	10.6	NA	21.4	—	—	—	25.6	19.1
1986	—	—	—	NA	NA	27.3	32.3	—	—	—
1987	—	—	15.3	NA	—	—	—	53.5	23.8	—
1988	—	18.5	—	NA	NA	50.7	44.9	—	—	—
1989	23.0	—	11.3	—	—	—	—	51.5	30.8	31.7
Average	21.3	21.9	10.1	19.1	15.8	33.7	47.4	48.9	33.5	32.0
Median	24.0	25.7	9.9	19.1	21.4	29.2	47.1	51.5	36.8	22.9

Sources: For Albuquerque, Dallas, San Diego, San Jose, and Chicago, respective Offices of the City Clerk. For Austin, "Elections, 1924–1979" (City of Austin, Public Information Office, 1979), 1981–1989, Office of the City Clerk; San Antonio, L. L. Sanders, "How to Win Elections in San Antonio: The Good Government Way, 1955–1971" (M.A. thesis, St. Mary's University, 1979), and Juanita Hernandez, "Chicano Mobilization in San Antonio City Politics, 1972–1981" (senior thesis, Harvard University, 1981); *San Antonio Express*. For New Haven, *New Haven Register*. For New York, *New York Times*. For Phoenix, *Phoenix Gazette*.

taking "the steam out" of the ACT effort.[14] In Dallas an African-American was appointed to fill a vacancy on the city council (although the CCA withheld a nomination from him in the succeeding election). In Austin by the middle of the 1960s, African-Americans had been "moderately upgraded in city employment, Negro leaders have been appointed to city boards, city services are being improved in the Negro areas, and city facilities have been desegregated."[15]

Concessions were offered to democratize local politics. In Dallas the CCA initiated a "grass roots" nominating system in which districts nominated candidates for the CCA slate. (Candidates for the city council were designated by district but elected by voters citywide). The limits of this system were quickly demonstrated as the CCA rejected two grass roots nominees from affluent North Dallas in 1965, placing other names on the CCA ticket. Two years later the CCA platform included a promise of adding two more districts to the city charter, with the understanding that these would accommodate minority representation. In 1968 voters approved expanding the council from nine to eleven seats, and the next year an African-American was elected to the city council on the CCA ticket. San Jose also appointed minority representatives to the city council, and direct election of the mayor was initiated in 1967. In Austin the city council was increased from five to seven members in the same year.[16]

Local administrations also accepted, and sometimes endorsed, statutes protecting civil rights and federal initiatives for physical rebuilding and the alleviation of poverty. In Phoenix the administration of Milton Graham enacted both an open-housing ordinance and a public accommodations ordinance, banning segregation. The city council also created a Human Rights Commission in 1963.[17] Despite protests against federal intervention and resistance to sharing authority over local policy decisions, the money provided by urban renewal, the war on poverty, and model cities programs was seductive. Phoenix, San Diego, San Jose, Albuquerque, Austin, Dallas, and San Antonio all participated in these programs.

In Albuquerque the People's Committee for Better Government provided an interlude of more liberal administrations. People's Committee governments invested in solving the Valley's flooding problems and also built five small parks in Valley neighborhoods (one of which was outside

[14] Goodall, "Phoenix," 124.

[15] Olson, "Capital City," 35.

[16] Frank Staniszewski, "Ideology and Practice in Municipal Government Reform: A Case Study of Austin" (Austin: University of Texas, Studies in Politics, series I, no. 8, 1977), 43.

[17] Luckingham, *Phoenix*, 213–14.

city limits).[18] To demonstrate its responsiveness to the citizenry, the People's Committee initiated community visits by commission members to listen to neighborhood "gripes" (although, confronted with complaints, one commission member declared, "I'm not going to drop down [sic] to these meetings to discuss your problems if we're going to hear what the terrible old city hasn't done.")[19] Although Albuquerque accepted urban renewal, War on Poverty, and Model Cities funds, commitment to federal initiatives was uneven. Plans to refurbish downtown with urban renewal monies were more aggressively and successfully pursued than War on Poverty efforts.[20] In Austin, too, government support for facilities improvements was more certain than programs for alleviating poverty. This could hardly have been unpopular: paving and draining were the first priority of residents of poverty areas.[21]

In San Antonio the participatory impulses of the War on Poverty and Model Cities were overwhelmed by government's commitment to building. Bricks and mortar were good priorities for the growth machine and not controversial to other citizens. Building schools became the first priority of the programs, and as late as 1980 it was new school building that people first thought of when asked about Model Cities.[22] Another construction project, Apache Creek Improvement, although it was meant to alleviate flooding, required moving hundreds of families and dozens of businesses. Although there were funds for housing rehabilitation, the required lot size disqualified most residents of the Model Cities area. With War on Poverty funding, some social services were briefly available, including day care, enabling welfare mothers to pursue job training or employment. Most such initiatives, however, were controversial.[23]

[18] Interview with Harry Kinney, July 1994.

[19] Wood, "Transformation," 261. The speaker was Pete Domenici.

[20] Ibid., 260–61, 288–89.

[21] Staff and neighborhood representatives in the Model Cities program proposed expanding mobile and neighborhood health clinics, providing temporary housing for families whose homes were being rehabilitated, Spanish lessons for police officers, and an ombudsman service, all of which were rejected by the city council. The proposal submitted to HUD including paving, sidewalks, fire stations, day-care services, a community service center, housing, job training for twenty-four men, a program for runaway youth, and a community-relations program for police. Cecelia Babcock Smith, "The Austin Model Cities Program" (M.A. thesis, University of Texas at Austin, 1970), 18–19, 68–72.

[22] Sister Frances Jerome Woods, *The Model Cities Program in Perspective: The San Antonio, Texas, Experience* (Washington, D.C.: Government Printing Office, 1982), 161–62, 169.

[23] Hostility to public housing and bilingual education were matters of law: the city charter provided that no public housing could be built in urban renewal areas; state legislation prohibited bilingual instruction for more than an hour a day. Woods, *San Antonio*, 187. The Phoenix effort for the War on Poverty was a public-private partnership christened Leadership and Education for the Advancement of Phoenix (LEAP), which became a city

In San Diego, Mayor Frank Curran's administration was more concerned than its predecessors with the problems of lower-income neighborhoods. Curran himself, as a council member, had represented the city's poorest areas. Curran created an Economic Development Corporation to promote industrial growth and create jobs and accepted Model Cities and War on Poverty funds as well. Although the city began both Head Start and job-training initiatives, and despite the involvement of more than eleven thousand residents in community action meetings, here as elsewhere there was little to show for War on Poverty efforts. In San Ysidro the two issues of greatest community concern were a proposed freeway and the placement of many Spanish-speaking children in an educational track for the mentally retarded. Community protest against the freeway did not stop its construction, although protest did result in more adequate public housing for displaced families. Progress was made on the schools issue, with the assistance of the director of the local community action agency.[24] Here as elsewhere academic chroniclers of the War on Poverty observed that there was no "culture of poverty"; rather, poverty-area residents were simply "middle class without money." And here as elsewhere there was "no . . . evidence that financial resources of any group, governmental or private, have been committed . . . toward alleviating poverty." The program's legacies were improved service delivery and Head Start.[25]

Although War on Poverty funds were accepted, commitments were ambivalent and uncertain, and their impermanence was frustrating. One administration in Albuquerque embraced Urban Renewal, the next abandoned it; one administration in San Jose pursued Model Cities funds, the next rejected them. During the mildly liberal administration of Harry Akin in Austin (1967–69), the city both pursued Model Cities funds and passed a fair-housing ordinance (1968). The ordinance was repealed the

department in 1966. In July 1967 LEAP reported "52 job placements out of 250 contacts." Even program supporters claim little for it in retrospect. Bradford Luckingham, *Minorities in Phoenix* (Tucson: University of Arizona Press, 1994), 175–76. In 1970 John Crow reported, in Arizona, "exclusivity is an attitude which pervades formal and informal decision situations." As a result, "arguments from the poor [that they should be represented] are not so much responded to in kind but are met with incredulity and bafflement." "Urban Politics in Arizona," in *Politics in the Urban Southwest*, ed. Robert D. Wrinkle (Albuquerque: University of New Mexico, Institute for Social Research and Development, publication no. 81, September 1971), 32.

[24] Donald Kurtz, "Politics, Ethnicity, and Integration: Mexican-Americans in the War on Poverty" (Ph.D. diss., University of California, Davis, 1970), 198–99.

[25] Wayman Crow, "The War on Poverty on San Diego County," (typescript, Western Behavioral Sciences Institute, La Jolla, 1968), 47, vii, x.

next year by referendum, and in the succeeding election those who had supported it were defeated.[26]

At the same time that there was widespread disappointment with the War on Poverty and related efforts, federal initiatives became entwined with local civil rights activism, amplifying the voice and political presence of the poor and communities of color. In San Antonio, city bureaucrats attended meetings on the Hispanic west side, where most "had never set foot before," and federal programs also gave neighborhood leaders access to the city council, agency officials, and municipal department heads.[27] By 1970 in San Diego, the Anglo elite's complacent assessment of the local housing supply, school system, and economic opportunities, described by David Greenstone in 1960, had been replaced by more sober evaluations. Local elites now viewed poverty and race relations as the city's most pressing problems.[28]

Enhancing the political presence of poor communities meant more than raising the consciousness of local elites. Federal requirements increased representation both in the municipal workforce (minority hiring was pressed on San Jose under threat of losing General Revenue Sharing funds)[29] and on boards and commissions (in Albuquerque community residents successfully demanded representation on the Urban Renewal Board).[30] More important over the long run, just as their planners in Washington imagined, War on Poverty initiatives contributed to the political organization and mobilization of poor communities.

City governments were not successful in containing the political efforts or establishing the political targets of community activists. In San Jose, where the local administration hoped to use Model Cities funds to "insulate city hall" from political attack, advocacy groups organized under the Model Cities program were in the 1980s "a strong political force."[31] In

[26] Cecelia Babcock Smith, "Model Cities," 40.

[27] Juanita C. Hernandez, "Chicano Political Mobilization in San Antonio City Politics, 1973–1981" (senior thesis, Harvard College, 1981), 44.

[28] Wayman Crow, "War on Poverty," x.

[29] Rufus P. Browning, Dale Rogers Marshall, and David H. Tabb, *Protest Is Not Enough: The Struggle of Blacks and Hispanics for Equality in Urban Politics* (Berkeley: University of California Press, 1984), 177.

[30] Wood, "Transformation," 287.

[31] Writing about San Jose and Oakland, political scientists Browning, Marshall, and Tabb offered a description that suits San Antonio, Dallas, Phoenix, and San Diego as well. Local governments were "economic development conservative, meaning that they favored the vigorous use of government to undertake large-scale economic development activities, but opposed using government to redistribute benefits to minorities." In San Jose, city officials succeeded at using federal initiatives "to insulate city hall from minority demands . . . and divert minority discontent away from city hall and towards the leaders of Model

Phoenix and San Antonio, younger political leaders moved without pause from campus activism to community politics. In Phoenix activists graduating from Arizona State University helped to found Chicanos por la Causa (CPLC), which assisted boycotts of Phoenix Union High School. There parents and students objected that minority students were encouraged to pursue "manual rather than intellectual development," which "produces and perpetuates economic-racial discrimination."[32] Support of the local Catholic church and other agencies meant federal funding reached CPLC without the assistance of the city government, which preferred to work with older organizations.[33] CPLC "initiated many community service programs, including housing, counseling . . . and health clinics," and by 1981 CPLC boasted an operating budget of $6.3 million. Some CPLC alumni pursued careers in the Arizona state legislature; others, less formally, served as effective brokers between the Mexican-American community and Anglo leaders.[34] Similarly, in San Antonio the Coalition for Barrio Betterment, the Mexican American Youth Organization, and the Mexican American Unity Council (MAUC) all received assistance from War on Poverty or Model Cities initiatives, the Ford Foundation, or the Catholic church and continued as activist organizations long after the War on Poverty was over.[35]

Like cities elsewhere in the United States, the big cities of the Southwest were targets of increased civil rights activity in the courts, in public protest, and in negotiations among community leaders. Younger leaders in communities of color took up agendas long pursued by their elders: an end to police brutality, improved opportunities in municipal employment, higher quality schooling, representation among teachers and administrators in the pubic schools, better city services, low-income housing, and open housing ordinances.

In 1969, for example, the Mexican American Legal Defense and Education Fund (MALDEF) won a suit claiming discriminatory employment practices by the San Antonio city government. In Albuquerque the Chi-

---

Cities agencies." Rufus Browning, Dale Marshall, and David H. Tabb, "Implementation and Political Change: Sources of Local Variations in Federal Social Programs" *Policy Studies Journal* 8, no. 4 (1980): 618. But their later assessment, quoted above, saw greater gains for Hispanics as a consequence of the War on Poverty.

[32] Luckingham, *Phoenix*, 216–17.

[33] Interview with Christine Marin, November 15, 1994. By contrast, Phoenix city government chose the NAACP, to which government officials had longstanding ties, to administer the Head Start program. Luckingham, *Phoenix*, 218, 215. For a similar account of Catholic activism on behalf of a Mexican-American community in Los Angeles, see Isidro D. Ortiz, "Chicano Urban Politics and the Politics of Reform in the Seventies," *Western Political Quarterly* 37, no. 4 (December 1984): 56–77.

[34] Luckingham, *Phoenix*, 218.

[35] Hernandez, "Chicano Mobilization," 41.

cano Police Officers Association brought suit against the police department, claiming it discriminated in hiring and promotion. Although the
judge dismissed the case, he warned the city to exercise greater vigilance
in hiring and promotion to avoid more time in court.[36]

Education was a prominent focus for protest and political action. In
San Diego in the spring of 1969, there was a widespread boycott of
schools by Mexican-Americans, protesting the poor education provided.[37] In Phoenix in the same year, Chicanos por la Causa protested
the channeling, by the high school, of Hispanic children into education
for manual employment.[38] In Dallas in 1967, African-Americans
joined forces with dissatisfied Anglo parents to take over the school
board.[39]

Although the municipal administrations of the 1960s and 1970s were
more accommodating than their predecessors in the 1950s, whatever
concessions were offered were viewed as "valuable but peripheral."[40]
There remained compelling reasons to be unhappy with big-city reform.
Poorer communities were cursed with flooding whenever there were
heavy rains in Albuquerque and San Antonio; paving and sewerage were
also sadly deficient in Austin, Phoenix, and San Diego. There were unmet
demands for low-income housing, minority hiring by city government,
and better training of police officers; there was displacement by urban
renewal, and everywhere bitter dissatisfaction with public schooling for
children of color. And not least, there were the discriminatory arrangements of city politics.

Contests in Court

The 1965 Voting Rights Act was the beginning of a series of changes in
the legal environment that dramatically affected the course of big-city
reform. The act abolished literacy tests for five years in places where
voter registration was less than 50 percent of voting age residents. Although the act did not abolish the poll tax (which had been outlawed in
federal elections by the Twenty-fourth Amendment), it did instruct the
attorney general to challenge the constitutionality of poll taxes in state

---

[36] *Albuquerque Journal*, February 8, 1974, 1.

[37] Donald Kurtz, "War on Poverty," 257.

[38] Luckingham, *Phoenix*, 217.

[39] *Wall Street Journal*, November 17, 1967, 26; see also Lee Clark, "Battle of Ideas in
Dallas," *Texas Observer*, May 10, 1967, 13–14.

[40] David Olsen reported that Black leaders in Austin found the city's concessions "valuable but peripheral" ("Capital City," 35).

and local elections. In 1966 federal courts struck down the poll tax in Texas and three other states.[41]

Resistance to these federal dicta was intense. In Texas in the immediate wake of the abolition of the poll tax, the state passed legislation requiring annual voter registration.[42] The new law required voters to register during the four months ending January 31 to vote in elections the following November. This law was ruled unconstitutional in 1971, the court declaring that "it is beyond a doubt that the present Texas voter registration procedures tend to disenfranchise multitudes of Texas citizens otherwise qualified to vote." Four years later the Texas legislature passed yet another registration law that required all voters to register anew. This law was immediately challenged and its implementation enjoined.[43]

In the early 1970s there were still high barriers to voting in Arizona, and there was resistance to lowering them. In 1971 the state enacted a "purge law" requiring voters to reregister. In the same year, Arizona joined a suit in federal court defending the validity of its literacy test. Arizona's literacy test was, by some reports, "selectively applied, especially in counties with significant numbers of Mexican American citizens." Lawyers for Arizona argued that the literacy-test ban was "a blow at the foundation of the state's governmental system," which would be imperiled "if even one illiterate voter were allowed to cast a ballot." Bowing before the inevitable, Arizona repealed its literacy law in 1972. Registration remained difficult. In addition to early closing, "lassitude among registration officials toward reaching those never a part of the electorate and living perhaps a hundred miles from the registration center, and passive dependence on voluntary deputy registrars from the parties" also kept the Arizona's voter registration below 65 percent, the lowest in any northern or western state.[44]

[41] Chandler Davidson, "The Voting Rights Act: A Brief History," in *Controversies in Minority Voting, The Voting Rights Act in Perspective*, ed. Bernard Grofman and Chandler Davidson (Washington, D.C.: Brookings Institution, 1992), 17.

[42] Bryan D. Jones and Delbert A. Taebel, "Urban Politics in Texas," in *Politics in the Urban Southwest*, ed. Robert D. Wrinkle (Albuquerque: University of New Mexico, Institute for Social Research and Development, Publication no. 81, September 1971), 17.

[43] Robert Brischetto, David R. Richard, Chandler Davidson, and Bernard Grofman, "Texas," in *Quiet Revolution in the South: The Impact of the Voting Rights Act, 1965–1990*, ed. Chandler Davidson and Bernard Grofman (Princeton: Princeton University Press, 1994), 240.

[44] John E. Crow, "City Politics in Arizona," 28–29. Crow reported the "more important barrier is the intimidation felt by many Indians and Mexican Americans with modest formal education in English . . . trying to pass [literacy] tests in the presence of a fast-talking or indifferent registration clerk." Opposition to repeal of literacy testing, 32. Repeal of the literacy law, Luckingham, *Minorities in Phoenix*, 48. Luckingham also reports challenges to Mexican-Americans at the polls (49).

The effects of the arrangements of big-city reform were made more apparent once the white primary (1944), poll tax, and literacy testing were abandoned. Even when these unabashedly exclusionary devices were gone, big-city reform—in particular, citywide elections and the nonpartisan slating group—posed high barriers to political efficacy for communities of color. Fraga's research on San Antonio, Abilene, and Dallas argued that nonpartisan slating groups "structured the vote" in at-large elections "to virtually guarantee the success of white, middle- and upper-class voters in city elections."[45] Studies of other cities demonstrated the strong relationship between citywide elections and the absence of descriptive representation.[46]

One symptom of political malaise was racially polarized voting. In Phoenix when the Charter Government Committee lost precincts, it was on the African-American south side; in Albuquerque support for the Albuquerque Citizens' Committee was fragile at best in the Hispanic Valley, and when more of the Valley was annexed to the city, ACC ascendancy was doomed. In Austin poor blacks and whites alike supported insurgent voices on the city council. In San Antonio voting was also racially polarized. Fraga has shown that of ninety-two Good Government League candidates for the city council between 1955 and 1975, seventy-seven (83.7 percent) were the first choice of Anglo voters, while only twenty-five (27.2 percent) were the first choice of Mexican-American voters, and nine (22.5 percent) were the first choice of African-American voters. Examining support for Hispanic candidates nominated by the Good Government League, Fraga found that 72 percent were the first choice of Anglo voters, but only 44 percent were the first choice of Hispanic voters, who preferred insurgent Hispanic candidates.[47]

In San Diego too election outcomes faithfully reflected the political preferences of Anglos rather than Mexican-Americans or blacks. There city council members were nominated in their home districts, but were required to win elections citywide. This system was known in Cleveland as the "black beater." The system beat African-Americans because those militant enough to win nomination in their own districts were too militant to be elected by the citywide electorate. In San Diego, the fourth district's first choice nominee in 1987 lost citywide to another African-

[45] Luis Fraga, "Domination through Democratic Means: Nonpartisan Slating Groups in City Electoral Politics," *Urban Affairs Quarterly* 23, no. 4 (1988): 550.

[46] Peggy Heilig and Robert J. Mundt, *Your Voice at City Hall* (Albany: State University of New York Press, 1984), 5–8 summarizes this research.

[47] "During the period 1961–1975, the predominantly Mexican-American portion of [San Antonio] consistently voted against GGL candidates" (Charles L. Cotrell and R. Michael Stevens, "The 1975 Voting Rights Act and San Antonio, Texas," *Publius* 8, no. 1 [Winter 1978]: 84). Luis Fraga, "Domination," see especially 544–46.

American candidate who had the backing of the African-American political establishment.[48]

Voting-rights legislation provided three openings for challenging these arrangements. One was the concept of "vote dilution," which required some clarification through case law. The second was Section 5 of the Voting Rights Act, which required "pre-clearance" of changes in voting arrangements by the Justice Department. A third opening was provided by the extension of voting-rights protections to language minorities. At-large elections quickly became targets of civil rights advocates under these provisions. In Dallas Albert Lipscomb sought relief from the at-large electoral system on the grounds that it "constitute[d] a dilution of racial minority strength."[49] The addition of "language minorities" greatly expanded the geographic reach of the law to include all of Texas and Arizona[50] and was also important for California. In San Diego the Chicano Federation coordinated legal challenges to election systems in San Diego, San Diego County, Chula Vista, and National City.[51] In Austin MALDEF and MAUC brought suit against the city's at-large election system in 1976.[52] Dallas, San Diego, and Austin were not exceptional; much of the campaign for districts (and later, to redraw the lines of districts) was conducted in federal courts.

The same provisions created openings for escalating challenges to citywide elections in San Antonio. Between 1970 and 1974 the city annexed eighty square miles of neighboring territory; these annexations constituted fully a quarter of the city's territory in 1974. Because the annexations were on the north side of the city, they were additions of overwhelmingly Anglo communities, and because the Mexican-American population of San Antonio hovered around 52 percent, annexations threatened to dilute their voting strength. Civil rights organizations were of course well aware of this threat. Even before the annexations, MAL-

[48] Dean Schloyer, "Ethnic Politics in a Sunbelt City: The Case of San Diego" (M.A. thesis, University of California, San Diego, 1993), 25. In Houston between 1959 and 1979, nine African-American or Mexican-American candidates won their districts but lost the general election to the city council. Jaime Davila, "Houston City Politics: The 1979 Change from At-Large to Single-Member Council Districts and Its Effect on Mexican-Americans" (senior thesis, Harvard University, 1982), chap. 2, pp. 15–17. For the "black beater" in Cleveland, see Lee Sloan, "Good Government and the Politics of Race," *Social Problems* 17 (Fall 1969): 161–74.

[49] Jones and Taebel, "Urban Politics in Texas," 13.

[50] Davidson, "Voting Rights Act," 36. The same change also brought Alaska and scattered counties in other states under Section 5.

[51] Schloyer, "Ethnic Politics," 27.

[52] Frank Staniszewski, "Ideology and Practice in Municipal Government Reform: A Case Study of Austin" (Austin: University of Texas, Studies in Politics, series 1, no. 8, 1977), 52.

DEF had challenged San Antonio's citywide elections as a vote-diluting device that "resulted in disparities of public service, and lead to inequitable minority representation not only on the city council but also on appointed city boards and commissions." Once language minorities were brought under Voting Rights Act protections, San Antonio was required to submit its annexations to the Justice Department for preclearance as an alteration of voting arrangements. MALDEF, the Mexican American Equal Rights Project, the National Reapportionment Rights Project, and neighborhood advocates all submitted briefs to the Justice Department arguing the ill effects of the annexations.[53] The attorney general found these arguments persuasive and concluded that the institutional arrangements of San Antonio's city government, in conjunction with the annexations, did abridge the right to vote of the city's minorities. "One way to remedy this situation," he proposed, "would be to adopt a system of fairly drawn single member wards. Should that occur, the Attorney General will reconsider the matter upon receipt of that information."[54] Despite complaints about federal intervention, the city council placed a referendum proposing district elections on the ballot for January 15, 1977.

Federal rulings made inevitable and quick, outcomes that the institutions of local government made likely in the long run. It was not only communities of color that felt neglected by city government. Anglo middle-class neighborhoods, always the most ardent supporters of big-city reform, also became disaffected. There were good reasons for their disenchantment: the attention of municipal administrations was focused on annexation and expansion; city council members lived clustered in a few neighborhoods; amenities were scarce enough that there were not enough to go around; taxes were going up. On each of these counts, big-city reform alienated its core constituents.

Rewriting the Rules

There were three sources of dissatisfaction with big-city reform in the 1970s and 1980s. First was the desire for descriptive representation, or more precisely (since dominant NPSGs had sometimes nominated diverse slates), that the first-choice candidate of minority communities be elected. Second was the desire for neighborhood representation to increase services provided or influence policies that seemed detrimental to particu-

[53] Hernandez, "Chicano Mobilization," 72–73.

[54] Quoted in Charles L. Cotrell and R. Michael Stevens, "The 1975 Voting Rights Act and San Antonio, Texas: Toward a Federal Guarantee of a Republican Form of Local Government," *Publius* 8, no. 1 (Winter 1978): 79–89, 86.

TABLE 8-2
Population of Southwestern Cities, 1970–1990

	1970	1980	1990
Albuquerque	243,751	330,537	384,736
Austin	251,817	345,496	465,422
Dallas	844,189	904,078	1,006,877
Phoenix	581,600	789,704	983,403
San Antonio	654,289	785,880	935,933
San Diego	696,769	875,538	1,110,549
San Jose	445,779	573,822	782,248

Sources: U.S. Bureau of the Census, *County City Data Book, 1970* (Washington, D.C.: Government Printing Office, 1972), 15.

U.S. Bureau of the Census, *County City Data Book, 1980* (Washington, D.C.: Government Printing Office, 1983), ix.

U.S. Bureau of the Census, *County City Data Book, 1994* (Lanham, Maryland: Bernam Press, 1994), table 3, p. xxvii.

lar neighborhoods. The third was support for managed, controlled, or limited growth, which would mean sharp changes in the direction of public policy.

The antigrowth impulse itself had two strains. One was a desire to lower taxes and restrict the area to which services had to be provided; the second was concern to secure the quality of the natural environment. Inadequate public services were an old story in Mexican-American neighborhoods. Two members of Albuquerque's charter revision committee in 1971, Phoebe Chavez and Orlando Padilla, both from the city's Valley/West End area, "said their neighborhoods did not feel represented in city government." More, "they argued that historically the Heights has developed at the expense of the Valley."[55]

Dissatisfaction with public services was, by the late 1970s, not confined to disadvantaged neighborhoods. As shown in tables 8-2 and 8-3, population and, more importantly, geographical growth continued at a rapid pace through these decades. The result was that local governments were responsible for areas well beyond their capacity to provide services. In Phoenix residents in the northwest quadrant of the city intermittently

[55] *Albuquerque Journal,* June 24, 1971, 1, 5. Padilla and Chavez were supported by the Valley's representatives in the state legislature, who promised to have that body impose districts on the city, were the referenda to fail. "Eight Valley Legislators Back Charter Changes": "If we'd had districting since 1917 when the present charter was written we would have had the flooding problems of Barelas and San Jose solved 35 or 40 years ago," claimed Duven Lujan, legislative adviser to the GI Forum. *Albuquerque Journal,* June 25, 1971, 1–2.

TABLE 8-3
Land Area of Southwestern Cities, 1970–1990 (square miles)

	1970	1980	1990
Albuquerque	82.2	95.3	132.2
Austin	72.1	116.0	217.8
Dallas	265.6	333.0	342.2
Phoenix	247.9	324.0	419.9
San Antonio	184.0	262.7	333.0
San Diego	316.9	320.0	324.0
San Jose	136.2	158.0	171.3

Sources: U.S. Bureau of the Census, *County City Data Book, 1970* (Washington, D.C.: Government Printing Office, 1972), 15.

U.S. Bureau of the Census, *County City Data Book, 1980* (Washington, D.C.: Government Printing Office, 1983), ix.

U.S. Bureau of the Census, *County City Data Book, 1994* (Lanham, Maryland: Bernam Press, 1995), table 3, p. xxvii.

offered support to insurgent candidates. One voter there complained, "the present City Council members don't campaign here, but they don't mind collecting taxes here." Communities resented both the paucity of city services ("My street hasn't been swept in two years") and the absence of neighborhood voices from the planning process. In northwest Phoenix the galvanizing issue was siting of the expressway.[56] Disaffection was not confined to northwest Phoenix. A survey conducted in 1975 showed that fully 50 percent of Phoenix residents polled opposed citywide elections for the city council. Overwhelming majorities of those polled thought the mayor (still an unpaid amateur) should be a full-time, paid official (95 percent) and council members should be full-time as well (57 percent).[57]

Beyond criticism that big-city reform left various constituencies aside, there was criticism of local government's wholehearted commitment to growth and annexation. Some antigrowth sentiment was grounded in the difficulties of paying for an ever expanding metropolis. In Austin the ambitious growth pursued by city government was destructive of the natural environment on one hand, and depleted the city treasury on the other, limiting provision of amenities like libraries. As one observer said, local government pursued policies "that played the whole against the sum of its parts. Neighborhoods found themselves isolated victims of

[56] *Arizona Republic*, December 2, 1982, X-3. Lack of neighborhood representation was also an issue in San Jose. Trounstine and Christensen, *Movers and Shakers*, 105.

[57] David R. Berman and Bruce D. Merrill, "Citizen Attitudes toward Municipal Reform Institutions: A Testing of Some Assumptions," *Western Political Quarterly* 29, no. 2 (June 1976): 273–83.

solutions which caused problems with increased . . . taxes, deteriorating environmental quality." There the Neighborhoods Council (an umbrella group for community organizations) offered an analysis that faulted the city's growth strategy for "serving the interests of a small elite, at the expense of Austin Citizens." The inability of the city to secure approval of general obligation bonds from the electorate between 1976 and 1982 demonstrated that dissatisfaction was widespread.[58]

In San Diego antigrowth sentiment had a long history, only in the 1980s joined to a desire for rewriting the rules. In the 1970s Pete Wilson campaigned for mayor and won by promising, among other things, managed growth. Wilson proved himself a tough negotiator with developer interests on several highly visible issues. The electorate also passed growth-control referenda (although these were ineffective). Rising taxes and thinning services spread over rapidly expanding development gave antigrowth and managed-growth advocates ready audiences in the 1980s.[59] An "alliance of neighborhood groups and slow growth activists" placed a proposition for district elections on the ballot in 1988.[60] One Albuquerque politician dismissed antigrowth sentiment as antitax sentiment. Yet unmanaged growth was destructive of the natural environment, and some Albuquerque residents wanted surrounding mountains protected from development. In San Jose antigrowth sentiment took shape in the slogan "Let's make San Jose better before we make it bigger."[61] In San Antonio too proponents of controlled growth joined in support of district elections.[62]

The common ground of the various discontents with big city reform was not easily found. There was agreement that the current system was unsatisfactory. On that basis, and as a matter of convenience, insurgents of different sorts found themselves assembled under the big tent of campaigns to change the rules of local politics.

[58] Timothy Raymond Mahoney, II, "Neighborhoods and Municipal Politics: A Case Study of Decentralized Power Systems: Austin, Texas (Spring 1981)" (M.A. thesis, University of Texas, Austin, 1983), 80, 84, 89.

[59] Harold Keen, "The Wilson Era: San Diego's New Power Structure," *San Diego Magazine* 25, no. 7 (May 1973); Nico Calavita, "Growth Machines and Ballot Box Planning: The San Diego Case," *Journal of Urban Affairs* 14, no. 1 (Winter 1992): 1–24.

[60] Schloyer, "Ethnic Politics," 39. This initiative was independent of the Chicano Federation lawsuit against San Diego. Hispanics and African-Americans supported the proposition despite strained relations with slow-growth advocates.

[61] This was a campaign slogan of mayoral candidate Janet Gray Hayes in 1974 (she won). Trounstine and Christensen, *Movers and Shakers*, 104.

[62] Sidney Plotkin, "Democratic Change in the Urban Political Economy: San Antonio's Edward's Aquifer Controversy," in *Politics of San Antonio: Community, Progress, and Power*, ed. David R. Johnson, John A. Booth, and Richard J. Harris (Lincoln: University of Nebraska Press, 1983), chap. 8.

In striking contrast to other organized efforts to change the rules, the National Municipal League was peripheral to institutional change. Changes in city charters creating districts were not heralded by the *National Civic Review*, as adoptions of commission and city-manager charters had been earlier in the century. Nor did the *Review* headline the court and Justice Department decisions affecting local political institutions. The Model City Charter remained unchanged from 1964 through 1990, when the League published the Seventh Model City Charter. Again endorsing the city manager (with or without a mayor) and nonpartisanship, the charter listed alternative arrangements for city council—citywide election, mixed systems, and districts. Essays in the *National Civic Review* insisted that (court or no court) it was hardly obvious that districts were superior to citywide elections. Admitting that the Seventh Model City Charter allowed a choice of city council arrangements, one historian of structural reform wrote in the *National Civic Review* that the league continued to endorse the "at-large principle."[63]

Those involved in local politics were not so complacent about long-standing premises of reform city government. Proponents of district elections argued government would be more democratic, accountable, representative, and accessible; that the costs of campaigns would be lower and that public policy would be more equitable if districts were adopted. Opponents argued that local government was not broken and so needed no fixing. Some opponents saw Armageddon approach as districts would bring corruption, ward politics, social division, and "brown power."

Supporters of district elections for the city council argued that districts would make local government more democratic—more open, representative, accessible, and accountable—assuring citizens of both direct representation of neighborhood interests and of the accountability of city officials. "Electing council members from eight equal districts brings the selection of our city government out in the open," argued Terry Goddard in Phoenix. "Under the present system, a small group of self-appointed manipulators control who is elected to the City council. These men have operated under the assumption that they and they alone know what is best for the city."[64] "What it really means is it will bring politics closer to

[63] National Civic League, *Model City Charter*, 7th ed. (Denver, 1992); Howard D. Hamilton, "Choosing a Representation System: More than Meets the Eye," *National Civic Review* 69, no. 8 (September 1980): 427–34; William N. Cassella, Jr., "Representative Government: Expressing, Interpreting, and Legislating the Will of the People" (317–22), and James H. Svara, "The Structural Reform Impulse in Local Government: Its Past and Relevance to the Future" (323–43), both in *National Civic Review*, 83, no. 3 (Summer–Fall 1994), 337, cites "the importance of the at-large principle."
[64] *Arizona Republic*, November 28, 1982, A14.

the people and . . . this means democracy to me" argued state representative Frank Madla in San Antonio.[65]

Advocates of district elections claimed that if districts were adopted the costs of campaigning for office would be lowered. "Under the present system" argued proponents of districts in Phoenix, "City council candidates must influence hundreds of thousands of voters citywide. This encourages mass media campaigns instead of personal contacts. Special interests who can make large campaign contributions are assured access to the City Council, while individual citizens and neighborhoods are excluded."[66] In San Antonio it was argued, similarly, that districts would do away with the "money politics" of expensive citywide elections, while compensating city council members would change a system which did not allow "any but financially independent people to serve."[67]

In Albuquerque in 1971, environmentalists sponsored Proposition 4, which enjoined and empowered the city council to "protect and preserve environmental features such as water, air, and other natural endowments, insure the proper use and development of land, and promote and maintain an esthetic and humane urban environment." Environmentalists saw a connection between a professional city council and the pursuit of their goals, "People who are professional, full-time elected leaders naturally [sic] will be more responsive to our environmental needs and to all the needs of the city."[68]

Finally, districts promised to make public policy more equitable. Districts will "give an equal voice to the different communities in the city, and will insure a . . . uniform growth policy in San Antonio."[69] And there was no need to worry about the appearance of "Eastern-style" bossism. Advocates of district elections argued that the city manager and civil service together insured the city against patronage politics. In San Antonio, city council member Glen Hartman "said the city manager form of government bolstered by an effective civil service system forms a safeguard against any give-away of municipal jobs."[70]

Opponents of district systems most frequently argued that local government had done a good job, while change was risky. B. J. McCombs, who owned a large business in San Antonio, opposed the change to dis-

[65] *San Antonio Express*, January 7, 1977, 3A.

[66] Pamphlet published by the Phoenix city clerk's office, quoted in *Arizona Republic* November 28, 1982. Since votes cast never exceeded eighty thousand between 1970 and 1982, "hundreds of thousands" was an exaggeration.

[67] *San Antonio Express*, January 11, 1977, 3A.

[68] The text of the proposition, which passed, is from the *Albuquerque Journal*, June 30, 1971, A2. Ibid., June 23, 1971, 1.

[69] *San Antonio Express*, January 5, 1977, 3A.

[70] Ibid., January 13, 1977, 3A.

tricts, "asserting San Antonio has enjoyed good city government under the at-large plan."[71] In Albuquerque, former commissioner Richard Bice insisted that "the present at large system of electing city officials has worked well in the past 'and we should keep it.'"[72]

Opponents of district systems tended to be more apocalyptic in their rhetoric than advocates of change, as evidenced by this commentary in the *Phoenix Gazette* in November of 1975. "The issues boil down," reported one writer, to the following choice:

> Has the Charter Government Committee—which has helped elect every mayor and all but two councilmen in the last 26 years—outlived its usefulness? Or should the CGC continue guiding City Hall with its hand-picked candidates, in an effort to discourage professional politicians from taking over and turning Phoenix into a ward-boss city of potential corruption?

On another page the paper editorialized,

> When Phoenicians vote . . . in tomorrow's election they will be deciding whether this city follows its pattern of quality growth or embraces drastic changes that already have led to ruin elsewhere. . . .
> Proposition 101 proposes a mongrelized ward system for Phoenix. . . . Ward government would serve only to divide a city that, because of fast growth, still needs most of all to be pulled together into a cohesive community.[73]

Later, opponents of changes in Phoenix's city government accused supporters of "an attempt to inject 'Eastern style' politics into local government."[74] The *Arizona Gazette* was hardly alone in arguing that boss- and patronage-style ward politics loomed on the horizon if districts were adopted. In Austin, "Conservatives strongly opposed any districting, which [they claimed] would 'end progressive government in favor of bossism and political bartering and trade-outs.'"[75] Incumbent San Antonio councilman Phil Pyndus threatened that "Ward politics will return to San Antonio. . . . Backroom wheeler-dealer deals will occur between individual councilmen."[76] Another opponent of districts in San Antonio

[71] Ibid.

[72] *Albuquerque Journal*, June 24, 1971, 1.

[73] *Phoenix Gazette*, November 3, 1975, 19 (news account), 6 (editorial).

[74] *Arizona Republic*, November 28, 1982, A1; "The test," argued the *Republic*, "is whether voters want a small, elitist group to concoct a mechanism that ultimately will enable union bosses to seize control of city hall through an easier system of electing their own. Voters should not be fooled" (ibid., A14).

[75] Staniszewski, "Ideology and Practice," 50. This was 1975.

[76] *San Antonio Express*, January 6, 1977, 34A. In San Antonio ward politics found a defender. County Judge Blair Reeves argued that ward politics "worked well for Chicago under the late strong Mayor Richard Daley." *San Antonio Express*, January 5, 1977, 3A.

painted a similar picture. Once the "ward chief gets a grip on the voters no one dares file against him because if they do they'll receive no garbage pickup and no fire protection and will receive traffic tickets." Worse, a "patron" system would be introduced into the city as a " 'Brown Mafia' composed of dishonest Mexican-American politicians will be further entrenched if the . . . districting plan passes."[77]

It was also argued that electing council members from districts was undemocratic because voters were denied the opportunity to vote for or against most council members. "We have in essence said to Austin minorities," argued charter revision committee member Bill Youngblood (dissenting form the majority report) " 'Yes, you have voting rights, so long as you vote for one only of 10 city council members.', Are not 90 percent of the voting population in Austin denied the opportunity to vote on all of their elected city council members?"[78] In San Diego the *Union* argued that districts were unnecessary for minority representation: "It could be that they believe election by district somehow might relieve any racial imbalances on the council and give minority groups a greater voice in their city. But they have a voice now—the same voice all of us have."[79]

Defenders of citywide elections argued that district elections would be divisive. In San Antonio, one opponent claimed, districts would "create 'ten little cities' competing with one another for . . . funds and facilities."[80] Even if district representatives were honest, their perspective on decisions would be narrow. "Unfortunately," wrote a dissident on Austin's Charter Revision Committee, "the district system can lead to a deterioration in the decision making ability of the council. Important decisions affecting the entire city [will] be determined by myopic trade-offs for parochial politics."[81] In Albuquerque the chairman of the city commission said that the experience of running for office on a citywide basis left him "more convinced than ever that districting is not right for Albu-

[77] These claims were made by Armandina Saldivar at a press conference for Texans for Freedom, which was heading the opposition to the districting plan. *San Antonio Express*, January 12, 1977, 3A.

[78] The same argument was made in Phoenix: "We oppose pure districts because every citizen will automatically lose his right to vote for all City Council Members. . . . Instead . . . voters can vote for only one. This is the least representative form of city government" (statement by six incumbent members of the city council, *Arizona Republic*, November 28, 1982, A14). And in San Antonio: "You have nine councilmen representing you now. By Jan. 16, you may have only one." *San Antonio Express*, June 6, 1977, 4A.

[79] November 3, 1969, B6. Quoted in Schloyer, "Ethnic Politics."

[80] *San Antonio Express*, January 11, 1977, 3A.

[81] Minority Report, City of Austin, Charter Revision Commission, February 25, 1976, 13. Quoted remarks were from Royal Masset.

querque. It would produce a polarization of officials dedicated to diverse interests."[82]

Sometimes the character of the opposition persuaded voters to favor district elections. In San Antonio, when the Alliance for a Better City (an elite group that had long supported the Good Government League) announced that it had raised $30,000 to fight districting, one newspaper columnist remarked that this was "like having Herbert Hoover announce he is backing your 1932 congressional race." "What this means," a district supporter argued, "is the developers are trying to maintain control of the city."[83] In Phoenix one man declared he voted for districts because "The *Arizona Republic* is against it."[84]

Much more important, proponents of districts held the trump card: failure to adopt districts could mire local government in years of wrangling with the justice department, or with minority lawsuits in the courts. The Austin Charter Revision Committee was warned by Jose Garza, Texas Counsel for MALDEF, that "Austin's history of electing a Chicano and a Black is not a guarantee that the election system in Austin is constitutional. . . . a Court will look at the minority voters and if they have been consistently allowed . . . to elect representatives of their choice."[85] Under the headline "What if 10–1 plan is beaten?" the *San Antonio Express* reported:

> There is no way of telling what will happen to the spring city elections if voters Saturday reject single member council districts.
>
> "I don't have my Ouija Board," City Attorney Jim Parker said Wednesday after he was asked how the U.S. Justice Department would react if the change fails.
>
> City legal authorities say it is possible that a charter defeat might cause the Justice department to go to court and halt the April elections. . . . [and perhaps] also a projected improvement bond vote.[86]

As in other refoundings, usually more than one round of voting was required. In San Diego district elections were proposed and defeated four times between 1969 and 1981; in Albuquerque districts were proposed and defeated in 1971. In San Antonio and Houston districts were defeated in straw polls before passing. In Dallas there was considerable jockeying about the number of citywide council members in proposed

[82] *Albuquerque Journal*, June 26, 1971.

[83] *San Antonio Express*, January 7, 1977, 3A.

[84] Roddy Stinson in the *San Antonio Express*. January 6, 1977, 3A; in Phoenix, *Arizona Republic*, December 2, 1982, X3.

[85] Final Report, City of Austin, Charter Revision Commission, March 7, 1984, 10.

[86] *San Antonio Express*, January 13, 1977, 3A.

mixed systems. In Phoenix there was a brief petition campaign for a 5-5 system. In Austin the suit against the city was dropped as community leaders settled on a "gentlemen's agreement" for minority representation on a council elected citywide. District elections won referenda in Albuquerque in 1974, Dallas in 1976, San Antonio in 1977, San Jose in 1978, Phoenix in 1982, and San Diego in 1988.[87]

And All the Crowd

Dramatic political changes appeared in the immediate aftermath of changes to district elections. More candidates ran for open seats; issues were more prominent in campaigns, portraits of districts, neighborhoods, and the concerns of their residents appeared in the news; candidates boasted their familiarity with neighborhoods they hoped to represent. Newly elected city councils were more racially diverse than the city councils of big-city reform.

All of these changes have given local politics a populist appearance. More, since antigrowth or managed growth advocates were prominent in rewriting the rules and sometimes on new councils as well, the pure entrepreneurial regimes of big-city reform have been brought to an end. This does not mean, of course, that the actors who have made up the growth machine are gone, but rather that proponents of growth are challenged by demands for environmental caution and social equity as they are in cites elsewhere. James Fenimore Cooper wrote, "When property rules, it rules alone; but when the poor are admitted to have a voice in government, the rich are never excluded."[88] To popular challenges growth machines continue to bring tremendous and often victorious resources.

In the first postchange election, many candidates put themselves forward for the city council. In Phoenix there were fifty-one candidates for eight council seats in 1983; in Dallas, there were nineteen candidates for eight seats in 1975; in Albuquerque the first election after charter revision brought 155 candidates for the mayoralty and nine council seats, in San Antonio sixty-nine candidates sought seats on the city council and another nine competed for the mayoralty.[89]

[87] Voting was very close in Phoenix, San Antonio, and San Diego; overwhelmingly in favor of districts in Albuquerque and Dallas (the last, under immediate threat of court order).

[88] James Fenimore Cooper, *Democracy, Liberty, and Property*, ed. Francis Coker (New York: Macmillan, 1942), 513.

[89] *Dallas Morning News*, April 1, 1975, 1; *Arizona Republic*, October 3, 1983, 1; *Albuquerque Journal*, May 5, 1974, A8; Hernandez, "Chicano Mobilization," 78.

Candidates boasted their intimacy with neighborhood problems. In Phoenix twenty-four-year-old Paul Johnson felt "comfortable seeking the council seat from the area he grew up in. . . . 'I don't know the problems in South Phoenix,'" he admitted, "'but I know the problems in Sunnyslope and District 3.'" In Dallas's Fifth District, candidate William Cothurm, "capitalized on his closeness to the neighborhood being well known . . . from boyhood and his previous days on the council and his accessibility. He walked the district door to door."[90]

Issues figured more prominently in municipal campaigns than in the past. Against a backdrop of a generation or more of statesmen whose campaigns centered on the claim that nothing was broken (so no fixing was required), this is not surprising. The *Arizona Republic* headlined the concerns of each district in the 1983 council race; the *Dallas Morning News* profiled the districts and the issues council candidates campaigned on in 1976, and the *Albuquerque Journal* ran a series of accounts of districts, candidates, and issues in 1974.

The personnel of city councils changed. In San Antonio the first election after charter revision produced a city council of five Hispanics, one African-American, and four Anglos. In Albuquerque too Hispanic representation increased. African-Americans seem assured of two seats on the Dallas council since the charter change. But there were disappointments. In San Antonio in subsequent elections, the number of Anglos on the council increased; in the district intended for Mexican-American representation in San Diego, the first elected representative was an Anglo; in Dallas Hispanics were unable to win either any of the districts or one of the citywide seats, and there too African-Americans were disappointed to control only two of ten seats on the city council.

Perhaps more disappointing, stable electoral and governing coalitions have failed to appear. This makes sense in light of the uneasy coalitions that supported changing the rules; as one author said, "motley" hardly begins to describe the groups supporting change. The absence of stable governing coalitions is revealed in the practices of city councils. In *Your Voice at City Hall*, Peggy Heilig and Robert Mundt studied the change to district elections in eleven cities. Among other things, they discovered that newly constituted city councils showed no obvious or sustained pattern of voting alliances among council members.[91]

[90] *Arizona Republic*, October 3, 1983, 1; *Dallas Morning News*, April 2, 1975. Neighborhoods were jealous of their prerogative of choosing a representative, and the appearance of PACs or "outside" money brought negative publicity for the candidate who courted them.

[91] Heilig and Mundt, *Your Voice at City Hall*, chap. 7. The authors tested a long list of hypotheses about candidates for office and their behavior on the city council once elected. They found that despite an anticipated democratization of who ran for office (and despite

The political relations of communities of color and antigrowth advocates, central supporters of changes to districts in every city, demonstrate
the challenge of building cohesive popular coalitions. Dean Schloyer observed in San Diego that anti-growth leaders "were rarely distinct from
their opponents on other issues. To characterize the anti-growth movement as either liberal or exclusionary is to misperceive [sic] their goals."
In the campaign for districts in San Diego, supporters of managed
growth, anxious not to offend Anglos who did not support increased
representation of minorities, distanced themselves from questions of better representation of African-Americans and Hispanics if districts were
adopted. After districts were adopted, the Sierra Club insisted that divisions between themselves and African-American leaders were minor, but
NAACP officials were open about their anger.[92] Similarly, in Phoenix,
San Diego, and Albuquerque, affluent and middle-class neighborhoods
seeking to repair slights in service provision may not consent to service
equalization policies of which they are not likely to be the beneficiaries.

Worse, in some ways the agendas of antigrowth advocates and communities of color are inherently antagonistic: the poor need growth and
opportunity, while antigrowth advocates want a smaller and higher quality pie. The difference in priorities came to the fore in Austin in 1980.
Austin's growth-management plan mapped a corridor for industrial development. When Motorola chose to locate a plant in Austin, the company selected a site that was not in the growth corridor. In intense debate
in the city council, African-American and Hispanic council members
voted to allow Motorola the site it chose. Charles Urdy "expressed dis-
may at the possible environmental impacts" of the Motorola plant "but
said that the jobs which the plant will provide were crucial to the Austin
unemployed." "There are pockets of poverty and unemployment in the
this city which we must address." Agreeing, council member John Trevino said that although he opposed industrial location not in accord with
the plan, he supported Motorola. "Motorola will be able to provide job
opportunities for a lot of our folks."[93]

---

the rush of candidates immediately after the change to districts), broadly speaking the class
background of officials did not change, nor did campaign spending or turnout. Heilig and
Mundt observed that council members from disadvantaged districts more often took the
role of an aggressive ombudsman, provoked by their constituents' more frequent requests
for help. On changes in policy direction, Heilig and Mundt thought that even in San Antonio, with its well-organized Hispanic majority, little had been accomplished (152).

[92] Schloyer, "Ethnic Politics," 30. For antagonism between antigrowth advocates and
civil rights leaders during the campaign for districts, ibid., 39. For the dispute between the
Sierra Club and the NAACP, San Diego Union, November 9, 1988, B1, 10.

[93] Daily Texan, City Council Profiles, July 1981, in the election files of the Austin History Center.

The absence of stable governing coalitions does not mean that life on city councils is without order. The common organizing principles of contemporary city councils are equity among districts, deference to district representatives on issues affecting their district, and devolution of policy decisions to individual council members.

Decisions about policy priorities can be decentralized to districts by allocating money to districts but leaving spending decisions to district representatives. In San Diego in 1994, for example, the Council voted to dedicate 40 percent of its $16.3 million Community Development Block Grant (CDBG) funds to citywide programs that served the poor, while the remaining 60 percent was given to council members. Each member's prerogative is to select from among competing CDBG applications submitted by various organizations and programs.[94] Similarly, city councils in San Jose and San Antonio allocate development monies with a view toward equity across districts.

Even growth has become, to some extent, a decentralized, district-administered issue area. In Phoenix and Albuquerque, an end to decades of annexation as the foremost growth strategy has forced developers to redevelop and fill in vacant spaces and so, inevitably, to conflict with neighborhoods. In Albuquerque there is legislation requiring developer consultation with neighborhood groups. Although the city council is the court of last resort for disputes between developers and neighborhoods, the council member representing the affected district is in practice arbiter of these disputes. Vincent Griego described one contentious meeting between a developer and the neighbors of the proposed development. The developer wanted a large project, while current residents argued for a smaller project on the grounds that the proposal was out of scale with the neighborhood as a whole, and that the impact on traffic and parking would be high. The developer, adamantly opposed to downsizing, threatened to go to the city council. At this point in the meeting, Griego stood up and explained that in this instance *he* was the council, and the developer would have to negotiate. "Here we have the developer who wants everything," Griego explained, "and I have to tell them you can't have everything. . . . you have to put something that's compatible with the people."[95]

[94] Districts with the most low-income residents received the biggest share, affluent areas received considerably less. *San Diego Union-Tribune*, May 29, 1994, B1 and B3.

[95] Council members see themselves as part of the effort to formulate and pursue growth strategies. In San Diego, Juan Vargas has taken strong positions on San Diego's growth strategy, arguing for building on the trade anticipated as a consequence of NAFTA. Interview with Ralph Inunza (staff to Vargas) June 7, 1995 (by the author and Katherine Underwood). In Albuquerque, Vince Griego and Steve Gallegos worked together to recruit Hyatt Hotels to the city, and to convince Hyatt to hire minorities and residents of particular neighborhoods. Author's interview with Vincent Griego, May 18, 1994.

What are the consequences of changing the rules for public policy? The major policy change Heilig and Mundt found was the more equitable delivery of routine services. Each council member can boast a long list of concrete improvements delivered to his or her district. In Albuquerque, representatives of the Valley can point to new or renovated libraries, cultural, community, and family centers, a new public park to adjoin a public school, a new theater and dance hall (this from a bond issue that received support citywide), a nationally recognized program to assist single mothers, $2 million annually for paving and street maintenance, another $2 million annually for improving drainage. In San Diego too representatives of less advantaged districts can boast new police and fire stations, neighborhood service centers, libraries, and some low-income housing.[96]

Heilig and Mundt argued that the better distribution of routine services is not a minor matter for those formerly deprived of these services. From a popular point of view, routine services are what local government is about. Libraries, schools, police and fire protection, health centers, and even parks contribute to quality of life and life chances for community residents.

If the provision of services is not trivial for residents, neither is it a trivial consideration for the city budget. Where communities have been generally excluded from public services, getting to equity is likely to be an expensive and long-term project. In this context, despite elaborate council norms suggesting all politics is distributive, the very presence of representatives of previously underserved communities poses the threat of redistribution. Even so, the fact that getting to equity is on the agenda of city government means that, with the creation of district systems, the "new normalcy" has finally reached the big cities of the Southwest.[97]

In San Antonio there is evidence of broader changes in policy direction. This is so for three reasons. First, Hispanics are a majority of the city's population. Second, the Hispanic community is politically organized in Communities Organized for Public Service (COPS), an umbrella organization for community groups founded with assistance from Saul Alinsky's Industrial Areas Foundation. Third, divisions among San An-

---

[96] Griego interview, *San Diego Union Tribune*, January 29, 1995, G2, April 24, 1994, H11.

[97] Charles Hamilton argued that the enfranchisement of people of color by the civil rights acts was likely to bring in its wake demands for collective benefits requiring increased government activism. Hamilton coined the term "new normalcy" to describe politics in this era, when the needs underlying these demands and the necessity for response were widely and publicly acknowledged. Charles Hamilton, "Political Access, Minority Participation, and the New Normalcy," in *Minority Report*, ed. Leslie W. Dunbar (New York: Pantheon, 1984), 3–25.

TABLE 8-4
Ethnic Composition of Southwestern Cities, 1990

	Anglo	Hispanic	Native American	Asian	Black
Albuquerque	58.3	34.5	3.0	1.7	3.0
Austin	61.7	23.0	0.4	3.0	12.4
Dallas	47.7	20.9	0.5	2.2	29.5
Phoenix	71.8	20.0	1.9	1.7	5.2
San Antonio	36.2	55.6	0.3	5.4	7.0
San Diego	58.7	20.7	0.6	11.8	9.4
San Jose	49.6	26.6	0.7	19.5	4.7

Source: U.S. Bureau of the Census, Census of Population, 1990: General Population Characteristics (Washington, D.C.: Government Printing Office, 1992), Arizona, table 61, 144; California, table 61, 619, 623; New Mexico, table 61, 153–54; Texas, table 61, 690–691, 707, 756.

tonio's business leaders provided the Hispanic community with powerful allies for redirecting growth policies. COPS insisted on low-income housing as a component of redevelopment sites formerly planned exclusively for commercial uses. COPS and Mexican-American representatives on the city council also redirected city monies from new development on the affluent north side to redevelopment in the older downtown and south side. Even with these changes, critics argue that the majority's coalition with the growth machine has not delivered nearly enough to communities, neighborhoods, and ordinary voters.[98]

If this analysis of policy change in San Antonio is correct, it suggests that prospects for similar changes elsewhere are slim. Other southwestern cities have much smaller communities of color (table 8-4); these communities are not joined in umbrella organizations that promote their interests; and prospective allies are scarce.

Changes in candidates, campaigning, and elected officials were symptomatic of profound changes in the political environment that was once big-city

[98] Sekul, "Communities Organized"; Robert Brischetto, Charles Cotrell, and R. Michael Stevens, "Conflict and Change in the Political Culture of San Antonio in the 1970s," in Politics of San Antonio: Community, Progress, and Power, ed. David R. Johnson, John A. Booth, and Richard J. Harris (Lincoln: University of Nebraska, 1983), chap. 4. Dallas presents the other end of the spectrum, with maximum disappointment: after the adoption of districts, the mayor and city manager seemed to arrogate more decision-making to themselves, making the city council less powerful once district representatives were at the table. Heilig and Mundt, Your Voice at City Hall, 36–37. See also Arnold Fleischmann, "The Change to District Elections in Dallas" (typescript in the Supplementary Information of the Austin City Charter Revision Commission, March 7, 1984).

reform. Big-city reform was distinguished by well organized political leaders who presided over a system of secret negotiations and skewed rewards and claimed to act for the "good of the whole city." The aggressive support of growth by municipal government was unquestioned. The electorate was a small, and not very representative, fraction of the adult population. A majority of the electorate seemed content with, or even enthusiastic about, the amenities and services local government delivered.

Subsequent to the adoption of districts, the big cities of the Southwest present quite different political environments. The tightly organized NPSGs that led local politics have dispersed. Unlike other refoundings, which were championed by well-organized political and economic leaders, the most recent change of rules was supported by broad, uneasy coalitions. The goals of those supporting new rules were not the same; as a result the policy direction implied by rewriting the rules is uncertain. The absence of clear policy direction also distinguishes the most recent rewriting of the rules from other refoundings.

Today politics in southwestern cities is less distinctive than it once was. District elections have changed the face of local politics, brought big-city reform and pure entrepreneural regimes to an end, and introduced issues of equity into political debate. Big-city reform has left legacies in city managers, civil service, nonpartisanship, the professionalism of public bureaucracies, and popular values and expectations. Participation in local politics, at least as measured in turnout for local elections is, in some cities, considerably higher than in the 1950s and 1960s.

All the issues of coalition building and governance posed by the towering diversity and economic dilemmas of American cities are now faced in the Southwest. Unlike local politics in the era of big-city reform, in this political setting neighborhoods of every color, proponents of growth, environmentalists, and managed growth advocates alike must settle for representation, negotiation, and bargaining. It may be that for the first time since reformers set to work seven generations ago, municipal reform will become a popular and democratic style of local politics. It's all over but the shouting.

Nine

Morning Glories

THE LEGACIES of the municipal reform movement are found in every city in the United States. Bureaucracies and civil service, the independent authority and commission, voter registration, nonpartisanship—these are the reminders of generations of campaigning against corruption, favoritism, and party rule. In the older cities of the East, where reform campaigns began, reformers were seldom blessed with victory at the polls. By contrast, in the towns and cities of the Southwest, municipal reformers everywhere designed the institutions of local politics, and advocates of good government ruled for most of this century. Their efforts shaped political life in cities larger and richer than any Plunkitt dreamed of.

The origins of the municipal reform movement were in the big cities of the United States before the Civil War. As soon as the urban boss appeared, municipal reformers joined battle for control of the cities. The program of municipal reform reflected ongoing opposition to urban politics as usual. To wrest control of city government or to improve the quality of local government required disabling the political machine. The party boss and the allegiance of the great mass of voters to him and his party were the foundation of machine rule. To disengage the boss from his supporters, reformers championed nonpartisanship, citywide elections, civil service, and government by the "best men."

Fashioned to fight the shame of the nation's big cities, the program of municipal reform found its greatest appeal elsewhere. The ambitious little towns of the Southwest were welcoming settings for the proponents of municipal reform. Lacking infrastructure, capital, or strategies for economic advance, town leaders organized to secure investments and utilities from large corporations; prisons, universities, and designation as county seat or state capital from states; help with dams, irrigation, and harbors from the federal government. In 1964 *Fortune* wrote that Dallas was "really an enormous heavier-than-air machine that has just got off the ground and been maintained in permanent flight by the efforts of its business leaders. Without those efforts the city would have experienced only scrub growth, for there was essentially no reason for Dallas' existence."[1] Virtually the same account has been written of Houston, Phoe-

---

[1] Richard Austin Smith, "How Business Failed Dallas," *Fortune* 70 (July 1964): 160.

nix, Albuquerque, San Diego, Los Angeles, and Austin. Each city has its stories of the foresight, energy, and inventiveness of those who founded and built the town in defiance of nature's meager endowments for settlement and growth.

Town leaders also recognized that "no farsighted executive . . . dares risk his concern . . . to . . . an indifferent and mismanaged city administration." Security and prosperity required not only success with outsiders but also more efficient and powerful local governments. Town governments needed regular revenues sufficient for paving, grading, and schools and credit ratings strong enough to allow borrowing for larger capital investments. The model charters of the National Municipal League provided town leaders with designs for reorganizing their city governments.

Hardly promising for anything else, the little towns of the Southwest were fertile ground for good government. There the advocates of good government were advantaged, and its opponents disadvantaged, by regional characteristics. Experienced at uniting to lobby investors and higher governments, town leaders were well organized to campaign for municipal reform. More, local municipal reformers were men who hoped to tie their communities more closely to national investors; their claims to leadership rested in part on their successes negotiating with outsiders. When these local heroes asked for new city charters, they were not refused, and it was rational for voters to support them. Just as regional characteristics empowered advocates of reform, so they disabled likely opponents. Not least among the reasons reformers were successful in the Southwest is that (west of Texas) there were no bosses to oppose them, no strong party organizations claiming the allegiance of working-class and poor voters. Democratic and Republican party leaders had little stake in protecting a large electorate. Suffrage restriction thinned the ranks of those (like organized labor) who could be expected to oppose municipal reform. In addition, working men were even more geographically mobile than in the East, making them an unstable base for political organization. The result was that towns across the region adopted nonpartisanship, commission, and city-manager charters before the First World War.

Initially, town leaders were altogether pleased with their new governments. In Houston, Mayor Ben Campbell boasted that the city council was unified in its efforts for "the upbuilding of the whole city" and "the reason . . . is . . . our present form of city government."[2] Municipal honeymoons were not long lived, as the governments provided under reform charters proved disappointing to municipal reformers. The commission

[2] Ben Campbell, "The Commission Form of Government," in *Texas Municipalities* 2, no. 1 (April 1915): 36.

form failed to halt the collusion of city officials and interest groups, the courting of constituent interests, or patronage employment. At best collusion among commissioners might create a "ring" that governed coherently; more often competing cliques and individuals worked to keep themselves in office. City manager government was equally difficult to institutionalize, as city councils were loathe to give up management prerogatives.

Instead of the businesslike, apolitical governments reformers imagined, local politics in the interwar Southwest took two forms. One pattern, the more common, offered a bewildering array of leaders and factions, hastily assembled and equally short-lived alliances, rather like political life in the states described by V. O. Key in *Southern Politics*. Phoenix and San Diego are examples. The other pattern featured a sunbelt centralizer who overcame institutional adversity to create political order; this happened in Houston, Austin, and Albuquerque. Sunbelt centralizers opposed commission and city-manager government and presented a populist image to voters, campaigning as friends to organized labor and people of color. Each built a local organization as well as a popular following that secured repeated reelection. As one reformer said of Boss Pendergast, the function of sunbelt centralizers was to "control the popular vote." Sunbelt centralizers were aggressive and ambitious city builders who pursued growth successfully and so also maintained the support of the business community. Whatever surprises commission and manager governments held for their initial supporters, reform regimes in the interwar period secured central elements of the reform agenda: restricted participation, the erosion of partisan organizations, and local governments that were "frugal and sparing." If some advocates of good government were disappointed, they were entitled only to minimum regrets.

Despite the achievements of local government, business leaders were anxious about the course of city government following the Second World War. As defense spending increased in the 1940s, and new economic dangers and opportunities were forecast for the postwar period, businessmen became increasingly concerned that local economies were not well positioned for postwar growth (or worse, recession), and local government was ill-equipped to manage postwar challenges. By the 1940s local governments did not have adequate taxing powers to finance expanding infrastructure or provision of amenities, nor were the propertied voters who controlled the financing of additional debt inclined to approve new bonds. Spending was as problematic as getting: suburbs and older neighborhoods alike complained of neglect; neither wanted government to have general taxing powers that would allow spending neighborhood money someplace else. In some cities police and fire departments were demoralized, inefficient, too autonomous from the center. At the same time, the desire to annex suburbs, direct growth, and attend to fraying downtowns energized local elites to become more attentive to city government. In addition, migrants from the North and Midwest added new constituencies receptive to municipal reform. As a result, in the 1940s and 1950s there was another successful round of reform campaigning and charter revision.

Between 1945 and 1955 city governments in the Southwest were refounded. For reformers, a half century of reform government in southwestern cities seemed to teach two lessons. The first was that reformers could write the rules to win the game of local politics. This they carefully did, maintaining and occasionally enhancing the arrangements that created a small political community: suffrage restrictions, difficult registration procedures, citywide elections, nonpartisan politics. The second lesson was that new charters would not on their own insure the governments reformers desired. Unwilling to "permit the work we have done to be wasted by turning the government over to the politicians," reformers organized nonpartisan slating groups to design public policies, campaign, and sponsor candidates for office. Like the nation's founders in the 1790s, urban leaders found political parties distasteful in principle but extremely useful in practice.

The cities of the Southwest at midcentury were the setting for big-city reform. The distinguishing characteristics of big-city reform politics were very low participation, rhetorical narrowness, lack of competition at the polls, government by men who claimed to be civic statesmen rather than politicians, and carefully targeted distribution of limited amenities. Political life revolved around an apparent consensus on the priorities of local government, the aggressive pursuit of growth and annexation, and the distribution of amenities to middle class neighborhoods.

The key accomplishment of big-city reform in this period was the creation of political communities that looked rather like Winnetka (if less affluent), despite governmental agendas substantially more ambitious and social settings that were considerably more diverse. Most of the politically active population (one in five or six adults, whiter and more affluent than the city population as a whole) shared the short political wish list Banfield and Wilson described for Winnetka: excellent schools, parks, libraries, and other community services provided with businesslike efficiency (measured in low taxes) and perfect honesty.

They shared as well the values Dorothy Cline described for residents of the Heights in Albuquerque. Here, she wrote, was reform's natural constituency, the well-educated middle class of the corporate, scientific, and research communities. Heights residents wanted a government like themselves, "professionally trained, politically neutral executives, utilizing scientific, technical knowledge and modern business methods."[3] The capture of the public schools by Heights residents exemplifies their role in the political community more generally. Disappointed with the quality of public high schools, the newly arrived, well-educated Heights residents organized to persuade other local leaders of their views and to dramatically revise the curricula of Albuquerque's public high schools. In this they had the support of the city's major employer of professionals and engineers.

The same events provide evidence of the lacunae in the goodness of good government: fewer college preparatory courses were available in the Valley high schools than the Heights high schools. In the Valley the Technical Vocational Institute was established to provide "marketable vocational skills" to those who were "not going on to college." Similarly, the same government that subsidized developers (and with them, their middle-class customers) did not construct public housing, or provide libraries, parks, or sewers in the Valley. Heights residents in Albuquerque, and the core constituencies of other reform regimes, could feel politically efficacious, valued, comfortable. Whether what was at stake was taxes, streets, schools, parks, or libraries, they were well served by local politics and government.

The institutional arrangements that insured victory at the polls insulated political leaders from the citizenry to such an extent that incumbents failed to perceive the progressive alienation not only of those who had long been politically excluded, marginal, or critical, but also of their most valued constituents. Everywhere the first alarms were sounded by the civil rights movement. In San Antonio, Dallas, and Houston, civil rights activism in the courts forced changes in the rules of local politics, changing city councils from citywide election to election from districts. In the same years incumbents suffered defections from the affluent Anglo constituencies who had been reliably supportive through the 1950s and 1960s. In San Jose, Phoenix, Albuquerque, San Diego, and Austin, it was Anglo, middle class, antigrowth, managed-growth, neighborhood, and environmental advocates who were most prominent in movements to dismantle citywide elections. If the federal government was the enforcer, issues of race only made inevitable what the practice of local politics made likely.

The new political order created by these efforts did not entirely abandon the institutions and practices of municipal reform. As advocates of greater democracy and representation reassured those who feared

[3] Dorothy I. Cline and T. Philip Wolfe, "Albuquerque: The End of the Reform Era," in *Urban Politics in the Southwest*, ed. Leonard Goodall (Tempe: Arizona State University Press, 1967), 13.

"eastern-style politics," the city manager, civil service, and nonpartisan-ship remain in place. The goals and priorities of local politics and the coalition that will chart their course are uncertain. The groups most strongly supportive of rewriting the rules of local politics—communities of color and advocates of managed growth—have little else in common. The usual suspects constituting growth coalitions are still in the cities of the Southwest, as are the imperatives to maintain healthy local econ-omies. Nevertheless, the change to districts has, at a minimum, been an equalizing force in the provision of public services, and brought, at last, the new normalcy to the cities of the Southwest.

The course of municipal reform in the Southwest was shaped by the re-gion's strategic location at the turn of the century, by the institutional arrangements reformers designed, and by the "racial fault lines" of American politics. The strategic location of the Southwest—its late entry into the corporate economy and the national political community—permanently marked the political life of the region's cities. The lack of resources for development provoked the organization of local economic leaders for the aggressive pursuit of growth. The weakness of political parties both paved the way for nonpartisan local politics and left vulner-able the populations that elsewhere were protected by disciplined party organizations. Thus in the Progressive Era town governments were cre-ated that secured the foundations of big-city reform: low participation, low tax rates, absence of corruption, minimal social provision, and gov-ernment in the service of growth.

At mid-century the "new convergence of power" in the Southwest took the form of elaborating the arrangements of big-city reform. The nonpartisan slating group formalized both the organization and the po-litical role of business leaders. Barriers to participation restricted the po-litical community. Migration of well-educated, middle class families pro-vided constituents for big-city reform. In this way, the institutional arrangements reformers put in place created small, relatively homoge-neous political communities in the midst of metropolitan areas that were quite diverse. The same rules, because they made victory at the polls possible with a narrow base of support, insulated the leaders of big-city reform from accumulating discontents. The result was that eventually a plurality of voters failed to support the status quo, and instead endorsed a change in the rules.

Across these events, considerations of race have influenced the design of political institutions, and the goals and outcomes of urban public poli-cies. Because racial considerations were, from the beginning, a part of the program of municipal reform, righting racial inequities required chang-ing the institutions of reform government. The most recent redesign of the electoral arrangements of southwestern cities is a product both of civil rights struggles and of the spreading discontent among big-city reform's central constituents.

This review of the course of reform suggests solutions to the puzzle posed by reform's agenda: how, having designed institutions to distance residents from government, could reformers organize consent? The solution changed across the century. In the first period, reform was not institutionalized as reformers planned. The extra-institutional arrangements of the interwar period allowed some patronage and personal machine-building. Sunbelt centralizers opposed the Klan in Austin and Houston and supported unions in Austin, Houston, and Albuquerque; in the context of restricted participation and a generally hostile political environment, these few concessions were important.

For big-city reform, the solution was the exclusion of most potential voters and the shrewd distribution of community amenities to affluent and middle-class neighborhoods. From the point of view of political leaders, the logic of this system, as Steven Erie argued for machine politicians in power,[4] commanded conservation of the reliable electorate rather than the expansion of the electorate to include new voters and communities. The same logic meant that over time, as cities expanded but the base of support did not, reform government suffered a loss of popularity. The denouement of big-city reform showed it proved almost impossible to sustain consent without exclusion. Big-city reform worked best, not incidentally, for the small political community it created.

Adding the West to City Politics

There are lessons to be drawn for the study of city politics from this survey of the course of reform in the big cities of the Southwest. Machine and reform alike bear reappraisal; some amendments and caveats can be offered to growth-centered approaches to city politics; adding the West to the study of city politics also suggests a more prominent role for institutions in the study of cities and some rethinking of political culture.

We may begin with the archetypes that have long been the organizing concepts of city politics, machine and reform. I have presented here an account of the development of reform governance over the course of this century in the big cities of the Southwest. To the arguments already presented about the style, substance, and limits on big-city reform, I offer a

[4] Steven P. Erie, *Rainbow's End: Irish-Americans and the Dilemmas of Urban Machine Politics, 1840–1985* (Berkeley: University of California Press, 1988), chap. 3, "Guardians of Power."

few additional observations. Although professionalized public bureaucracies are a legacy of municipal reform everywhere, the service-
providing bureaucracies did not become in the Southwest the "islands of
functional power"[5] that they became elsewhere. I have not encountered a
single instance of a runaway or rogue bureaucracy, while I have found
several instances (San Antonio's libraries, Phoenix public housing, education in Albuquerque, Dallas, and San Diego) of professional priorities
and logic brought effectively in line by the consensus of political and
economic leaders. Those bureaucracies that could generate their own income, the legally autonomous development and port authorities, are a
different matter. These "growth bureaucracies," like the Department of
Water and Power in Los Angeles or the port authorities in San Diego and
Houston, maintain substantial autonomy from elected officials.[6]

Public employees have not exercised the political influence in the
Southwest that they have in machine-descendant cities. Leaders in big
reform cities have for the most part been hostile to municipal unions;
indeed, one consequence of midcentury refounding was that municipal
employee associations in several cities lost ground. In several cities the
city manager implemented these policies. Before World War II, labor
leaders corresponded with one another about the predispositions of
particular managers (and no doubt after the war, too, although I have
not found the correspondence). Big-city reform being inhospitable to
municipal employee organizations, it is not surprising that these came
to be counted among the supporters of rewriting the rules in the last
two decades.

Students of urban growth and regimes will benefit from adding the
West to their study of city politics. The growth machines of the nation's
older cities were dominated by downtown interests, as the theories of
growth and of regime politics have been. In the Southwest, developers—
whose interests ranged further and further from the center over time—
have dominated the growth machine, with important results for the
agenda of city politics. In the nation's older cities, urban renewal and
downtown development were the most prominent effort of local governments in the 1950s and early 1960s. In the Southwest redevelopment was
more contentious among elites, not simply for fear of "federal intervention," but because outlying interests were not persuaded of the importance of rebuilding downtown. Another consequence of developer prom-

---

[5] The phrase is from Theodore Lowi, "Machine Politics Old and New," *Pacific Interest*,
no. 9 (Fall 1967): 87. "The modern city is now well run but ungoverned because it has . . .
become comprised of islands of functional power before which the modern mayor stands
impoverished."

[6] See chapter 7 for accounts of the San Antonio libraries and public housing in Phoenix.

inence has been that these economic leaders had, for decades, natural residential constituencies supporting their vision of growth. More recently, in several cities disadvantaged neighborhoods near the center and central business interests have joined to form downtown coalitions to press their claims for municipal priorities and spending.

Attention to the West provides opportunities to understand the practice of creating growth strategies. Across these cases of "pure entrepreneurial regimes," various "growth machines" have been in the ascendant. Despite the awareness of the major actors here of competitive pressure, they have not always pursued *maximum* growth, as other considerations have affected the construction of growth strategies.[7] Early in the century, Austin, for example, chose a white-collar development strategy that excluded industrial recruitment. In the same years, San Diego staked her future on the navy in part because the navy promised an exclusively Anglo labor force (a reason altogether ironic in the 1990s, when the armed forces are among the best integrated large organizations in the United States). The same strategy restricted San Diego's growth options later on, as the navy's control of land and particularly the waterfront brought veto power over port development, airport construction, and other plans. Elsewhere too, growth theorists may recognize path dependence as a determinant of growth strategies, past decisions as constraints on current options.

Whatever theoretical claims may be made about growth's costs and benefits, whether growth strategies generate consensus or not is an empirical question. The more fragile and uncertain the local economy, the more persuasive arguments supporting growth strategies are likely to be to the general public. The narrative has shown that uncertainty early in the century helped southwestern urban leaders build support for growth, and with it, municipal reform. Even so, there were always dissenters, resisters, and proponents of alternate strategies.

Another empirical question is how well unfettered pursuit of growth served the ordinary citizens. Here the results are mixed. Certainly there were many who prospered in the pure entrepreneurial regimes of southwestern cities. By contrast, John Mollenkopf has shown that the income distribution in southwestern cities was more unequal than in northeastern cities in 1970,[8] and I have provided evidence about inequity in

---

[7] For a similar argument about New Orleans, see Michael Peter Smith and Marlene Keller, " 'Managed Growth' and the Politics of Uneven Devleopment in New Orleans," in *Restructuring the City: The Political Economy of Urban Redevelopment*, ed. Susan S. Fainstein, Norman I. Fainstein, Richard Child Hill, Dennis Judd, and Michael Peter Smith (New York: Longman, 1983), 126–66.

[8] John H. Mollenkopf, *The Contested City* (Princeton: Princeton University Press, 1983), 247.

the delivery of urban services. Thus, although some thrived as southwestern cities expanded, for many others in the Southwest, rising tides provided only wet feet.

The pressures toward growth may be the beginning or even the premise of local politics, but they are not the whole story of city politics, even in pure entrepreneurial regimes. Emphasis on the pursuit of growth has increased attention to elites in local politics to the neglect of popular politics and the arrangements that enhance the role of the many in political decisions. Adding the big reform cities of the West to the study of city politics should increase scholarly sensitivity to the political supports of the pursuit of growth and the political institutions that organize the delivery of its benefits.

Machine politics also merits reevaluation in light of big city reform. It is an axiom of the contemporary study of city politics that machines suppress participation, especially the participation of minorities. Rufus Browning, Dale Marshall, and William Tabb, for example, recently placed urban machines as the first barrier to the political incorporation of minorities in city politics. Boston, New York, and Chicago, they argued, "present characteristics that were not found in . . . California cities and that constituted additional barriers to minority mobilization and incorporation. . . . a party, or 'machine' . . . [has] co-opted minorities into their organization." Others have been more harsh, claiming that machine politics "demobilized" or "dismantled" the African-American vote.[9]

From the perspective of the big cities of the Southwest, machine politics does not look nearly so antiparticipatory. Even if, as Browning and his co-authors claim, "the machine attempts to prevent the formation of multiracial challenging coalitions through cooptation,"[10] machine politics must be judged a veritable school of politics for working-class and minority voters, compared to big-city reform.

Voter turnout is the most readily available indication of this, and a

[9] Steven Erie argues, "In Chicago, the machine used the welfare state to dismantle and control the Black vote," "the machine relied on the expanding welfare state to demobilize the black vote" (*Rainbow's End*, 169). See also William J. Grimshaw, *Bitter Fruit: Black Politics and the Chicago Machine, 1931–1991* (Chicago: University of Chicago Press, 1992). And similarly, Mike Royko, *Boss: Richard J. Daley of Chicago* (New York: New American Library, 1971), chap. 7, and Milton Rakove, *Don't Make No Waves . . . Don't Back No Losers: An Insider's Analysis of the Daley Machine* (Bloomington: Indiana University Press, 1975), 256–91.

[10] Rufus Browning, Dale Rogers Marshall, and David H. Tabb, "Has Political Incorporation Been Achieved? Is It Enough?" in *Racial Politics in American Cities*, ed. Rufus Browning, Dale Rogers Marshall, and David H. Tabb (New York: Longman, 1990), 216–17.

telling one. Turnout in machine-descendant cities, for most of this century, greatly outpaced turnout in big reform cities. This is hardly accidental. Party workers and leaders continued to have incentives to get out the vote, be present in the neighborhoods, contact voters, and be responsive to voters' contacts. The result was, comparatively speaking, a highly participatory form of local politics.

Recent events provide evidence of this (as well as a good example of the "tool kit" understanding of political culture). When Carol Mosely Braun won the Illinois Democratic primary race for the U.S. Senate, her first comment to her cheering supporters was "we know how to do this." Media coverage emphasized Braun's status as the first African-American woman elected to the Senate, but of course she is also the first African-American *Democrat* elected to the Senate (despite the fact that the overwhelming majority of African-American voters have supported the party since FDR). When Braun reminded her audience "we know how to do this," she was referring to the tremendous repertoire of political skill accumulated over seventy years of electoral practice and organization of the African-American community in Illinois, especially Chicago. Chicago blacks fought their way first into the Republican machine in the 1920s, and then into its successors (all Democratic machines). Thus despite opposition to her candidacy on the part of party leaders, Braun was able to win first the Democratic nomination and then the election. It should surprise no one that the first African-American Democrat, in the Senate, like the first African-American Democrat in the House, came from Chicago.

Adding the West to the study of city politics suggests some additional revisions in thinking about local politics and government. For example, frequently authors rely on the "conservative" political culture of the West or South, compared to more "liberal" political cultures in the East to explain differences in politics and policy. We need to problematize these assumptions about political culture, not because they are without foundation, but because we should explain how they came about. Institutional arrangements are sure to play some role here. The boundaries of cities are a good example. Suppose New York City were bounded as Phoenix was in 1965, and the suffrage equally restricted. Could John Lindsay have been elected mayor of New York if Westchester, Nassau, western Connecticut, and the city's New Jersey suburbs all cast ballots in the mayoral election? If only one in six or one in ten adults voted? If an even smaller proportion of African-Americans and Hispanics voted? It may well be that regional differences in sentiment are less striking than differences in political arrangements, with consequences for political discourse, identity, and expectations.

Big-City Reform

The municipal-reform movement began in the big cities of the Northeast in the middle of the nineteenth century; municipal reformers saw all their dreams and programs realized in the big cities of the Southwest in the middle of the twentieth century. My aim in *Morning Glories* has been to trace the growth and development of reform governance in the Southwest, and to place the history of big-city reform alongside the more familiar stories of the Progressive Era campaigns for social and structural reform, and post–World War II reform government in the suburbs.

The big-city reform regimes of midcentury seem, in their perfection, illusions, and demise rather like Pullman, Illinois. George Pullman designed the city to house his workforce as well as the factory that manufactured railroad sleeping cars. Pullman had high hopes that his beautifully designed town would promote a "different type" of worker and bring with it industrial peace. "Believing that 'everything depends upon surroundings,' Pullman anticipated that the removal of people from the city to his town would bring about a transformation in their values and ways." The *Boston Herald* agreed, reporting, "With such surroundings . . . the disturbing conditions of strikes and other trouble that periodically convulse the world of labor would not need to be feared here."[11]

Pullman planned the city to return 6 percent on his investment in building it, even as his sleeping-car business was a profitable industrial investment. There were no elected officials in the town and no political life to speak of. Pullman was managed by a company officer who employed a corps of assistants and "managed for the best interests of the whole community." In Pullman's view, "as long as the town . . . is owned by one association there is little necessity of agitating the subject of its control by any municipal government."[12] Although the occasional reporter denounced Pullman as a "slave pen," most press coverage was very positive, emphasizing the physical beauty and handsome accommodations of the town, as well as the apparent contentedness of its residents.

For all its beauty and calm, however, the town proved disappointing. Pullman did not publicly acknowledge it, but he was never able to earn 6 percent on his investment in the town, despite the fact that the "company did not let the real estate market influence its rents."[13] Similarly, big-city

---

[11] Stanley Buder, *Pullman: An Experiment in Industrial Order and Community Planning, 1880–1930* (New York: Oxford University Press, 1967), 77; for *Boston Herald*, 70.
[12] Buder, *Pullman*, 107.
[13] Ibid., 89–91, 132–33.

reform promoted fiscal illusions. Governments extravagant in their support of developers claimed to be frugal and sparing, boasted the transfer of service provision to county government as they claimed to provide for the good of the whole, and pointed to a bottom line of low taxes. Government debts mounted nevertheless.

Second, there were those never accommodated in the houses Pullman built. At the southern edge of town, there were brick works employing 250 men housed in "wood frame dwellings which were distinctly inferior to the accommodations offered the other residents."[14] Although Pullman had made no accommodation for these workers in the town proper (and tours of the village avoided its far south side), they were as integral to the town's economy as the neat little homes and tenements Pullman built for workers, foremen, and managers. Similarly, the contented political communities of big-city reform were not the whole of their metropolitan setting. These settings included diversity, inequality, and inequity; diversity, inequality, and inequity were the unacknowledged realities of the cities of big-city reform.

Finally, the great Pullman strike of 1894 provided proof that however pleasing the town, it could not create industrial peace. No more did the governments of big reform cities eliminate politics, provide for the good of the whole with businesslike efficiency, or raise their diverse and sprawling communities up on a prosperous tide.

What was the setting in which big city reform flourished? What were the conditions in which reformers' wish list was institutionalized?

The first condition for big-city reform government was exclusion. It is no accident that the affluent suburb became the paradigmatic representation of reform governance. The restricted, middle-class, Anglo electorate was the popular foundation of big city reform. This was not because their working-class fellow citizens were self-regarding or abided corruption happily, but because expanding the political community is at least potentially redistributive and expensive. Subsidies for growth, for industrial recruitment, and even more for geographic expansion left little in local treasuries for amenities or public services. These were carefully targeted to government's greatest beneficiaries and most reliable supporters.

A second condition for big-city reform was prosperity. Prosperity was key to the creation of jobs, expansion, and a high standard of living. Big reform cities were home to pure entrepreneurial regimes both because their most likely challengers were excluded from political life, and because sustained prosperity made geographic expansion and the provision of infrastructure and amenities possible. The same prosperity perhaps made big-city reform politicians overconfident in the expansive 1950s,

---

[14] Ibid., 58–59.

220

CHAPTER NINE

1960s, and even in some places the 1970s, as they annexed more territory than they could afford or manage to serve.

Paul Peterson has argued that there is a popular consensus supporting the pursuit of growth because growth is in the interest of the whole community. Along these lines we may say that big reform cities enjoyed a long Petersonian moment after the Second World War. Big-city reform governments created a "growth community." There was a consensus on growth, which seemed to raise all the boats in the small political communities of big-city reform. Not only were developers made rich, but also the home buyers in their newly constructed communities benefited materially (in lower housing costs) from the priorities of the growth machine. The same residents, of course, enjoyed good schools, public libraries, parks, and pools. This was the common experience of residents in the Heights in Albuquerque, the north side of Phoenix, and the west side of Austin. In these communities and communities like them across the Southwest, residents had good reasons to be contented with local government.

This was not a scenario that could be extended without limit. One limit was spatial and economic. The viability of the growth community was dependent on continuously expanding the boundaries of the city. If bonds helped to finance developers and build the streets and infrastructure for new residents, they were paid off by ever more residents added to the city's tax rolls. Eventually, however, spatial growth reached limits, either because cities ran up against other incorporated or otherwise independent areas or because environmentalists imposed boundaries. Then taxes could only go up, or subsidies down or both. Even earlier, local government's political reach overextended its service-delivering grasp, even for middle-class Anglo communities. Once this happened the growth consensus of big-city reform's small political community was threatened.[15]

The second limit was political. The beneficiaries of these governments were the same middle-class constituents who so generously rewarded big-city reform with their votes. Yet their contented community lived within larger, more diverse, communities of sprawling southwestern metropolises. The neighborhoods excluded from amenities, services, and representation protested, petitioned, organized, mobilized, and finally, changed the rules of local politics. Big-city reform worked best for the

---

[15] These arrangements seem in retrospect something of a Ponzi or pyramid scheme, dependent on an ever-expanding base. The Revenue Anticipation Bonds [sic] of the Lindsay and Beame administrations in New York City betray comparable optimism. The revolution of rising expectations in the 1960s was probably not, as some thought at the time, among the nation's poor, but among its city-builders.

small political community its rules created; reformers wrote the rules to win the game. The same rules, however, insulated local government from the accumulating discontents of the communities it served less well. This was surely the intention of midcentury city-builders who carefully created the "wieldy constituencies" of big-city reform.

The institutional arrangements of local politics became the target of communities dissatisfied with local government. The criticisms of minority and Anglo neighborhoods, environmentalists, and advocates of managed growth echoed the opponents of municipal reform at the beginning of the century. In the Progressive Era, commission government was feared as too centralized; citywide elections opposed because they threatened to deprive workers, Spanish-speakers, and neighborhoods of representation.[16] In the interwar period and after, city-manager government was characterized as "class government," city managers were denounced as potential autocrats, their proposed governments feared as expensive and antilabor.[17] Later citywide elections became the target of civil rights activists, who recognized in these arrangements barriers to the representation of the preferences of communities of color. Eventually both the federal government and a majority of local voters also became persuaded that big-city reform was intolerably undemocratic. The result, changing the rules for electing members of the city council, was accompanied by changes in campaigning and representation, in the substance, style, and implementation of public policy.

More than cities elsewhere in the United States, the big cities of the Southwest continue as the legatees of the municipal-reform movement and the big-city governments it created. Like city governments elsewhere, city governments in the Southwest boast professional bureaucracies, civil service, the absence of patronage and corruption. Here too are city managers, whose efforts are crucial to adjusting the priorities of municipal bureaucracies to new institutional arrangements (or resisting that change, as in Dallas). Nonpartisanship also continues to distinguish local politics in the big cities of the Southwest. Without the organizing discipline of party, both voters and council members fall back on geography to define their interests.

Finally, big cities in the Southwest govern a much larger portion of their metropolitan areas than big cities in other regions. As David Rusk has argued, this greater reach positions city government better to avoid or assuage the ills of our times: segregation, the appearance of an underclass, the deterioration of public education, the unexamined pursuit of

[16] See *supra*, chapter 3.
[17] See *supra*, chapter 5.

growth.[18] Whether there is the political will to accomplish these tasks is yet unknown.

In 1986 the National Municipal League appointed a committee to develop a strategic plan for the organization. In November the committee proposed, and the league adopted, new goals and a new name. The league's central task, the mission statement read, "is to assist, motivate, and enable citizens, and to serve as the national forum in which they can exchange ideas and strategies for the strengthening of self-government." Echoing earlier campaigns, the mission statement claimed that the "lifeblood of America's communities is a civic ethic articulating a vision of the common good" and the league rechristened itself the National Civic League. Lifting the banner of its next crusade, the league declared its dedication to helping citizens make government "more efficient and responsive to the needs of all members of society."[19] The reader tempted to jeer at these lonely cranks might reflect on how foolish it must have seemed, a century ago, to vow an end to the shame of the cities.

---

[18] This is the argument of David Rusk, *Cities without Suburbs* (Baltimore: Johns Hopkins University Press, 1993).

[19] "Letter from the League: Changes Afoot," *National Civic Review* 76, no. 1 (January–February 1987), 5–9.

Appendix

Notes on the Choice of Cases

MORNING GLORIES constructs an account of the course of reform in the big cities of the Southwest. By the "Southwest" I mean Texas, Oklahoma, New Mexico, Arizona, and California. At the outset I hoped to study cities in each of these states, and perhaps Colorado, but the logistics of long distance travel quickly persuaded me that this was too ambitious and, except for an occasional mention, neither Oklahoma nor Colorado cities are included here.

My general rule was to choose the largest cities with city-manager government, nonpartisanship, and citywide elections. This was both because my goal was to construct a narrative about big-city reform and because the larger cities seemed more likely to offer better libraries and historical collections. For New Mexico that meant Albuquerque, and for Arizona, Phoenix. In California, San Jose and San Diego were the largest city-manager cities.

I broke the size rule for Texas. The largest city manager cities there are Dallas and San Antonio. I have included some original research on Dallas, although I rely heavily on Robert B. Fairbank's excellent historical essays. San Antonio has received considerable scholarly attention, and I have relied both on published accounts and on the excellent scholarship of Heywood T. Sanders. I chose Houston initially because of the archives at the Houston Public Library, the city's strong industrial base (unusual for the Southwest), and the city's decision to reject the city-manager form. My second choice was Austin, also boasting an excellent public library (the Austin History Center) and also unusual for its early choice of a white-collar growth strategy.

Chapters 1–4 focus on San Diego, Albuquerque, Phoenix, Houston, and Austin. Chapters 5 through 8 survey the experience of seven cities: Albuquerque, Austin, Dallas, Phoenix, San Antonio, San Diego, and San Jose. Where it has been available, I present data on all seven cities for population growth, government expenditures, turnout in municipal elections, and provision of amenities. This is close to a complete set of big reform cities in the Southwest, with (in addition to Oklahoma City and Tulsa), only Fort Worth, Oakland, and Long Beach excluded. For the heyday of big-city reform, the first two decades after the Second World

War, I focus on Albuquerque, Austin, and Phoenix to describe electoral arrangements, popular support, and distribution of amenities.

I should also note some paths not taken. In a world of unlimited resources, an interesting investigation would have compared the few big southwestern cities that did not choose reform government (El Paso, Tucson, Houston, Los Angeles, San Francisco) to the big-reform cities.

One reader asked why I had not taken a "national sample" of big-city reform. More resources would not have helped here: outside the Southwest, big-city reform, although it may have existed de jure, hardly existed de facto. The reform charters of Cincinnati, Portland, and Seattle, for example, were overwhelmed by the presence of political parties. The reform charters of Memphis, Norfolk, and Birmingham were subordinated to the politics of race. One city outside the Southwest in which municipal reformers got most of what they wanted was Toledo, Ohio, where politics looked very much like it did in the big reform cities studied here. The interested reader may want to peruse Jean L. Stinchcombe, *Reform and Reaction: City Politics in Toledo* (Belmont, Calif.: Wadsworth, 1968).

Bibliography

Books

Abbott, Carl. *The Metropolitan Frontier: Cities in the Modern American West*. Tucson: University of Arizona Press, 1985.

———. *The New Urban America: Growth Politics in Sunbelt Cities*. Chapel Hill: University of North Carolina Press, 1981.

Allen, Ivan. *Mayor: Notes on the Sixties*. New York: Simon and Schuster, 1971.

Almaguer, Tomas. *Racial Fault Lines: The Historical Origins of White Supremacy in California*. Berkeley: University of California Press, 1994.

Banfield, Edward C., and James Q. Wilson. *City Politics*. New York: Vintage, 1966.

Bensel, Richard Franklin. *Sectionalism and American Political Development, 1880–1980*. Madison: University of Wisconsin Press, 1984.

Berman, David R. *Reformers, Corporations, and the Electorate: An Analysis of Arizona's Age of Reform*. Niwot: University Press of Colorado, 1992.

Bernard, Richard M., and Bradley Robert Rice, eds. *Sunbelt Cities: Politics and Growth since World War II*. Austin: University of Texas Press, 1983.

Blackford, Mansel G. *The Politics of Business in California, 1890–1920*. Columbus: Ohio State University Press, 1977.

Bridges, Amy. *A City in the Republic: Antebellum New York and the Origins of Machine Politics*. New York: Cambridge University Press, 1984.

Browning, Rufus, Dale Rogers Marshall, and David H. Tabb. *Protest Is Not Enough: The Struggle of Blacks and Hispanics for Equality in Urban Politics*. Berkeley: University of California Press, 1984.

Buder, Stanley. *Pullman: An Experiment in Industrial Order and Community Planning, 1880–1930*. New York: Oxford University Press, 1967.

Bunche, Ralph. *The Political Status of the Negro in the Age of FDR*. Chicago: University of Chicago Press, 1973.

Childs, Richard S. *The First 50 Years of the Council-Manager Plan of Municipal Government*. New York: American Book–Stratford Press, 1965.

Cline, Dorothy I. *Albuquerque and the City Manager Plan, 1917–1948*. Albuquerque: University of New Mexico Press, 1951.

Davidson, Chandler, and Bernard Grofman, eds. *Quiet Revolution in the South: The Impact of the Voting Rights Act, 1965–1990*. Princeton: Princeton University Press, 1994.

Donnelly, Thomas C., ed. *Rocky Mountain Politics*. Albuquerque: University of New Mexico Press, 1940.

Eakins, David W., ed. *Businessmen and Municipal Reform: A Study of Ideals and Practice in San Jose and Santa Cruz, 1896–1916*. San Jose: San Jose State University Press, 1976.

Ebner, Michael H., and Eugene M. Tobin, eds. *The Age of Urban Reform: New*

Perspectives on the Progressive Era. Port Washington, N.Y.: Kennikat Press, 1977.

Elkin, Stephen. *City and Regime in the American Republic.* Chicago: University of Chicago Press, 1987.

Embry, Jessie L., and Howard A. Christy, eds. *Community Development in the American West: Past and Present Nineteenth and Twentieth Century Frontiers.* Provo: Brigham University Press, 1985.

Erie, Steven P. *Rainbow's End: Irish-Ameicans and the Dilemmas of Urban Machine Politics, 1840–1985.* Berkeley: University of California Press, 1988.

Ethington, Philip. *The Public City: The Political Construction of Urban Life in San Francisco, 1850–1900.* New York: Cambridge University Press, 1995.

Evans, Peter B., Dietrich Rueschmeyer, and Theda Skocpol, eds. *Bringing the State Back In.* New York: Cambridge University Press, 1985.

Fairbanks, Robert B., and Kathleen Underwood, eds. *Essays on Sunbelt Cities and Recent Urban America.* College Station: Texas A & M University Press, 1990.

Gershenkron, Alexander. *Economic Backwardness in Historical Perspective.* Cambridge: Harvard University Press, 1962.

Goble, Danney. *Progressive Oklahoma: The Making of a New Kind of State.* Norman: University of Oklahoma Press, 1980.

Goodall, Leonard, ed. *Urban Politics in the Southwest.* Tempe: Arizona State University Institute of Public Administration, 1967.

Gottlieb, Robert. *Empires in the Sun: The Rise of the New American West.* New York: G. P. Putnam's Sons, 1982.

Grantham, Dewey. *Southern Progressivism: The Reconciliation of Progress and Tradition.* Knoxville: University of Tennessee Press, 1983.

Greenstone, J. David, and Paul E. Peterson. *Race and Authority in Urban Politics: Community Participation and the War on Poverty.* New York: Russell Sage, 1973.

Grofman, Bernard, and Chandler Davidson, eds. *Controversies in Minority Voting: The Voting Rights Act in Perspective.* Washington, D.C.: Brookings Institution, 1992.

Hamilton, Charles. "Political Access, Minority Participation, and the New Normalcy." In *Minority Report,* ed. Leslie W. Dunbar, pp. 3–25. New York: Pantheon, 1984.

Harrigan, John J. *Political Change in the Metropolis.* New York: HarperCollins, 1993.

Hawley, Willis D. *Nonpartisan Elections and the Case for Party Politics.* New York: Wiley, 1973.

Heilig, Peggy, and Robert J. Mundt. *Your Voice at City Hall.* Albany: State University of New York Press, 1984.

Hofstadter, Richard. *The Age of Reform.* New York: Vintage, 1955.

Holli, Melvin G. *Reform in Detroit: Hazen S. Pingree and Urban Politics.* New York: Oxford University Press, 1969.

Johnson, David R., John A. Booth, and Richard J. Harris. *The Politics of San Antonio: Community, Progress, and Power.* Lincoln: University of Nebraska Press, 1983.

Judd, Dennis R., and Todd Swanstrom. *City Politics, Private Power and Public Policy*. New York: HarperCollins, 1994.

Karnig, Albert K., and Susan Welch. *Black Representation and Urban Policy*. Chicago: University of Chicago Press, 1980.

Kelso, Paul, *A Decade of Council-Manager Government in Phoenix, Arizona*. Tucson: University of Arizona Press, 1960.

Key, V. O., Jr. *Southern Politics in State and Nation*. New York: Vintage, 1962.

Lasswell, Mary. *John Henry Kirby: Prince of the Pines*. Austin: Encino Press, 1967.

Lee, Eugene C. *The Politics of Nonpartisanship: A Study of California City Elections*. Berkeley: University of California Press, 1960.

Logan, John R., and Harvey L. Molotch. *Urban Fortunes: The Political Economy of Place*. Berkeley: University of California, 1987.

Lotchin, Roger. *Fortress California, 1910–1961: From Warfare to Welfare*. New York: Oxford University Press, 1992.

———. "Power and Policy: American City Politics between the Two World Wars" in *Ethnics, Machines, and the American Urban Future*, ed. Scott Greer, 1–50. Cambridge: Schenkman, 1981.

Luckingham, Bradford. *Minorities in Phoenix: A Profile of Mexican American, Chinese American, and African American Communities, 1860–1992*. Tucson: University of Arizona Press, 1994.

———. *Phoenix: The History of a Southwestern Metropolis*. Tucson: University of Arizona Press, 1989.

———. *The Urban Southwest: A Profile History of Albuquerque, El Paso, Phoenix, and Tucson*. El Paso: Texas Western Press, 1982.

Marston, Mary Gilman. *George White Marston: A Family Chronicle*. San Diego: Ward Ritchie Press, 1956.

McComb, David G. *Houston: A History*. Austin: University of Texas Press, 1981.

McDonald, Terrence J., and Sally K. Ward, eds. *The Politics of Urban Fiscal Policy*. Beverly Hills: Sage, 1984.

Miller, Char, and Heywood T. Sanders, eds. *Urban Texas: Politics and Development*. College Station: Texas A & M University Press, 1990.

Mohl, Ray, ed. *Searching for the Sunbelt: Historical Perspectives on a Region*. Knoxville: University of Tennessee Press, 1990.

Mollenkopf, John. *The Contested City*. Princeton: Princeton University Press, 1983.

Montejano, David. *Anglos and Mexicans in the Making of Texas, 1836–1986*. Austin: University of Texas Press, 1987.

Nash, Gerald. *The American West Transformed: The Impact of the Second World War*. Bloomington: Indiana University Press, 1985.

Olson, David A. *Nonpartisan Elections: A Case Analysis*. Austin: University of Texas Press, 1965.

Orum, Anthony M. *Power, Money, and the People: The Making of Modern Austin*. Austin: Texas Monthly Press, 1987.

Osofsky, Gilbert. *Harlem, the Making of a Ghetto: Negro New York, 1890–1930*. New York: Harper & Row, 1971.

Perry, David C, and Alfred J. Watkins, eds. *The Rise of the Sunbelt Cities*. Beverly Hills: Sage, 1977.

Peterson, Lorin. *The Day of the Mugwump*. New York: Random House, 1961.

Peterson, Paul E. *City Limits*. Chicago: University of Chicago Press, 1981.

Pietsch, Louis Robert, et al. *The Austin Electric Railway System*. Austin: University of Texas, 1906.

Platt, Harold L. *City Building in the New South: The Growth of Public Services in Houston, Texas, 1830–1910*. Philadelphia: Temple University Press, 1983.

Plotkin, Sidney. "Democratic Change in the Urban Political Economy: San Antonio's Edwards Aquifer Controversy." In *The Politics of San Antonio, Community, Progress, and Power*, ed. David R. Johnson et al., pp. 257–174. Lincoln: University of Nebraska, 1983.

Pourade, Richard F. *City of the Dream*. Vol. 7 of *The History of San Diego*. La Jolla: Copley Books, 1977.

———. *Gold in the Sun*. Vol. 5 of *The History of San Diego*. San Diego: Union-Tribune, 1965.

———. *The Rising Tide*. Vol. 6 of *The History of San Diego*. San Diego: Union-Tribune, 1967.

Rice, Bradley Robert. *Progressive Cities: The Commission Government Movement in America, 1901–1920*. Austin: University of Texas Press, 1977.

Riker, William. *Liberalism against Populism*. Prospect Heights: Waveland Press, 1982.

Riordan, William L. *Plunkitt of Tammany Hall*. New York: Bedford, 1994.

Rogin, Michael Paul, and John L. Shover. *Political Change in California*. Westport: Greenwood, 1970.

Rosenstone, Steven J., and John Mark Hansen. *Mobilization, Participation, and Democracy in America*. New York: Macmillan, 1993.

Sale, Kirkpatrick. *Power Shift: The Rise of the Southern Rim and Its Challenge to the Eastern Establishment*. New York: Random House, 1975.

Shefter, Martin. *Political Crisis, Fiscal Crisis: The Collapse and Revival of New York City*. New York: Basic Books, 1985.

Sibley, Marilyn McAdams. *The Port of Houston: A History*. Austin: University of Texas Press, 1968.

Silverberg, Helene. "'A Government of Men': Gender, the City, and the Origins of Political Science." In *Gender and American Social Science: The Formative Years*, ed. Helene Silverberg. Princeton: Princeton University Press, forthcoming.

Simmons, Marc. *Albuquerque: A Narrative History*. Albuquerque: University of New Mexico, 1982.

Smith, Constance E. *Voting and Election Laws*. New York: Oceana, 1961.

Smythe, William E. *History of San Diego, 1542–1907*. San Diego: History Co., 1908.

Steinmo, Sven, Kathleen Thelen, and Frank Longstreth. *Structuring Politics: Historical Institutionalism in Comparative Analysis*. New York: Cambridge University Press, 1992.

Stone, Clarence. *Regime Politics: Governing Atlanta, 1946–1988*. Lawrence: University Press of Kansas, 1989.

Stone, Harold A., Don K. Price, and Kathryn H. Stone. *City Manager Government in Nine Cities*. Chicago: Public Administration Service, 1940.

Tabb, William, and Larry Sawers. *Marxism and the Metropolis*. New York: Oxford University Press, 1978.

Thomas, Robert D., and Richard W. Murray. *Progrowth Politics: Change and Governance in Houston*. Berkeley: IGS Press, 1991.

Trounstine, Philip J., and Christensen, Terry. *Movers and Shakers: The Study of Community Power*. New York: St. Martin's Press, 1982.

Wade, Richard C. *The Urban Frontier: Pioneer Life in Early Pittsburgh, Cincinnati, Lexington, Louisville, and St. Louis*. Chicago: University of Chicago, 1964.

Wallerstein, Immanuel. *The Modern World System*. New York: Academic Press, 1974.

Weinstein, James. *The Corporate Ideal in the Liberal State, 1900–1918*. Boston: Beacon Press, 1968.

Welch, Susan, and Timothy Bledsoe. *Urban Reform and Its Consequences: A Study in Representation*. Chicago: University of Chicago Press, 1988.

Wood, Robert C. *Suburbia: Its People and Their Politics*. Boston: Houghton Mifflin, 1959.

Woods, Sister Frances Jerome. *The Model Cities Program in Perspective: The San Antonio, Texas, Experience*. Washington, D.C., Government Printing Office, 1982.

Wrinkle, Robert D., ed. *Politics in the Urban Southwest*. Albuquerque: University of New Mexico, Institute for Social Research and Development, 1971.

Yearly, C. K. *The Money Machines*. Albany: State University of New York Press, 1970.

Articles and Pamphlets

Alford, Robert R., and Eugene C. Lee. "Voting Turnout in American Cities." *American Political Science Review* 62, no. 3 (1968): 796–813.

Austin, City of. "Elections, 1924–1979." Austin: City of Austin Public Information Office, 1979.

Austin Chamber of Commerce. "Progressive Austin Has It." Austin: Chamber of Commerce, ca. 1920.

Berman, David R., and Bruce D. Merrill. "Citizen Attitudes toward Municipal Reform Institutions: A Testing of Some Assumptions." *Western Political Quarterly* 29, no. 2 (1976): 273–83.

Blodgett, Terrell, and John Parr. "Letter from the League: Changes Afoot." *National Civic Review* 76, no. 1 (1987): 5–8.

Brashear, S. H. "Mayor's Message, Feburary 1900." Houston: City of Houston, February 5, 1900.

Bridges, Amy. "Another Look at Plutocracy and Politics in Antebellum New York City." *Political Science Quarterly* 97, no. 1 (1982): 57–71.

Bromley, David, and Joel Smith. "The Historical Significance of Annexation as a Social Process." *Land Economics* (August 1973): 294–309

Browning, Rufus, Dale Rogers Marshall, and David H. Tabb. "Implementation and Political Change: Sources of Local Variations in Federal Social Programs." *Policy Studies Journal* 8, no. 4 (1980) 616–32.

Calavita, Nico. "Growth Machines and Ballot Box Planning: The San Diego Case." *Journal of Urban Affairs* 14, no. 1 (1992): 1–24.

Cassella, William N., Jr. "Representative Government: Expressing, Interpreting, and Legislating the Will of the People." *National Civic Review* 83, no. 3 (1994): 317–22.

Cotrell, Charles L., and R. Michael Stevens. "The 1975 Voting Rights Act and San Antonio, Texas." *Publius* 8, no. 1 (1978): 19–99.

Doti, Lynne Pierson, and Larry Schweikart. "Financing the Postwar Housing Boom in Phoenix and Los Angeles, 1945–1960." *Pacific-Historical Review* 58, no. 2 (1989): 173–94

Ehrlich, Karen Lynn. "Arizona's Territorial Capital Moves to Phoenix." *Arizona and the West* 23, no. 2 (1984): 231–42.

Farbar, Jerome H. "The Houston Chamber of Commerce." *National Municipal Review* 2, no. 1 (1913): 104–7.

Fleischmann, Arnold. "The Politics of Annexation: A Preliminary Assessment of Competing Paradigms." *Social Science Quarterly* 61, no. 1 (1986): 128–42.

———. "The Territorial Expansion of Milwaukee, Historical Lessons for Contemporary Urban Policy and Research." *Journal of Urban History* 14, no. 2 (1988): 147–76.

Fraga, Louis. "Domination through Democratic Means: Nonpartisan Slating Groups in City Electoral Politics." *Urban Affairs Quarterly*, 23, no. 4 (1988): 528–55.

Gideon, Samuel Edward. "Austin and the Austin National Bank, 1890–1940." Austin: Austin National Bank, 1940.

Hamilton, Howard D. "Choosing a Representation System: More Than Meets the Eye." *National Civic Review* 69, no. 8 (1980): 427–34.

Hays, Samuel P. "The Politics of Municipal Reform in the Progressive Era." *Pacific Northwest Quarterly* (1961): 157–69.

Isaac, Paul E. "Municipal Reform in Beaumont, Texas, 1902–1909." *Southwestern Historical Quarterly* 78, no. 4 (1975): 409–30.

Journal of Arizona History, editors of. "Water for Phoenix: Building the Roosevelt Dam." *Journal of Arizona History* 18, no. 3 (1977): 279–94.

Keen, Harold. "The Wilson Era: San Diego's New Power Structure." *San Diego Magazine* 27, no. 7 (1973): 77–85, 120–38.

Kelley, Stanley, Jr., Richard E. Ayres, and William G. Bowen. "Registration and Voting: Putting First Things First." *American Political Science Review* 61, no. 2 (1967): 350–79.

Krenkel, John H. "The Founding of the Salt River Water Users Association." *Arizona and the West* 23, no. 1 (1984): 82–90.

Lee, Eugene C. "City Elections: A Statistical Profile." *Municipal Year Book, 1963.* Chicago: International City Managers' Association, 1963, 74–84.

Lee, Lawrence B., "William E. Smythe and San Diego, 1902–1908." *Journal of San Diego History* 19, no. 2 (1973): 10–24.

Lineberry, Robert, and Edmund Fowler. "Reformism and Public Policies in American Cities." *American Political Science Review* 61, no. 3 (1967): 701–16.

Long, Walter E. "Something Made Austin Grow." Austin: Chamber of Commerce, 1948.

March, James G., and John P. Olsen. "The New Institutionalism: Organizational Factors in Political Life." *American Political Science Review* 78, no. 3 (1984): 734–49.

Martin, Roscoe C. "The Municipal Electorate: A Case Study." *Southwestern Social Science Quarterly* 14, no. 3 (1933): 193–237.

McCuiston, Edward H. "The Commercial Secretary." *Texas Municipalities* 4, no. 4 (1917): 141–43.

Mitchell, J. Paul, "Boss Speer and the City Functional: Boosters and Businessmen versus Commission Government in Denver." *Pacific Northwest Quarterly* (October 1979): 155–64.

Molotch, Harvey L. "The City as a Growth Machine: Towards a Political Economy of Place." *American Journal of Sociology* 82 (1976): 309–33.

National Civic League, "Model City Charter," 7th ed. Denver: National Civic League, 1992.

National Municipal League. "The Cincinnati Plan of Citizen Organization for Political Activity." New York: National Municipal League, 1934.

———. "Citizen Organization for Political Activity." New York: National Municipal League, 1949.

Pratt, John W. "Boss Tweed's Public Welfare Program." *New York Historical Society Quarterly* 45 (1961): 196–211.

Rhinehart, Marilyn D. "A Lesson in Unity: The Houston Municipal Workers' Strike of 1946." *Houston Municipal Review* 4, no. 3 (1982): 137–52.

Rice, Bradley R. "The Galveston Plan of City Government by Commission: The Birth of a Progressive Idea." *Southwestern Historical Quarterly* 78, no. 4 (1975): 366–408.

Salisbury, Robert. "Urban Politics: The New Convergence of Power." *Journal of Politics* 26, no. 4 (1964): 775–97.

Schweikart, Larry. "Financing the Urban Frontier: Entrepreneurial Creativity and Western Cities, 1945–1975." *Urban Studies* 26, no. 1 (1989): 177–86.

Shefter, Martin. "Regional Receptivity to Reform: Legacy of the Progressive Era." *Political Science Quarterly* 98, no. 3 (1983): 459–83.

Sloan, Lee. "Good Government and the Politics of Race." *Social Problems* 17 (1969): 161–74.

Smith, Richard Austin. "How Business Failed Dallas." *Fortune* 70 (July 1964): 157–218.

Smythe, William E. "Responsible Government for California." *Out West* 26, no. 5 (1907) 456–61.

Starbird, George. "The New Metropolis: San Jose bewteen 1942 and 1972." San Jose: Rosecrucian Press, 1972.

Surrat, J. E. "Cooperation between City Officials and Chambers of Commerce in City Building." *Texas Municipalities* 4, no. 4 (1917): 138–40.

Svara, James H. "The Structural Reform Impulse in Local Government: Its Past and Relevance to the Future." *National Civic Review* 83, no. 3 (1994): 323–43.

Swidler, Ann. "Culture in Action: Symbols and Strategies." *American Sociological Review* 51, no. 2 (1986): 273–86.

Wilson, Marjorie Haines. "Governor Hunt, the 'Beast,' and the Miners." *Journal of Arizona History* 15, no. 2 (1974): 119–38.
Wolfinger, Ray, and John Osgood Field. "Political Ethos and the Structure of City Government." *American Political Science Review* 60, no. 1 (1966): 306–26.

Unpublished Papers

[Austin] Charter Revision Commission. "Final Report." Austin City Council, March 7, 1984.
———. "Supplementary Information" Austin City Council, March 7, 1984.
Barta, Carolyn Jenkins. "The *Dallas News* and Council-Manager Government." M.A. thesis, University of Texas at Austin, 1970.
Beibel, Charles. "Making the Most of It: Public Works in Albuquerque during the Great Depression, 1929–1942." Typescript, Albuquerque Museum, 1986.
Brown, Brent Whiting. "An Analysis of the Phoenix Charter Government Committee as a Political Entity." M.A. thesis, Arizona State University, 1968.
Crow, Wayman. "The War on Poverty in San Diego County." Typescript, Western Behavioral Sciences Institute (La Jolla), 1968.
Davila, Jaime. "Houston City Politics: The 1979 Change from At-large to Single-Member Council Districts and Its Effect on Mexican-Americans." Senior thesis, Harvard University, 1982.
Dixon, Ruth B. "Predicting Voter Turnout in City Elections." M.A. thesis, University of California, Berkeley, 1966.
Fleischmann, Arnold. "The Change to District Elections in Dallas." Typescript in the Supplementary Information of the Austin City Charter Revision Commission, March 7, 1984.
Gray, Kenneth E. "A Report on the Politics of Houston." Mimeograph, Joint Center for Urban Studies of the Massachusetts Institute of Technology and Harvard University, 1960.
Greenstone, J. David. "A Report on Politics in San Diego." Mimeograph, Joint Center for Urban Studies of the Massachusetts Institute of Technology and Harvard University, 1962.
Hales, William M., Jr. "Technological In-migration and Curricular Change: Educational Politics in Albuquerque, 1945–1965." Ph.D. diss., University of New Mexico, 1970.
Hemphill, Floylee Hunter. "Mayor Tom Miller and the First Year of the New Deal in Austin, Texas." M.A. thesis, University of Texas at Austin, 1976.
Hernandez, Juanita. "Chicano Mobilization in San Antonio City Politics, 1973–1981." Senior thesis, Harvard University, 1981.
Koch and Fowler. "A City Plan for Austin, Texas." mimeograph, 1928.
Konig, Michael Francis. "Toward Metropolis Status: Charter Government and the Rise of Phoenix, Arizona, 1945–1960." Ph.D. diss., Arizona State University, Tempe, 1983.
Kotlanger, Michael John. "Phoenix, Arizona: 1920–1940." Ph.D. diss., Arizona State University, 1983.
Kurtz, Donald. "Politics, Ethnicity, and Integration: Mexican-Americans in the War on Poverty [in San Diego]." Ph.D. diss., University of California, Davis, 1970.

Lacy, Sara. "Austin, 1900–1915." Typescript draft for the Federal Writer's Project Guide to Austin, 1938.

Mahoney, Timothy Raymond, II. "Neighborhoods and Municipal Politics: A Case Study of Decentralized Power Systems: Austin, Texas (Spring 1981)" M.A. thesis, University of Texas, Austin, 1983.

Mawn, Geoffrey Padraic. "Phoenix, Arizona: Central City of the Southwest, 1870–1920." Ph.D. diss., Arizona State University, 1979.

Miller, Grace Louise. "The San Diego Progressive Movement, 1900–1920." Ph.D. diss., University of California, Santa Barbara, 1976.

Nicolaides, Becky, "Battle on the Crabgrass Frontier: Society and Political Struggle in a Working Class Suburb of Los Angeles, 1929–1930." Paper delivered at the annual meeting of the Organization of American Historians, Anaheim, 1993.

Rockstroh, Stephen. "An Analysis of Phoenix Municipal Administration, 1881–1952." M.A. thesis, Arizona State University, 1952.

Sanders, Heywood. "Beyond Machine and Reform: The Politics of Postwar Development in Sunbelt Cities." Paper prepared for delivery at the annual meeting of the American Political Science Association, Washington, D.C., 1984.

———. "The Creation of Post-War San Antonio: Politics, Voting, and Fiscal Regimes, 1945 to 1960." Paper prepared for the annual meeting of the Southwestern Social Science Association, San Antonio, Texas, March 1991.

———. "Rethinking Lineberry and Urban Service Delivery: Politics, Dollars and Libraries in San Antonio." Paper prepared for the annual meeting of the Urban Affairs Association, Indianapolis, April, 1993.

Sanders, L. L. "How to Win Elections in San Antonio the Good Government Way, 1955–1971." M.A. thesis, St. Mary's University, 1975.

Schingle, Michael J. "Albuquerque Urban Politics, 1891–1955: Aldermanic vs. Commission Government." Senior thesis, University of New Mexico, 1976.

Schloyer, Dean. "Ethnic Politics in a Sunbelt City: The Case of San Diego." M.A. thesis, University of California, San Diego, 1993.

Smith, Cecelia Babcock. "The Austin Model Cities Program." M.A. thesis, University of Texas, Austin, 1970.

Smith, Joseph C. "The Phoenix Drive for Municipal Reform and Charter Government, 1911–1915." Typescript, Arizona Historical Foundation Manuscript Collection, Arizona State University, 1975.

Smith, Karen Lynn. "From Town to City: A History of Phoenix, 1870–1912." M.A. thesis, University of California, Santa Barbara, 1978.

Staniszewski, Frank. "Ideology and Practice in Municipal Government Reform: A Case Study of Austin." University of Texas at Austin Studies in Politics, Series I: Studies in Urban Political Economy, paper no. 8, 1977.

Stites, Kenneth, Jr. "A Study of Nonpartisanship: The 1963 Phoenix Municipal Primary Election." M.A. thesis, Arizona State University, 1964.

Stone, Daniel Edward. "The Evolution of Municipal Budgeting in the City of San Diego, California." M.A. thesis, San Diego State University, 1967.

Thorpe, Robert. "Council-Manager Government in San Jose, California." M.A. thesis, Stanford University, 1938.

Tinsley, James A. "The Progressive Movement in Texas." Ph.D diss., University of Wisconsin, 1953.

Underwood, Katherine. "Process and Politics: Multiracial Electoral Coalition Building and Representation in Los Angeles' Ninth District, 1949–1962." Ph.D. diss., University of California, San Diego, 1992.

Wood, Robert Turner. "The Transformation of Albuquerque, 1945–1972." Ph.D. diss., University of New Mexico, 1980.

Manuscript Collections

Ferguson Papers. Coronado Room, University of New Mexico Library.

Interviews. Phoenix Public History Project, Arizona Historical Society.

Lissner Papers. Stanford University.

Minutes of the Houston Charter Commission. Houston Municipal Research Center.

Minutes of the [San Diego] Board of Freeholders. City Clerk's Office, San Diego.

Neal Pickett Papers. Houston Municipal Research Center.

Oral History Collection. Labor History Archives, University of Texas at Arlington.

Oscar Holcombe Papers. Houston Municipal Research Center.

Political Campaign Collection. Houston Municipal Research Center.

Newspapers

Albuquerque Herald.
Albuquerque Journal.
Albuquerque Morning Journal.
Arizona Gazette.
Arizona Republic.
Arizona Republican.
Arizona Sun.
Austin American.
Austin American Statesman.
Austin Daily Statesman.
Dallas Morning News.
Facts and Figures (Houston).
Houston Chronicle.
Houston Defender.
Houston Post.
Houston Press.
Houston Labor Journal.
San Antonio Express.
San Antonio Light.
San Diego Sun.
San Diego Union.

Index

Action Citizens' Ticket (ACT, Phoenix), 177

Addams, Jane, 8

African-Americans: Austin community of, 91–92, 95; in Austin/Phoenix/Albuquerque (1960s), 144–45; "black beater" system used against, 189; campaigns promoting rights of, 139–40; challenges to big-city reform by, 178; community grievances of (San Diego), 169–70; disfranchisement of, 20; district election of, 201; educational segregation of, 168–69; electoral power of, 75; excluded from city services, 155; first female Democratic Senator among, 217; GGL's consultations with, 123; Houston community of, 87–90, 95; nomination of (1960s), 181–82; participation in machine politics (Chicago), 216–17; poll tax aimed at, 132; suffrage restrictions against, 66–67, 74, 89–90. *See also* discrimination; race; segregation

Age of Reform, The (Hofstadter), 21–22

Akin, Harry, 184

Albuquerque: advertising for settlers by, 35–36; antigrowth sentiment in, 194; challenges to big-city reform in, 176; commission manager government in, 82; defense spending solicitation by, 101; demographics (1960) of, 144–45; early history of, 31–32; ending of annexation by, 203; growth coalition in, 158–59; postwar description of, 151; postwar political community of, 171; Proposition 4 of, 196; public libraries in, 164; reform coalition in, 142–43; voter turnout (1960) in, 146–47

Albuquerque Booster, 47

Albuquerque Citizens' Committee (ACC), 123, 141, 142–43, 147, 167, 176

Albuquerque Herald, 84

Albuquerque Journal, 142, 161, 167, 201

Albuquerque Morning Journal, 31, 35, 64–65, 86

Alford, Robert R., 128, 130, 132

Alliance for a Better City (San Antonio), 199

annexation: ending of Phoenix/Albuquerque, 203; forcible, 156n.17; impact of, 155, 173; during postwar ear, 152–54

antigrowth movements, 191–92, 193–94, 202. *See also* growth

Apache Creek Improvement, 183

Arizona Gazette, 36, 60–61, 140, 177, 197

Arizona Republic, 201

Arizona Republican, 59, 61–62, 67, 81, 110, 157

Arizona Sun, 21, 139–40, 155

Arizona Voters' League (Phoenix), 139

Armstrong, Bob, 143

Association of City and County Employees (Houston), 108, 109

"at-large principle," 195

Austin: advertising for settlers by, 36; African-American community in, 91–92, 95; analysis of 1933 election in, 75; antigrowth sentiment in, 193–94; debate over Motorola plant in, 202; demographics (1960) of, 144–45; early history of, 31–32; federal lobbying by, 41–42; financial problems of, 105–6; municipal reform in, 67–68, 69–70; passage of council-manager plan in, 115–16, 117–18; politicization of commission plan in, 79; public libraries in, 164; reform coalition in, 143; reform government in, 93; voter turnout (1960) in, 146–47; white-collar growth plan (1940s) of, 100

Austin American, 115

Austin-American Statesmen, 42, 46

Austin Business League, 70

Austin Daily Tribune, 31

authority: under commission plan, 64; private resources and government, 28

Balboa Park (San Diego), 32, 49

Baldwin, A. C., 60, 114

Baldwin, George Johnson, 68

Banfield, Edward, 4, 5, 22, 25, 125, 134, 162, 210
Barnett, George, 37
Beard, Charles, 53
Bellamah, Dale, 159
Bellinger, Charles, 164
Bice, Richard, 197
big-city reform: campaigning/persuading under, 135–41; characteristics of, 125–26; civic statesmen of, 172–74; dissatisfaction/reform of, 181–87, 191–200, 213; election challenges to, 176–81; key accomplishments of, 210–12; limits of, 218–20; middle class and, 22, 25–26, 220–21; overview of, 6–12, 205–6, 218–22; political community of, 148–50; political machines and, 216; prosperity and, 219–20; public amenities under, 166; voter rules/turnout and, 130–35; voter turnout (1947–63) under, 133. See also municipal reform movement; reform government
Bigley, Charles, 124
"black beater" system, 189
Blessing, Elizabeth, 176–77, 178
Board of Education vs. Brown, 168
Board of Freeholders (San Diego), 105, 106
Book of the Month Club (San Jose), 124, 159, 160
Booth, John, 169
Boston's Citizens Ticket, 7
Bowers, W. W., 79
Brashear, Samuel, 44, 46
Braun, Carol Mosely, 217
Browne, T. W., 106
Browning, Rufus, 216
Brown vs. Board of Education, 168
Buchanan, James, 92
Busey, Ray, 157
business leaders: Chambers of Commerce, 47–51; developers as, 156, 214–15; governmental authority and, 27–28; municipal reform advocated by, 56; political lobbying of, 42–46; postwar efforts of, 102, 209–10; reform charters supported by, 74; in the Southwest before World War I, 34. See also elites; "growth machine"

Campbell, Ben, 41, 70, 208
Campbell, Walter, 68

Carver High School (Phoenix), 168–69
Central Labor Council of AFL (Phoenix), 107
Chamber of Commerce (Oklahoma City), 124
Chambers of Commerce (Southwestern cities), 47–51
Charter Government Committee (CGC, Phoenix), 119–20, 178, 197
Charter Revision Committee (Austin), 199
Charter Revision Committee (Phoenix), 105
charters: commissions appointed to study, 105; and defeat of city-manager, 115; impact on politicians of, 75, 78–83; impact of reform on, 73–75; municipal employees' opposition to, 107–8; and proposed provision on police activities, 108
Chavez, Fred, 142
Chavez, Phoebe, 192
Chicago, 76–77, 131, 133, 179–80, 217
Chicano Police Officers Association, 187
Chicanos por la Causa (CPLC), 186
Childs, Richard S., 16, 30
Christy, Lloyd, 39, 40
Chronicle, 52
Cincinnati, 120
Cincinnati Plan of Citizen Organization for Political Activity, The, 120, 121n.92, 127
Citizens' Charter Association (Dallas), 110, 119, 136, 137, 139, 176, 182
Citizen's League for the Preservation of Democratic Government (Houston), 113
Citizen's Union, 3
"City as a Growth Machine, The" (Molotch), 26
city councils: city manager combination with, 82; coalitions within, 201–2; district elections for, 195–96, 200; organizing principles of, 203; under reform government, 72
City Employees Unity Council (Phoenix), 107–8
City Limits (Peterson), 26, 27
City Manager, The (White), 105
city-manager campaigns: citizen actions following, 118–24; debate over, 113–15; defeats of, 115, 118; strategies/themes of, 110–13; successes of, 115–16, 117–18

city-manager government: Austin passage (1942) of, 115–16; benefits of, 111–12; creation of, 30; elections under early, 82–83; increasing adoption of, 101–3; institutionalized, 81–82; labor view on, 109; nature of, 72. *See also* government
City Plan (Koch and Fowler), 49
city politics: business and authority of, 28; economic growth and, 26–29, 97; new institutionalism and, 13–14. *See also* local politics; municipal reform
City Politics (Banfield and Wilson), 4, 5
City Politics, Private Power and Public Policy (Judd and Swanstrom), 5
city-wide elections, 103, 196, 198–99, 221. *See also* elections
civil rights: activism during 1960s for, 21; campaigns promoting, 139–40; complaints on violations of, 169–70; federal initiatives and, 185; institutional arrangements blocking, 175; NPSG response to activity of, 181; statutes protecting, 182; Voting Rights Act protection of, 187–91. *See also* discrimination; race; segregation
civil service protections, 108
Cline, Dorothy I., 171, 173, 174, 210
Coalition for Barrio Betterment, 186
Colorado River, 41–42, 92
Colorado River Improvement Association, 42
Colored Carnegie Library, 88
"Commercial Secretary, The" (*Texas Municipalities*), 47
commission government: arguments against, 62–65; benefits of, 58–62; described, 58; failures of, 104–5; politicization of, 79–81; Southwestern adoption of, 65–71; success of Galveston, 9, 57, 68
Commission on Human Relations (San Diego), 170
Committee of Seventy (1894), 3
Communities Organized for Public Service (COPS), 204–5
Community Development Block Grant (CDBG), 203
Conard, Grant, 78–79
Cooper, James Fenimore, 200
Cothurm, William, 201
Cotton, Oscar, 32
Cottrell, Edwin, 53, 105

Council-Manager Club (Austin), 110
Crossland, John, 88
Curran, Frank, 184

Daily Advertiser, 7
Daley, Richard J., 24
Dallas: challenges to big-city reform in, 176–77; city plan (1910) of, 49; description of early, 33; growth coalition in, 158; municipal problems of, 151; politicization of commission plan in, 79–80; power of private resources in, 28
Dallas Morning News, 66, 110, 111, 114, 117, 137, 140, 201
Davis, Clarence, 142
Day of the Mugwump (Peterson), 102
Dealy, George B., 110
Deep Water Committee (Galveston), 57
Democratic party: on commission government, 63; nonpartisanship advocated by, 60; political appointee's support of, 86; in Southwest region, 54–55
Deppe, James T., 119
De-Ro-Loc carnival (Houston), 36
developers, 156, 214–15. *See also* growth
discrimination, 169–70, 186–87. *See also* segregation
district elections: campaigns for, 195–200; political changes following, 200–206. *See also* elections
Dixon, Ruth B., 128, 129–30, 132
Domenici, Pete, 176
Donnelly, Thomas, 86

Earth, The (railroad magazine), 36
Economic Development Corporation (San Diego), 184
economic growth: big-city reform and, 219–20; city politics and, 26–29, 97; municipal reform and, 53–54; postwar, 101–3. *See also* growth
education. *See* public school systems
8-F Crowd (Houston), 124
elections: analysis of 1933 Austin, 75; campaigning under big-city reform for, 135–41; challenging big-city reform, 176–81; on city-manager plans, 115–18; city social characteristics (1960) and, 134; city-wide, 103, 196, 198–99, 221; competitiveness (1945–63) in

elections (*cont.*)
  selected, 135; district vs. city-wide,
  195–200; under early city-manager government, 82–83; impact of return to
  district, 200–206; voter turnout (1920–
  45) in, 76–78; voter turnout (1947–63)
  in, 133; voter turnout (1965–89) in,
  179–80; Voting Rights Act impact on,
  187–91; white man's primary system in,
  89–90, 189. *See also* voters
elites: city-manager plan support by, 118–
  24; concerns with poverty/race relations
  of, 185; municipal reform supported by,
  67; redevelopment interests by, 214; reform support by Austin, 70. *See also*
  business leaders
Elkin, Stephen, 28
ethos theory, 22–23

Facts and Figures (tabloid newspaper),
  113
fair-housing ordinance (1968, Austin),
  184–85
Federal Housing Act (1949), 157
Felicetti, Larry, 142
Ferguson, James, 41
Field, John Osgood, 17
Fisher, Lewis, 109
5-5 system (Phoenix), 200
Fletcher, Edward, 67
Fortune, 207
Foster, Hohen, 120, 137
Fowler, Benjamin, 39, 40, 49
Fowler, Edmund, 17
Fraga, Luis, 189

Galveston: commission plan success in, 9,
  57, 68; hurricane damage in, 40, 57;
  suffrage restriction in, 74
Garza, Jose, 199
Georgia, 113–14
Givens, Everett, 165–66
Glaab, Charles, 5
Goddard, Terry, 195
Goldwater, Barry, 120, 169
"good government," 173–74. *See also*
  municipal reform movement
good government clubs, 3
Good Government League (Houston), 53
Good Government League (San Antonio),
  119, 122, 123, 178, 181
Goodhue, Bertram, 32

Goodwin, Clarence, 124
government: commission, 9, 57–65, 79–
  81; elements of reform, 72–73; employ-
  ment/spending (1960) by, 159–62; impacts of reform charters on, 73–75;
  lobbying of higher, 37–42; during postwar era, 102–3, 209–10; reform for
  good, 52–54. *See also* city-manager
  government; reform government
Graham, Milton, 182
Grantham, Dewey, 53
"grass roots" nominating system (Dallas),
  182
Greenstone, David, 134, 185
Griego, Vincent, 203
growth: city politics and economic, 26–
  29, 97; as district-administered issue,
  203; financial costs of, 159–62; managing new residential, 106–7; movement
  for limited, 191–92, 193–94; municipal
  reform and economic, 53–54; postwar
  economic, 101–3; of postwar era, 152–
  59, 214–16; Southwestern coalitions
  for, 158; of transportation, 42–43. *See
  also* economic growth
"growth community," 220
"growth machine": in postwar Southwest
  cities, 152, 158–59, 161, 214–15; theory of, 26–27
Gurule, John, 176

Hague, Frank, 95
Harbor Board (Houston), 41
Hardy machine, 78
Harlem, the Making of a Ghetto (Osof-
  sky), 19
Harless, Richard, 177
Harper's Weekly, 57
Harrigan, John J., 5
Harris, J. B., 89
Harris County Houston Ship Channel
  Navigation District, 40
Harrison, Carter, 4
Harry Cordova project, 157
Hartman, Glen, 196
Hawley, Willis D., 129
Haynes, Harry, 63, 113
Hays, Samuel, 56
Head, Louis P., 117
Head Start, 184
Heard, Dwight, 39, 40
Heilig, Peggy, 201, 204

Hewlett, William, 99
Hirsch, Arnold, 173
Hispanics. *See* Mexican-Americans
Hofstadter, Richard, 21–22, 25, 56
Holcombe, Oscar, 83, 84, 87–90, 95, 116–17
Holmes, Charles B., 46
Holt, Oran T., 68
Holton, Frank, 107
Honesty, Economy, and Representation (HEAR), 177
Horton, Alonzo, 51
Houston: African-American community in, 87–90, 95; city-manager government in, 115–17; commission government in, 87–90; development of, 50; difficulties faced by (1913), 52; early history of, 31–32; federal lobbying by, 38; financial problems of, 105–6; harbor created in, 40–41; municipal reforms in, 68; return of strong-mayor plan to, 116–17; strike by municipal employees of, 116; suffrage restriction in, 74
Houston Charter Commission (1938), 74, 80, 106, 110
Houston Charter Commission (1942), 112
Houston Chronicle, 40
Houston Defender, 21, 139
Houston Labor Journal, 63–64
Houston Vocational School of Household Service, 89
Human Rights Commission (1963, Phoenix), 182
Hunt, George, 34
Hutcheson, Joseph C., 40

International City Managers Association (Chicago), 114

Jacson, Rev. Bertron M., 89
James, Herman G., 53, 105
Johnson, David, 35, 169
Johnson, G. Wesley, 50
Johnson, Lyndon, 92
Johnson, Paul, 201
Johnson, Tom, 4
Jonsson, Erik, 176, 177, 181
Judd, Dennis R., 5

Kansas City, 94, 113
"Kansas City capitalists," 68

Kapp, Russell, 142
Kelley, Stanley, 126, 127–28, 130
Kelso, Paul, 119
Kessler, George, 49–50
Kettner, William, 41
Key, V. O., 73, 83, 95–96, 98, 209
Kibbey, Joseph, 39, 40
Kinney, Harry, 176
Kirby, John, 68
Kirtland Air Force Base, 101
Knight, Alfred, 105, 119
Kober, Leslie, 120
Kober, Margaret, 122
Ku Klux Klan, 20, 88, 213

Labor Messenger, 116, 140
labor unions: on city-manager plans, 109, 117; Holcombe, 88, 108; police interference with (Houston), 108–9; sunbelt centralizers support of, 213. *See also* municipal employees
language minorities, 190–91
League of Texas Municipalities, 53, 70, 81
Lee, Eugene C., 128, 129–30, 132
Leslie, Warren, 33
Lindsay, John, 181, 217
Lineberry, Robert, 17
Lipscomb, Albert, 190
Lissner, Meyer, 79
literacy test ban, 187–88
literacy tests, 128, 132
lobbying: of higher governments, 37–42; of private resources, 42–46
local politics: efforts to democratize (1960s), 182–87, 211–12; impact of reformers' work on, 72–73; institutional approach to, 14–16; interaction between region and, 17–19; interest of municipal employees in, 107–8; racial considerations of, 20–21; over utilities, 43–46; ward elections and, 61; ward representation in, 61, 63, 72. *See also* city politics; government
Long, Emma, 140, 143, 147–48, 149, 169
Long, Walter E., 100, 105
Lotchin, Roger, 5, 100
Low, Seth, 4
low-income housing, 157, 184
Luce, Edgar, 67, 70

McClure's, 57
McCombs, B. J., 196

McDuffie, Milton, 155
machine descendants: defined, 31; voter
    turnout (1820–1945) in, 76–77; voter
    turnout (1947–63) in, 133; voter turn-
    out (1965–89) in, 179–80
machine politics: and African Americans,
    217; Boss Tweed's, 73, 93; built with
    municipal employees, 92; city-manager
    government and, 113–14; compared to
    big-city reform, 95–96, 149, 161–62,
    164, 167, 216–17; corruption of, 7;
    and employment and spending (1960),
    161; government financing under
    (1960), 161; public expenditures by
    (c. 1936), 96n.88; in San Francisco
    (1890s), 55n.6; theory of, 21–22; voter
    turnout (1920–45) under, 76–77; voter
    turnout (1947–63) under, 132–33; vo-
    ter turnout (1965–89) under, 179–80;
    working-class support of, 24–25. See
    also Chicago; machine descendants
Madla, Frank, 196
March, James G., 12–13
Mardian, Sam, 142, 158
Maricopa County (Arizona), 38–39
Marshall, Dale, 216
Marston, George, 67
Martin, Roscoe, 75, 91
Marxism, 13
Massey, Otis, 116
Maverick, Maury, 83
Maxwell, George, 39
May, Samuel C., 105
media: city-manager campaigns supported
    by, 110–12; public discourse rhetoric
    by, 140–41
Mexican American Equal Rights Project,
    191
Mexican American Legal Defense and Ed-
    ucation Fund (MALDEF), 186, 190–91,
    199
Mexican-Americans: in Austin/
    Phoenix/Albuquerque (1960s), 144–45;
    boycotts of Phoenix schools by, 186;
    challenges to big-city reform by, 178;
    channeled into manual education, 186,
    187; disfranchisement of, 20; district
    election of, 201; educational segregation
    of, 169; electoral power of, 75; ex-
    cluded from city services, 155; GGL's
    consultations with, 123; as "language

minorities," 190; low-income housing
    for, 157; low public awareness of, 170;
    nomination of (1960s), 181–82; po-
    larized voting by, 189; poll tax aimed
    at, 132. See also discrimination; race;
    segregation
Mexican American Unity Council
    (MAUC), 186
Mexican American Youth Organization,
    186
middle class: Houston's African-American,
    89; municipal reform and, 22, 25–26,
    220–21; public assistance to, 95–96; in
    Southwest municipal reform, 25
Miller, Char, 35
Miller, Tom, 84, 91–94, 95
Model Cities, 183–86
Model City Charter, 195
Mollenkopf, John, 28, 215
Molotch, Harvey, 26–27, 28
"morning glories," 3
Morning Journal, 60, 66
Motorola plant (Austin), 202
Mundt, Robert, 201, 204
municipal employees: limited political in-
    fluence of, 214; political machines built
    with (Albuquerque), 86; political ma-
    chines built with (Austin), 92; strike by
    Houston, 116; vested interest in govern-
    ment by, 107–8
municipal golf courses, 165–66
municipal parks, 165–66
municipal reformers: as "morning glo-
    ries," 3; nonpartisanship of, 16, 95; or-
    ganizations created by, 16
municipal reform movement: campaigning
    for, 57–65; early benefits of, 52–54;
    economic growth and, 53–54; goals of,
    72; historiography of, 4–5; institutional
    arrangements of, 172–74; legacies of,
    207; and major charter changes, 10;
    middle class and, 22, 25–26, 220–21;
    nineteenth-century campaigns of, 6–8;
    nonpartisanship of, 16, 95; overview of,
    175, 207–13; political coalitions
    (1960s) for, 141–48; political culture
    and, 21–26; Progressive Era history of,
    8–9; race consciousness within, 19–21;
    regional setting of, 54–57; in South-
    western context, 213–17; success of
    Southwest, 3–4; suffrage restrictions

and, 66–67, 208; supported by elites, 67; voter turnout under, 132. *See also* big-city reform; reform government
Municipal Year Book (1962), 128
Munro, William Bennett, 53, 105

NAACP, 169, 172, 202
National Civic Review, 195
National League of Municipalities, 9
National Municipal League: city-manager campaign support by, 110; commission government support by, 9, 57, 58; exclusion of women in, 8; on institutional change, 195; model charters of, 208; promotion of reform charters by, 69; strategic plan developed (1986) by, 222
National Municipal League (Phoenix), 53
National Municipal Review, 11, 52, 69, 70, 101, 115, 117
National Reapportionment Rights Project, 191
National Reclamation Act, 67
Native Americans, 20
New Deal programs, 92, 95
New Haven, Conn., 76–77, 131, 133, 179–80
"new institutionalism," 12–14
"new normalcy," 204
New York, 3, 69, 76–77, 131, 133, 179–80
Nolen, John, 49
nonpartisanship: of commission plan, 59–60; impact on turnout, 129–30; of municipal reformers, 16, 95; reform government move toward, 72–73; as Southwestern characteristic, 221; voter turnout and, 129–30
nonpartisan slating groups (NPSGs): for city-manager campaign, 111; compared to political parties, 121–22; continual ascendancy of, 149–50; election challenges to, 178, 181; nominees of, 136–41; organization of, 104; political institution of, 212; response of, to election challenges, 181; Southwestern cities with, 131; support by affluent Anglo voters of, 148; vote structured by, 189
No-Tsu-Oh Festival (Houston), 36

Oklahoma City, 31
Olsen, Johan P., 12–13

Olson, David, 131
one-party politics, 95
Orum, Anthony, 50
Osofsky, Gilbert, 19

Packard, David, 99
Padilla, Orlando, 192
Panama-California Exposition (1915), 31–32, 36–37, 41
Pannell, Victor, 115
Papago Park (Phoenix), 165
parochial schools, 166–67
Pendergast, Tom, 94, 113, 209
Pendleton, Joseph, 37
People's Committee for Better Government (Albuquerque), 176, 182–83
People's Municipal League (1890), 3
Perea, Jose Leandro, 42
Peterson, Arthur G., 53
Peterson, George, 105
Peterson, Lorin, 102
Peterson, Paul, 26, 28, 220
Phoenix: advertising for investors by, 100; advertising for settlers by, 36; boycotts of public school systems in, 186; challenges to big-city reform in, 177; citizen actions in, 119; city-manager government in, 81–82; demographics (1960) of, 144–45; district elections in, 195–201; early history of, 31–32; ending of annexation by, 203; growth coalition in, 158; Mardian elected as mayor of, 142; minorities excluded from services in, 155; passage of city-manager plan in, 117; postwar corruption in, 107; postwar political community of, 170–71; public libraries in, 164; voter turnout (1960) in, 146–47; water problems of, 38–39
Phoenix Charter Government Committee, 112, 147
Phoenix Gazette, 110, 142, 197
Phoenix Housing Authority (PHA), 157
Pittsburgh, 33
"Plans for Improving Science and Mathematics Teaching in New Mexico" (Sandia Corp.), 168
Plunkitt, George Washington, 3, 4
police departments: Albuquerque, 186–87; Austin, 92; Houston, 108–9

Political Change in the Metropolis (Harrigan), 5
political coalitions: district elections and building, 202–3; for growth, 158; for municipal reform (1960s), 141–48
political culture: of machine, 216; municipal reform and, 21–26; of political regimes, 23; region and, 217; theory of, 21–26; values within, 24
political institutions: and blocking civil rights, 175; of city-manager government, 81–82; municipal reform movement and, 172–74; National Municipal League on changes of, 195; new institutionalism and, 12–14; of NPSGs, 212; overview of, 12–17; political action through, 14–16; race and design of, 212–13; voters and rules of, 128–30
political parties: *The Cincinnati Plan* on, 120; compared to NPSGs, 121–22; municipal reformers on, 120–21; unique nature of Southwestern, 54–56; voter turnout and, 129–30
political regimes: of Dallas, 28; political culture of, 23
political rules: function of, 14; rewritten during 1970s/1980s, 191–200; voters and, 128–30
poll tax, 66, 131, 187–88
postwar economic growth, 101–3
Price, Dix, 119
Progress Committee (San Jose), 124
Progressive party, 56
property tax, 160, 172
Proposition 4 (Albuquerque), 196
protestant ethic, 22n.38
public discourse (rhetoric), 24, 140–41
Public Housing Authority, 157
public libraries, 162–65
public policy, 204–5
public recreation facilities, 165–66
public-regarding values, 25
public school systems: boycotts of Phoenix, 186; in the Heights of Albuquerque, 210–11; segregation within, 140, 166–69; textbook reform and, 170–74
public services: dissatisfaction with, 192–93; policy changes in, 204; private vs., 43–46; provided by developers, 156; in Southwestern context, 214; theory on level of sunbelt, 172n.62; as unavailable outside city limits, 155. *See also* utilities

public swimming pools, 165
Pullman, George, 218–19
"purge law" (1971), 188
Pyndus, Phil, 197

race: design of political institutions and, 212–13; discrimination due to, 169–70, 186–87; municipal reform and consciousness of, 19–21; segregation due to, 140, 157, 166–60. *See also* African-Americans; civil rights; Mexican-Americans
racial fault lines, 20
railroad transportation, 42–43
Reclamation Act (1902), 39
Red Roosters (Houston), 41
Reed, Thomas H., 53, 70
reform charters: immediate impacts of, 73–75; impact on politicians of, 75, 78–83; revised at midcentury, 10, 11, 101–3. *See also* charters
"Reformer, The" (Childs), 30
reform government: in big cities, 6–12; coalitions (1960) supporting, 141–48; "extra-constitutional" devices of, 98; financing (1960) of, 162; ideal of, 4; legacy of, 94–98; official employment/spending (1960) in, 161; political institutions and, 12–17; public expenditures by, 96n.88; in the suburbs, 4–5; of sunbelt centralizers, 73, 83–94; unique nature of Southwestern, 12. *See also* big-city reform; government; municipal reform movement
region: as historically strategic location, 18–19, 212; local politics and, 17–19; municipal reform in context of, 54–57; political culture and, 217
"Report on Politics in Detroit" (Greenstone), 134
Republican party: on commission government, 63; impact of nonpartisanship on, 70; nonpartisanship advocated by, 60; in San Diego, 79; in Southwest region, 54–55
residential growth management, 106–7. *See also* growth
Rice, Bradley, 57
Rice, Horace Baldwin, 68
Rivers and Harbors Committee, 40
Rizzo, Frank, 181
Roosevelt, Franklin D., 37

Roosevelt, Theodore, 40, 59
Roosevelt Dam, 39–40
Rosenzweig, Harry, 120, 169
Rusk, David, 221

Saavedra, Louis, 155
St. Louis, 33
Sale, Kirkpatrick, 18
Salisbury, Robert, 102
Salt River Valley, 38–39
San Antonio: antigrowth sentiment in,
    194; challenges to big-city reform in,
    177–78; challenges to elections (1970–
    74) in, 190–91; citizen's groups in, 119,
    122, 123; city-manager campaigns in,
    118; early history of, 31; policy direc-
    tion changes in, 204–5; public libraries
    in, 164–65
Sanders, Heywood, 172–73
Sanders, L. L., 122, 136
Sandia Corporation, 101, 167–68
San Diego: antigrowth sentiment in, 194;
    council-manager government in, 82; de-
    feat of council-manager plan in, 118;
    federal lobbying by, 38, 41; government
    corruption in, 58; grievances of African-
    Americans in, 169–70; growth coalition
    in, 159; impact of reform charter in,
    78–79; lobbying of private resources
    by, 42–43; as navy town, 100, 215;
    Panama-California Exposition (1915)
    of, 31–32, 36–37, 41
San Diego Union, 111, 114
San Jose: antigrowth sentiment in, 194;
    challenges to big-city reform in, 177;
    council-manager government in, 82; dif-
    ficulties faced by, 52–53; displaced as
    state capital, 38; early history of, 31;
    publicity campaign (1940s) by, 99
San Ysidro, 184
Saturday Evening Post, 158
Scheumack, Ward H. "Doc," 107, 119
Schloyer, Dean, 202
school segregation, 140
Section 5 (Voting Rights Act), 190
segregation: Brown vs. Board on school,
    168–69; of federally funded housing,
    157n.19; of public libraries, 163–64; of
    public recreation facilities, 166; school,
    140, 166–69. See also civil rights;
    discrimination
Sehon, John, 78

Sessions, Roy, 108, 115
Seventh Model City Charter, 195
Shefter, Martin, 18, 55, 56
Shipe, M. M., 67–68, 70
Short Ballot Organization, 16
Skocpol, Theda, 13
Skowronek, Steve, 13
"Small Businessman as Big Businessman,
    The" (Weinstein), 56
Smith, Karen Lynn, 50
Smythe, William, 67
Southern Politics (Key), 73, 83, 98, 209
Southwestern cities: advertising for settlers
    by, 35–37; city-building process in, 47–
    51; commission plan adopted in, 65–
    71; creation of political communities in,
    125–26; election competitiveness
    (1945–63) in, 135; ethnic composition
    (1990) of, 205; financial costs of
    growth in, 159–62; land area of (1970–
    90), 193; major charter changes in, 10;
    middle class political reform in, 25; mu-
    nicipal reform in context of, 54–57,
    213–17; overview of early, 31–35; pop-
    ulation of (1890–1920), 35; population
    of (1920–50), 97; population of (1950/
    1960), 153; population of (1970–90),
    192; postwar economic growth in,
    101–3; postwar financial problems of,
    105–6; postwar growth of, 152–59;
    private/public arrangements in, 28–29;
    public libraries (1960) in, 162–64; pub-
    lic vs. private utilities in, 43–46; social
    characteristics (1960) of, 134; strategi-
    cal location of, 18–19, 212; success of
    municipal reformers in, 3–4; unique na-
    ture of reform process in, 12, 29–30,
    221–22; voter turnout (1947–63) in,
    133
Spreckels, John D., 43, 51, 67, 78, 79
Staniszewski, Frank, 74
Stone, Clarence, 27–28, 56
strategic location, 18–19, 212
Suburbia (Wood), 4
suburbs: forcible annexation of, 156n.17;
    postwar annexation of, 152–54, 173;
    reform politics in the, 4–5
suffrage restriction: impact of, 74–75, 89–
    90; municipal reform and, 66–67, 208
sunbelt centralizers: characteristics of, 83–
    84; governance of, 93–94; growth strat-
    egies of, 97; pattern of, 73, 209; politi-

suffrage restriction (*cont.*)
cal order created by, 83–94; support of
unions by, 213
Swanstrom, Todd, 5
Swidler, Ann, 23

Tabb, William, 216
Tate, J. Waddy, 83
taxation: under commission plan, 64–65;
frugality and low, 96; for new resi-
dential growth, 106–7; poll, 66, 131,
187–88; property, 160, 172; voter re-
sponse to burden of, 176
Technical Vocational Institute (TVI), 168,
211
10-1 plan (San Antonio), 199
Tenth Ward Club (Austin), 92
Terrell Election law, 66
Territorial Fair (Albuquerque, 1890s), 36
Texas Municipalities, 47
Texas State University for Negroes, 88
textbook reform, 170–74
Thornton, Robert L., 100, 119, 158
Thunderbirds (Phoenix), 100
Tingley, Clyde, 78, 83–86, 122, 165
Tonto Basin Storage Reservoir (Roosevelt
Dam), 39
Torres, Pete, 178
transportation growth, 42–43
Trevino, John, 202
Tweed, Boss, 73, 93, 172–73

Ulivarri, Orlando, 142
United Negro College Fund, 88
Urban Fortunes (Logan and Molotch), 27
Urban Frontier (Wade), 19, 33
Urban League, 169–70
Urban Renewal, 182–83, 184
Urdy, Charles, 202
utilities: private vs. public, 43–46; pro-
vided by developers, 156; in South-
western context, 214; theory on level of
sunbelt, 172n.62; as unavailable outside
city limits, 155. *See also* public services

values: of business leaders, 56; of middle
class, 22, 171; within political culture,
24; public-regarding, 25. *See also* political culture
vote dilution, 190
voter registration requirements, 127–28,
187–88

voters: big-city reform and, 130–35; creating obstacles to, 127–28; institutional
rules and turnout of, 128–30; political
machine to control Black, 216n.9;
racially polarized, 189–90; responding
to tax burden, 176; rules regulating,
126–27; turnout (1960) in Austin/
Phoenix/Albuquerque, 146–47; turnout (1965–89) of, 179–80. *See also*
elections
Voting Rights Act (1965), 187–88, 190

Wade, Richard, 19, 33
Wagner-Stegall Act, 157
Wallerstein, Immanuel, 18
ward representation: abolition of, 72;
commission plan impact on, 63; election
issues for, 61; lasting legacy of (Austin),
92. *See also* district elections
War on Poverty, 176, 181, 183–86
Waters, George, 106
Webb, Del, 158
Webster, Ron, 119
Weinstein, James, 56
Westerfeld, Henry, 44
White, Leonard, 105
"white man's primary" system, 89–90,
189
"wieldy constituencies" principle, 16
Wilson, Bob, 100
Wilson, James Q., 4, 5, 22, 25, 125, 162,
210
Wilson, Pete, 194
Wilson, Woodrow, 41
Winnetka, 125, 162, 166–67, 210
Wolfinger, Raymond, 17
Wood, H. P., 41
Wood, Robert C., 4
Woodruff, Clinton Rogers, 53
Wooldridge, Alexander Penn, 68, 70, 81
working class, 24–25. *See also* middle
class
Wright, Herman, 108, 109

Yearly, C. K., 23
Youngblood, Bill, 198
Young Democrats (Phoenix), 119
Young Republicans (Phoenix), 119
Your Voice at City Hall (Heilig and
Mundt), 201

Zilker, Andrew, 83, 91–92

PRINCETON STUDIES IN AMERICAN POLITICS: HISTORICAL, INTERNATIONAL, AND COMPARATIVE PERSPECTIVES

Labor Visions and State Power: The Origins of Business Unionism in the United States by Victoria C. Hattam

The Lincoln Persuasion: Remaking American Liberalism by J. David Greenstone

Politics and Industrialization: Early Railroads in the United States and Prussia by Colleen A. Dunlavy

Political Parties and the State: The American Historical Experience by Martin Shefter

Prisoners of Myth: The Leadership of the Tennessee Valley Authority, 1933–1990 by Erwin C. Hargrove

Bound by Our Constitution: Women, Workers, and the Minimum Wage by Vivien Hart

Experts and Politicians: Reform Challenges to Machine Politics in New York, Cleveland, and Chicago by Kenneth Finegold

Social Policy in the United States: Future Possibilities in Historical Perspective by Theda Skocpol

Political Organizations by James Q. Wilson

Facing Up to the American Dream: Race, Class, and the Soul of the Nation by Jennifer L. Hochschild

Classifying by Race edited by Paul E. Peterson

From the Outside In: World War II and the American State by Bartholomew H. Sparrow

Kindred Strangers: The Uneasy Relationship between Politics and Business in America by David Vogel

Why Movements Succeed or Fail: Opportunity, Culture, and the Struggle for Woman Suffrage by Lee Ann Banaszak

The Power of Separation: American Constitutionalism and the Myth of the Legislative Veto by Jessica Korn

Party Decline in America: Policy, Politics, and the Fiscal State by John J. Coleman

The Origins of the Urban Crisis: Race and Inequality in Postwar Detroit
by Thomas J. Sugrue

*The Road to Nowhere: The Genesis of President Clinton's Plan
for Health Security* by Jacob Hacker

*Imperiled Innocents: Anthony Comstock and Family Reproduction
in Victorian America* by Nicola Beisel

Morning Glories: Municipal Reform in the Southwest by Amy Bridges

*The Hidden Welfare State: Tax Expenditures and Social Policy
in the United States* by Christopher Howard

*Bold Relief: Institutional Politics and the Origins of
Modern American Social Policy* by Edwin Amenta

*Parting at the Crossroads: The Emergence of Health Insurance in the
United States and Canada* by Antonia Maioni

*Forged Consensus: Science, Technology, and Economic Policy
in the United States, 1921–1953* by David M. Hart

*Faithful and Fearless: Moving Feminist Protest inside the Church
and Military* by Mary Fainsod Katzenstein

Uneasy Alliances: Race and Party Competition in America
by Paul Frymer

Stuck in Neutral: Business and the Politics of Human Capital Investment Policy
by Cathie Jo Martin